PRENTICE-HALL

Foundations of Economic Geography Series
NORTON GINSBURG, *Editor*

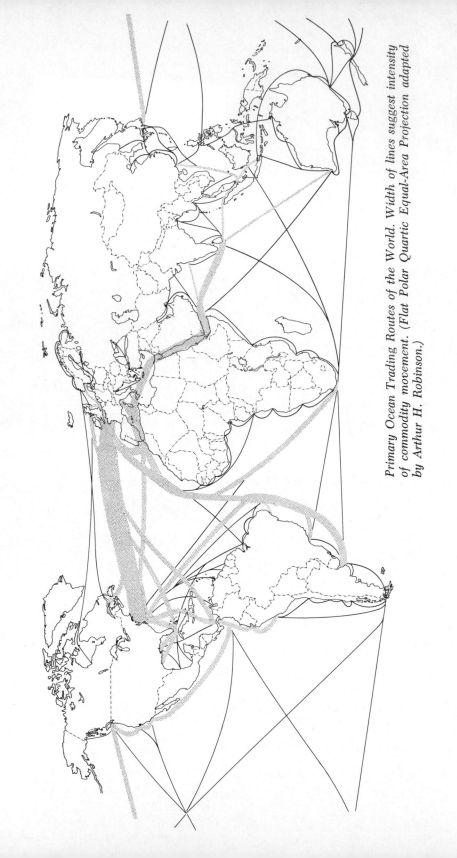

Primary Ocean Trading Routes of the World. Width of lines suggest intensity of commodity movement. (Flat Polar Quartic Equal-Area Projection adapted by Arthur H. Robinson.)

Geography
of
International
Trade

RICHARD S. THOMAN

Professor of Geography
Queen's University

EDGAR C. CONKLING

Associate Professor of Geography
Queen's University

PRENTICE-HALL, INC., Englewood Cliffs, N.J.

PRENTICE-HALL INTERNATIONAL, INC., London
PRENTICE-HALL OF AUSTRALIA, PTY. LTD., Sydney
PRENTICE-HALL OF CANADA, LTD., Toronto
PRENTICE-HALL OF INDIA PRIVATE LTD., New Delhi
PRENTICE-HALL OF JAPAN, INC., Tokyo

Foundations of Economic Geography Series

Among the various fields of geography, economic geography, per-haps more than any other, has experienced remarkable changes within the past twenty years—so many that it is almost impossible for one scholar to command all aspects of it. The result has been increasing specializa-tion on the one hand and, on the other, a fundamental need for bringing the fruits of that specialization to students of economic geography.

The *Foundations of Economic Geography* Series consists of several volumes, each focusing on a major problem in economic geography. It is designed to bring the student, whether novice or more experienced, to the frontiers of knowledge in economic geography, and in so doing, force-fully to demonstrate the methodological implications of current research —but at a level comprehensible even to those just becoming aware of the fascinating problems in the field as it is developing today.

Each volume stands as a contribution to understanding in its own right, but the series as a whole is intended to provide a broad cross-section of on-going research in economic geography, stemming from concern with a variety of problems. On the other hand, the series should not be regarded as a complete synthesis of work in economic geography, al-though the volumes explore in depth certain major issues of keenest interest to economic geographers and others in related fields to a degree impossible in textbooks that attempt to cover the entire field. At the same time, the student is brought face-to-face with the kinds of intellectual and conceptual problems that characterize economic geography in a way that no over-all survey can accomplish. Each volume thus provides a basis for an intensive exploration of issues that constitute the cutting edge of research in this most dynamic and demanding field of knowledge.

As time goes on and new volumes appear in the series, the original volumes will be modified in keeping with new developments and orientations, not only in economic geography, but in the field of geography as a whole. The first volume to appear in the series, Wilbur Zelinsky's *A Prologue to Population Geography,* acts as a bridge between economic and cultural geography and as a means for exploring ideas and methods concerning a problem of increasing interest to geographers and social scientists alike: the growth, diffusion, and distribution of populations throughout the world. Brian J. L. Berry's *Geography of Market Centers and Retail Distribution* attempts to fill a major lacuna in the literature of economic geography, as it lays down principles concerning the spatial distribution and organization of marketing in both advanced and lesser developed economies. In so doing, it provides a bridge between the geographies of consumption, production, and cities, and links them for perhaps the first time effectively through a theoretical system, still primitive, but far in advance of comparable formulations.

Gunnar Alexandersson's *Geography of Manufacturing* reflects the need for considering the historical-ecological settings within which manufacturing enterprises originate and flourish. Though superficially nontheoretical, it contains flashing insights into the extreme socioeconomic complexities that have resulted in the world pattern of manufacturing, and it is concerned with an interpretation of that pattern through an evolutionary-descriptive technique applied to selected industries and regions.

Richard S. Thoman and Edgar C. Conkling in their volume on international trade deal with a topic that has not been given the attention it deserves by economic geographers. By careful analysis of trade data and an imaginative use of graphic and tabular devices, they interpret the pattern and structure of international trade in terms of current monetary and economic blocs. The result is the first modern treatment of one of the basic types of international relations, and thereby an important contribution to the political as well as economic geographical literature.

The other volumes in the series, whether concerned with transportation, energy, resource management, water, wholesaling, or agriculture, display "bridging" qualities that transcend the narrow limitations of ordinary descriptive handbooks. All are concerned with the new and the fresh as well as the traditional, and with the transformation of a somewhat parochial field of scholarship into one that is interdisciplinary as well as innovative and pioneering.

NORTON GINSBURG

The University of Chicago

Preface

International trade has been neglected by geographers. Clearly, research is needed in the entire spectrum of possible ideas associated with the subject, ranging from critical evaluation of the composition, pattern, and trends of actual flows to, on the one hand, the creation of mathematical models and, on the other, the study of institutional "logistics and mechanics" facilitating or hindering the existing international demand-supply relationships. There is much room in this arena of interest for widely differing approaches and techniques, no one of which may offer a complete answer.

It is hoped that this little volume will be not only of immediate use in adding to basic geographical knowledge of trends in international trade up through the early 1960s, but also of longer-range value in stimulating much needed research into the topic. To maintain maximum comparability, the authors have relied heavily upon data from the *Yearbook of International Trade* for selected years, as well as additional United Nations statistical sources listed in the Bibliography, accepting the nomenclature of each volume as to specific meanings reported by each country. While aware of certain inconsistencies in such data, the authors have found no satisfactory substitute.

RICHARD S. THOMAN
EDGAR C. CONKLING

Contents

CHAPTER 1 *background considerations*

Present-day international trade rests on centuries of experience and stems from definite motivations or stimuli. This chapter, which combines an historical and economic view with a geographical one, contains appraisals of (1) selected background aspects of international trade and (2) possible causes and theoretical explanations of such trade.

Immediate Background

While deeply rooted in history, modern international trade is subject to such rapid and thorough change that we look to the distant past primarily for certain techniques which facilitate or restrict commerce. Our interest in this historical overview has therefore been limited to the past century (1865-1965), during which time a truly global trade evolved. The century can be divided into three unequal trading periods, marked by the beginning dates of the two world wars.

1865-1914: ESTABLISHMENT OF A WORLD-WIDE TRADE. The latter part of the nineteenth and early years of the twentieth centuries established for modern commerce a basic foundation of active trading routes and facilities reaching to all parts of the effectively occupied and utilized world. Prior to that time, "world trade" was in fact an exchange among places that did not include all of the occupied world. Ancient realms focusing on key points within and along the Mediterranean Sea and in the Far East and Muslim trade from the Near East in the seventh century AD are examples of earlier patterns which, though not small, were not world-wide. Even mercantile commerce of Europe and its offshoots in various parts of the world—trade that expanded in the seventeenth, eighteenth, and early nineteenth centuries when stimulated by the European phases of the Industrial Revolution—cannot be termed a world-wide commerce in the modern sense of the term. Not until the latter portion of the nineteenth century, dramatized by the Stanley-Livingstone meeting in 1871, was central Africa, the last remaining settled area of consequence, opened to outside influence and the foundation thus laid for a commerce that can be regarded as global.

The achievement of this objective resulted primarily from two movements, political colonization and the Industrial Revolution, of which one was to be short-lived as a major force and the other was to be intensified and expanded. Political colonialism, reaching the zenith of its power and influence in the period under examination, provided the energy and expansionist drive which established the necessary trading routes. It also provided a congeries of organizations, arrangements, and facilities, whether an intangible such as an accounting system or a material object such as a railway or a building, which were needed for international trade of the day and which could be built upon or adjusted to meet subsequent commercial demands.

However strongly motivated in a political sense, world commerce of the late nineteenth and early twentieth centuries never could have succeeded without the multitudinous benefits of the Industrial Revolution. One development of the late nineteenth century was of particular importance: the construction in the 1870's (accounts differ as to the specific year) of a transoceanic merchant vessel with a hull of steel, driven by a steam engine attached to a screw-type propeller instead of a paddle wheel. This new vessel, with its potential for carrying large cargoes efficiently over long distances, both symbolized and furthered the Industrial Revolution, enabling economies of scale to be realized on a world-wide basis.

This was a period of growth in trade. The reported value of all recorded exports, slightly less than $5 billion in 1867-1868,[1] had risen by slightly more than 4.7 times by 1913, even when measured at constant prices.[2] The annual rate of growth was especially high in the early part of the twentieth century, despite the calculation of that rate from an expanding base.

Western Europe remained dominant in both imports and exports (as measured by value) in this period, although the continent was confronted by rising competition from the United States and, in lesser measure, from Canada and Japan. By 1913, nearly 51 per cent of all recorded exports and almost 58 per cent of all imports involved Europe, especially western Europe.[3] Meanwhile the prevailing position of the United Kingdom in Europe was being challenged, especially by an energetic Germany and by the Netherlands. The relative position of France dropped somewhat during this period, while those of Belgium and Russia remained more or less stable.

Although detailed records of the composition of this trade are not readily available, there is evidence that intra-European movement of finished and semifinished materials was very important, especially when

---

[1] W. S. Woytinsky and E. S. Woytinsky, *World Commerce and Government* (New York: Twentieth Century Fund, 1955), p. 38.

[2] W. S. Woytinsky, "International Trade," *Encyclopaedia Britannica*, Vol. 22, p. 347A.

[3] *Ibid.*

measured by value. The railway, inland waterway craft, and coastwise ship were prime movers of this intra-European traffic. On the world scene, there was also a heavy flow—by ocean vessel—of primary materials. These included products from the farm, mine, and forest, moving from low and intermediate latitudes to the more heavily industrialized zones, and a counter-flow of manufactured goods. Coal became increasingly important as an item of commerce to strategically located bunkering stations as the steam ship became prominent as a carrier, frequently moving at cheap "return voyage" rates because extra space was available on vessels outbound from Europe. Coal also was a major commodity of shipment within Europe, moving from the few major fields to nations of import and to ports of re-export to bunkering stations and elsewhere.

1914-1939: FLUCTUATING CONSISTENCY AND EMBRYONIC CHANGE. The 25 years separating the outbreaks of the two world wars marked a very interesting, peculiar, yet important trend in the international commerce of the century. On the one hand, it was a period of fluctuation, especially in total volume, because of the impact of the world depression plus inter-war national power struggles and trade and monetary problems. On the other, it also was a period of relative consistency with respect to type of commodity exchanged, major trading partners, and prevailing trade routes. Meanwhile, beneath the veneer of conditions reflected by statistical reports, a number of changes began that were to affect rather drastically the international trade of the period to follow.

The fluctuations of trade associated with the world depression were extremely meaningful at the time but carried few implications for the present scene. International trade rose rapidly from 1914 to 1929, climbing by more than 50 per cent of the 1913 level, measured at constant prices. It plummeted during the depression years to a point below that of 1913. Subsequently it rose again, so that by the beginning of World War II it stood only slightly under its 1929 high.

Meanwhile, the basic pattern and composition of world trade did not alter drastically. Western Europe remained the primary focus, with other areas more or less continuing in the roles established for them before World War I, except as noted below.

During this period, however, seeds were sown that were to result in pronounced changes in international trade after the second war. First of all, Marxist Communism had survived its chaotic early years, was becoming a force in the Soviet Union, and was being accorded increasingly serious consideration in other parts of the world. Second, there was strong discontent within many colonies regarding the system of political colonialism focused on Europe, and by 1939 the first blows already had been struck against European-based colonialism as a political and economic force. Third, some European leaders had begun to realize that Europe's days as an economic power were numbered unless that continent, or at least the economic core of it, could function more or less as a single economic unit. Fourth, Europe declined slightly in relative world position in exports, and rather definitely in imports, during this period—with the United States, Canada, and Japan rising in almost direct proportion to

Europe's decline. Fifth, petroleum began to be substituted for coal as a major fuel, both on land and on sea, and the composition of world trade began to be affected accordingly. Sixth, finished and semifinished goods achieved increasingly high positions in import and export lists (to a degree, like petroleum, in preparation for World War II)—a trend that was to continue into the present period. Finally, these slight adjustments in trading partners and commodities meant a relative rise in the importance of North Atlantic and North Pacific trading routes as nations now called "technically advanced" intensified their trade with one another.

1940-1965: READJUSTMENT AND GROWTH.   To a certain extent, the fluctuations of the previous period continued after World War II in that the production facilities of much of Europe and Japan were so crippled during the conflict that nearly a decade passed before those countries were fully active in commerce again. Also important in this immediate postwar period was the temporary predominance of the United States, the only major victorious power whose economy had been stimulated rather than weakened during the closing phases of war. Total world trade therefore increased during and after the war, despite disadvantageous aftereffects in western Europe, the Soviet Union, and Japan. Indeed, as we shall document in Chapter 2, that increase since 1950 has been approximately 6 per cent per year when measured at constant prices.

Especially in the late 1950's and early 1960's, however, changes took place that have not yet left their full imprint on the world trading scene. These changes, most of which have been anticipated in preceding paragraphs, basically involved:

1. The emergence of the group of Communist, or centrally planned, economies which, although revealing internal discord and although only moderately prominent in total world trade at the time of this writing, contain as a group more than one-third of the world's people. Moreover, these countries are expanding in population, economic strength, and technology, and evidently aspire to an enlarged role in the international market place.

2. The establishment of the European Economic Community and the European Free Trade Association, as well as analogous groups in other parts of the world, as producing and trading realities rather than mere blueprints.

3. The collapse of political and economic colonialism in Africa and eastern Asia, and the equally hurried creation, from former colonies, of independent countries which in large measure are not expanding in economic growth as fast as most economically advanced countries.

4. Changes in technology, resource availability, and consuming patterns that resulted in more international trade in finished and semifinished manufactures, petroleum and its products, and iron ore and certain other raw materials.

Effect on trading patterns.   The world pattern of trading routes, considered in its total orientation rather than in the comparative size of its segments, has not altered significantly during this period except for the divisive effects of the Iron Curtain and the attracting effects of certain sites of petroleum and other strategic materials. Communist policies, whether with respect to other Communist nations or to non-Communist countries, change so rapidly and completely that a definite statement of trends is difficult to make. One cannot deny, however, that the presence of the Iron Curtain has affected the pattern of world trade that existed prior to World War II in that a new focal center, the Soviet Union, has been added to the previous primary trading nodes in western Europe, North America, and Japan. The role of Communist China in world trade cannot as yet be evaluated with any degree of precision.

On the whole, the new sites of mineral exploitation have not reoriented the basic outline of world trade routes, but they have added short, important extensions. The petroleum fields of the Middle East have been the leading sites in this category, attracting much tanker shipping to the eastern end of the Mediterranean Sea, the Persian Gulf, and, lately, the coast of northern Africa. Producing districts in the central Volga section (the "Second Baku") of the Soviet Union and in Alberta Province of Canada also have risen sharply in international as well as domestic significance, both relying upon land and inland waterway rather than oceanic transportation to carry outgoing materials from local oil fields. New sources of iron ore in the lower Orinoco River basin of Venezuela and in the upper Quebec/Labrador Provinces of Canada are outstanding among a variety of mining areas producing commodities other than petroleum that either have been added recently to the world's primary trading routes or have been expanded from a once minor position in those routes.

Although the basic patterns of world trade thus have not changed appreciably during this period, certain segments have grown faster than others. Most prominent of these is the North Atlantic Route between a revitalized western Europe and a dynamic North America. A second segment, more accurately a series of segments, connects Japan with North America across the Pacific and with western Europe via the Pacific-Panama Canal-Atlantic, or the Pacific-Indian Ocean-Suez Canal-Mediterranean-Atlantic. The Asian segment of this route from Japan reaches not only to Europe, but also to India and to Communist China, with an important branch extending to Australia.

Effect of European unification. Although involved in the changes just discussed, the volume of world trade that continues to originate and terminate in western Europe is sufficiently high to merit special consideration. We shall examine this trade in greater detail in Chapters 3 and 4, but shall make three general observations at this point: (1) Internal trade especially, but external trade also, of both the European Economic Community (West Germany, France, the Netherlands, Belgium, Luxembourg, and Italy plus certain associate members), and the European Free Trade Association (the United Kingdom, Norway, Sweden, Denmark, Austria, Switzerland, Portugal, and certain associate members) has increased rather dramatically within the 1955-65 decade; (2) the increases have been especially heavy in trade with other European nations and across the Atlantic with the United States and Canada; and (3) despite the fact that many former colonies have continued to trade with European nations that once ruled them, growth of commerce in such far-flung associations as the Commonwealth of Nations has not kept pace with growth of trade in the world as a whole. Although these trends represent trade diversion as well as creation, they are associated with marked growth in over-all world trade.

The Modern Basis for International Trade

Although most economies produce both goods and services, present international trade involves primarily the movement of goods. The provision of services, an activity which is becoming increasingly important as a source of livelihood in technically advanced countries and some underdeveloped countries, is predominantly a domestic function for most countries. Where considered a part of international trade, service activities involve mainly invisible exports and imports—spending by tourists and military personnel in foreign areas, accruals from foreign investments, charges for transporting people and goods to and from foreign places, and so forth.

Countries exchange goods for different reasons. Political dependencies, lacking freedom of choice, may trade because they have been requested to do so. Some independent nations may trade to obtain revenue from export tariffs, mining royalties, etc., from natural resources or primary activities under their jurisdictions. Some may trade to obtain primary materials and certain semi-manufactures needed for further processing. Others may be interested in the exchange of specialized types of finished product.

We may consider international trade basically as a reflection of vested interest decisions, each of which is expected to be favorable to the decision maker. In an economy that is state-owned or state-controlled, such decisions can be considered to reflect the calculated best interest of that particular state. Where a private or combination private-public economy functions under government supervision, such decisions reflect first of all the interest of the private organization and secondarily the national interest. Because private and semiprivate interests always are under government jurisdiction, however, their decisions are never entirely free from implications of government policy. When there is a conflict of interest, the wishes of the government usually can be expected to prevail.

The political element thus is never absent in a consideration of international trade. The size, shape, relative position, natural and human endowment, types of organization, degree of political independence, and political ideology or ideologies of specific countries are key factors to be considered in assessing international trading behavior.

Whatever its political connotations, however, international trade fundamentally is an economic phenomenon. Desire becomes demand only with the addition of purchasing power; this is true of countries as well as of individuals. Normal trade flows result directly from the existence of demand on the one hand and supply on the other. These economic realities enable countries to pursue their political policies of self-interest with varying degrees of success.

Therefore, in this book we shall consider the economic and political factors as directly basic to international trade, with all other considerations indirect and/or subordinate.

International Trade Theory

If international trade is fundamentally and directly an economic phenomenon, what theories exist to attempt its explanation? Economists long have been concerned with international trade theory, and their efforts have been classified by one author into two time periods: the classical and the modern.[4]

CLASSICAL THEORY

Initial effort.   Work in classical trade theory may be considered as extending from the writings of David Hume to those of Alfred Marshall —i.e., from 1752 to 1926.[5] A major contribution by Hume was the evaluation of the financial relationship between prices and circulation of money on the one hand and balance of payments on the other. Adam Smith, whose *Wealth of Nations* is considered the seminal work of economics as a discipline, regarded foreign trade as based on a number of conditions that included a vent for surplus, apparently recognizing the importance of differences among countries in resource base as well as the importance of division of labor and of unhindered movement of finished goods.[6] (This concept later was refined by David Ricardo, and substantially articulated by John Stuart Mill.)

The theory of comparative costs.   The most influential trade theory of the classical period, and indeed up to the present, has been the theory of comparative costs, sometimes called the theory of comparative advantage, propounded by David Ricardo (1772-1823). Assuming (1) a labor theory of value, (2) complete internal mobility of the factors of production, (3) complete external immobility among those factors, and (4) unlimited and unhindered international trade, Ricardo concluded that an economy should specialize in producing those commodities in which it has an advantage as measured by *comparative costs*. These comparative cost advantages are usually actual cost advantages, but need not be; if an economy can produce and sell both wheat and automobiles more cheaply than another economy, but its costs in producing wheat are definitely lower than in producing automobiles (and its comparative advantage thus higher in producing wheat than in producing automobiles), that

[4] Gottfried Haberler, *A Survey of International Trade Theory* (Princeton: Princeton University Press, 1961). For this section, works found especially useful in addition to the Haberler study include: Benjamin Higgins, *Economic Development* (New York: W. W. Norton & Company, 1959), pp. 345-383; Charles P. Kindleberger, *Foreign Trade and the National Economy* (New Haven: Yale University Press, 1962); Alfred Maizels, *Industrial Growth and World Trade* (London: Cambridge University Press, 1963); Bertil Ohlin, *Interregional and International Trade* (Cambridge, Massachusetts: Harvard University Press, 1933); Ragnar Nurske, *Patterns of Trade and Development* (New York: Oxford University Press, 1961).

[5] Haberler, *op. cit.*, p. 6 and p. 12.

[6] Kindleberger, *op. cit.*, p. 30; Hla Myint, "The Classical Theory of International Trade and the Underdeveloped Countries," *Economic Journal*, Vol. 68 (1958), 321-323.

economy may find an advantage in specializing in the production of wheat, allowing another economy to produce the automobiles. Both economies thus benefit.

The theory is dynamic, allowing for change over a period of time. With each economy specializing in goods and services in which it has comparative production advantages and constantly re-assessing its position in view of changing technology, trading conditions, etc., the resulting international trade would represent theoretically optimum patterns among trading countries. The adjusting action, however, may result in some marked shifts as to product specialty. For example, some types of agricultural production in such technically advanced countries as Australia, Canada, or the United States have become extremely efficient in output per person as farms have been increasingly mechanized and efficiently managed; but certain kinds of manufacturing in these countries, requiring high amounts of costly labor, have declined in relative advantage. Therefore, according to Ricardo's theory of comparative advantage, these countries may find it necessary to concentrate on the output of selected agricultural goods, allowing some other country—perhaps one with cheap yet efficient labor —to concentrate on those types of manufacturing which require large labor inputs!

The main conclusion of current importance to be drawn from Ricardo's theory is that, as long as the factors of production are not perfectly mobile internationally, product specialization by country can be expected to occur, and international trade will result unless artificial barriers are raised. Furthermore, such trade, according to the theory, would be mutually beneficial to participating countries.

John Stuart Mill refined the Ricardo theory further by considering comparative costs as setting limits of tolerance (in a two-commodity case) within which actual costs would range. These actual costs, in turn, would be determined by demand and supply. This concept was further refined at length by Alfred Marshall.[7]

MODERN ASPECTS.   Except in Communist countries, where the championing of the labor theory of value by Marx has been accepted somewhat dogmatically, modern theories of international trade have come to depend upon some alternative assessments of value. These alternatives have included real costs, opportunity costs, and a general equilibrium of total costs.[8] Even so, however, the theory of comparative costs continues to be useful. Indeed, two modern economists, Paul Samuelson and W. F. Stolper, hold that, within a series of very limiting assumptions, free international movement of goods is a perfect substitute for free international movement of the factors of production—land, labor, capital, and entrepreneurship.[9] The Heckscher-Ohlin theorem, also addressing Ricardo's theory, states that in the real world the factor endowments may

---

[7] Haberler, *op. cit.*, pp. 9-10.
[8] *Ibid.*, pp. 12-23. Real costs here were used in a special way to denote subjective costs directly associated with production. Opportunity costs refer to minimum costs at which a factor of production can be made available to an entrepreneur in view of alternative opportunities for employing that factor.
[9] *Ibid.*, p. 18.

exert an influence on the trade of countries, at least in an early stage of trading activity. For example, a country with an excellent resource endowment but a small labor supply may export resource-intensive products, while importing labor-intensive products. However, building on earlier work by Heckscher, Ohlin has argued that as free trade continues, it may result in a partial equalization of costs within participating countries among the factors of production, so that initial advantages in a specific factor are reduced. (It should be noted that Ohlin does not contend that a *full* equalization among factors of production will take place; this could happen only if there were complete mobility among the factors of production on an international basis.) [10] Work by W. Leontief has indicated that we may not yet be certain, pragmatically, of the degree to which specific factors of production enter into international trade. His initial application of input-output analysis to foreign trade of the United States has suggested that US participation in foreign trade may be based on a high degree of specialization of labor, rather than upon the more or less generally accepted concept of heavy capital investment—so that the US may be resorting to international trade to export certain surplus labor rather than products of certain capital-intensive industries.[11]

Of the various arguments attacking, defending, or adjusting Ricardo's theory of comparative costs, one of the most current and challenging is based on empirical evidence. Stated by Gunnar Myrdal, Raul Prebisch, H. Singer, and others, the argument notes that the gap between per capita income of the economically advanced and the less developed countries is widening rather than narrowing, due to continuing economic growth in the former group compared with economic stagnation, more or less, in the latter.[12] Furthermore, these scholars maintain, this widening gap may be caused by the fact that the terms of trade are turning against the less developed areas.[13] In short, the less developed areas must pay higher and higher prices for international purchases but do not enjoy correspondingly rising prices for goods sold into the international market place. The argument thus is a basic challenge to the theory of comparative costs because it suggests that, in fact, unrestricted international trade may be harmful to less developed economies participating in such trade. We shall have more to say of this idea in later chapters.

The foregoing overview of economic theories of international trade is suggestive rather than complete. The theories mentioned there are not universally accepted. Inasmuch as the discussion is devoted to general theories, it does not include the substantial and substantive work by econo-

---

[10] See especially: Bertil Ohlin, *op. cit.*; Haberler, *op. cit.*, pp. 16-17; Kindleberger, *op. cit.*, pp. 27-30, 48-49, 75-77; Paul Samuelson, *Economics* (New York: McGraw-Hill Book Company, 1964), p. 683.

[11] Wassily Leontief, "Domestic Production and Foreign Trade: The American Capital Position Re-Examined," *Proceedings of the American Philosophical Society,* September, 1953.

[12] See especially: Gunnar Myrdal, *An International Economy: Problems and Prospects* (New York: Harper & Row, Publishers, 1956), pp. 1-97; Benjamin Higgins, *Economic Development* (New York: W. W. Norton & Company, 1959), pp. 348-349.

[13] Terms of trade may be defined, in a somewhat oversimplified way, as a comparison of prices paid per unit of goods and services purchased with prices received per unit of goods and services sold.

mists in developing models for consumption, production, distribution and trade (including effects of technological change) for purposes of understanding trading problems and policies. The reader is referred to the bibliography, especially the works of Jacob Viner and the thorough treatment by John Chipman, for further discussion.

CHAPTER 2

the current trading scene

We have seen in the preceding chapter that the current international trading scene is one of readjustment and expansion after the close of World War II. In this chapter we shall take a closer look at such changes, viewing them in regard to trends in volume, pattern, and composition.

Volume

Despite the Cold War and other rivalries that might discourage international commodity exchange, the volume of world trade as measured by value is at an unprecedentedly high level. In 1964, the value of all reported exports was $170.67 billion.[1] As seen in Fig. 2.1, that value ap-

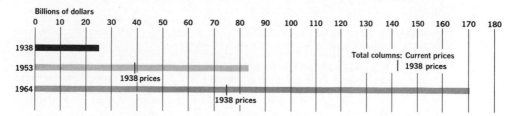

Fig. 2.1. *The Growth of World Exports from 1938 to 1964. In this and succeeding figures where 1953 and 1963/1964 values have been reduced to 1938 dollars, the method has been the application of the United States wholesale price index to the years under study. The technique yields general rather than exact results, inasmuch as the wholesale price index of a single country is applied to world conditions.*

proaches seven times the level of exports in 1938, if no allowance is made for currency inflation, and amounts to about three times the 1938 figure with allowance for inflation. The rate of growth in foreign trade has been about 6 per cent per year since 1950, considered at constant prices.[2] This

[1] United Nations, *Monthly Bulletin of Statistics* (June, 1965), p. *xii*.
[2] See especially: United Nations, *World Economic Survey, 1962*, Vol. 1, pp. 1-2. See also Fig. 2.1.

Table 2.1.   Trends in World Trading Patterns

Country or Area	Per Cent of World Imports			Per Cent of World Exports		
	1938	1953	1963	1938	1953	1963
United States	8.58	12.94	10.61	13.03	18.96	14.96
Canada	2.72	5.12	3.76	3.68	5.10	4.20
Latin America	6.06	7.74	5.42	7.27	9.22	6.33
Western Europe	50.49	39.14	45.35	39.31	34.85	41.21
EEC	20.19	18.38	25.04	18.55	17.76	24.46
EFTA	24.76	17.28	16.17	17.65	·14.52	14.17
United Kingdom	16.76	10.70	8.14	10.27	8.65	7.43
Japan	4.21	2.85	4.18	4.71	1.54	3.55
Australia, New Zealand, South Africa	5.03	3.80	3.32	3.78	4.06	3.21
Middle East °	2.83	2.98	3.20	2.34	3.42	4.26
Sterling Asia	5.55	5.14	4.50	6.72	5.04	3.78
Miscellaneous Asia °	3.74	3.16	2.12	4.55	2.27	1.71
Africa (other than Middle East and South Africa)	2.59	4.48	3.06	2.80	3.97	3.46
USSR	1.05	3.01	4.45	1.07 } 8.23 {		4.73
Eastern Europe °	3.55	4.36	6.23	7.60 }		6.31
China & Asian Bloc of Centrally Planned Countries	2.08	1.62	0.92	1.02	1.37	1.07
Sterling Area	28.91	21.60	19.30	23.11	21.47	18.20
Developed Areas	70.47	65.23	67.90	64.68	64.77	67.36
Less Developed Areas	21.62	23.96	20.50	25.15	25.60	20.52
Centrally Planned Areas	6.68	8.99	11.60	9.69	9.60	12.11

° The Middle East is here considered to be made of UAR Egypt, Sudan, Ethiopia, and French Somaliland in Africa plus all non-Communist Asian countries west of Pakistan (except Turkey, which here is included with western Europe). Miscellaneous Asia excludes the Middle East, Communist Asia, sterling Asia, and Japan. Yugoslavia is included with western Europe rather than the centrally planned group. Groupings are those of the original source.

Source: Calculated from the *Yearbook of International Trade Statistics, 1963*, United Nations, Tables A and B. Because of differences in the original source resulting from the use of general statistics by some reporting countries and special statistics by others, respective columns and certain subsections of columns do not always add to 100 per cent.

is approximately three times the average annual rate of world population growth, so that per capita trade obviously is rising.

Pattern

Non-Communist, developed economies continue to dominate the world trading pattern, accounting for over two-thirds of all exports and imports (Table 2.1). Indeed, three gigantic trading areas—the European Economic Community, the European Free Trade Association, and the United States—together send and receive over one-half of the value of all international trade. Less developed, non-Communist economies account for one-fifth of all exports and imports, and Communist nations for the remaining one-eighth.

Recent trends favor the centrally planned (Communist) economies and the non-Communist, developed economies at the relative expense of the less developed economies. Table 2.1 shows that the centrally planned group increased its trade rather significantly between 1953 and 1963, whereas the non-Communist, developed group experienced a smaller relative increase (although its rate is calculated from a larger base than trade of the centrally planned economies, and hence its growth rate would tend to be smaller). In contrast, trade of the less developed category rose so slowly between 1953 and 1963 as to result in a relative loss of trading rank. (Note the last three entries in Table 2.1.) Considered at constant prices, exports of all reporting countries rose by 6.4 per cent between 1950, and 1960, whereas exports from the centrally planned economies rose by 10.7 per cent, those from the non-Communist, developed economies rose by 6.9 per cent, and those from the less developed group rose by 3.6 per cent.[3]

Table 2.1 indicates differential rates of growth among the major members of each of the three major trading groups by showing relative changes in the sharing of world trade, and Fig. 2.2 shows patterns of total trade in 1963. Trade expansion within the centrally planned group has reflected especially the emerging status of the Soviet Union as both an importing and an exporting country. Eastern Europe also has increased its import trade since 1938, but it was relatively less active in exports in 1963 than in 1938. China and other centrally planned economies of Asia, considered as a group, have not exhibited a consistent trend as yet.

Among developed, non-Communist countries, EEC experienced a remarkable expansion of both imports and exports after 1953 within a western European complex that in 1963 imported a lower percentage of all trade, and exported only a slightly higher percentage, than in 1938. EFTA has declined relatively, its decline almost equal in percentage points to the decline of its major member, the United Kingdom. The United States and Canada enjoyed favorable trading positions in the aftermath of World War II, as reflected in the 1953 column of Table 2.1, but lost ground in a relative sense during subsequent years. Japan's position improved substantially after 1953, but ten years later it had not yet reached its 1938 relative level. Australia, New Zealand, and South Africa exhibited levels of trading activity in 1963 that were slightly below those of 1953 or 1938.

The relative decline of the non-Communist, less developed group is reflected in the trading patterns of each subgroup or bloc except the Middle East and Central Africa during the 25-year period under observation.

Finally, the sterling area, that group of large and small economically advanced and less developed countries, has experienced a rather pronounced relative decline since 1938. This decrease has been especially severe with respect to imports. In both imports and exports, however, the decrease has been greater in actual percentage points than has the relative decline of the United Kingdom upon which the sterling area is fo-

[3] *Loc. cit.*

Fig. 2.2. *The Gross Pattern of World Exports in 1963.*

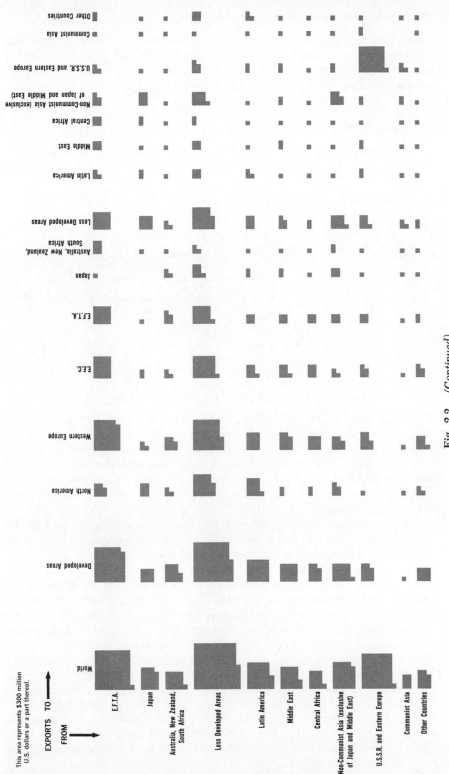

Fig. 2.2. (Continued).

cused. One may assume, therefore, that unless indirect effects of the relative reduction of United Kingdom trading activity has been felt in other parts of the sterling area, the losses here cannot be attributed wholly to relative commercial decline by the United Kingdom.

Composition

The composition of the world's trade and that of the three major trading blocs as grouped in this study are summarized in Figs. 2.3 and 2.4 and

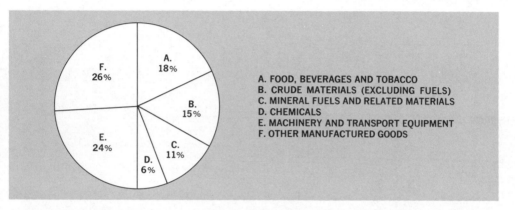

A. FOOD, BEVERAGES AND TOBACCO
B. CRUDE MATERIALS (EXCLUDING FUELS)
C. MINERAL FUELS AND RELATED MATERIALS
D. CHEMICALS
E. MACHINERY AND TRANSPORT EQUIPMENT
F. OTHER MANUFACTURED GOODS

Fig. 2.3.   *The Gross Structure of World Exports in 1963, in per cent by value.*

shown in detail in Figs. 2.5-2.10. Nearly three-fifths of that trade, measured by value, involves manufactures. Machinery and transportation equipment account for nearly one-fourth, manufactures other than chemicals for slightly more than one-fourth, and chemicals for slightly over 6 per cent. Agricultural foods, beverages, and tobacco account for about 18 per cent, crude materials other than fuels for nearly 15 per cent, and fuels for slightly over 10 per cent.

If one compares the commerce of the three major trading blocs as delimited in this chapter, using the world average as a norm, he finds some interesting similarities and differences (Fig. 2.4). Non-Communist, developed economies are below the world average in exports of food, crude materials, and fuels, but very much above that average in shipments of manufactured goods. Communist nations as a group are close to the world average in all categories but machinery, where they exceed the average by a small degree. Less developed economies, on the other hand, export mainly food, agricultural raw materials, ores, and fuels, and are far below the world average in exports of machinery and other manufactured goods. Partially because initial stages of processing take place near mines, the less developed countries approach the world average in the export of base metals much more closely than in other manufacturing categories.

It is not unexpected that the less developed economies are large importers of manufactured goods, particularly machinery. Significantly, however, the proportion of their imports involving food is almost as high as

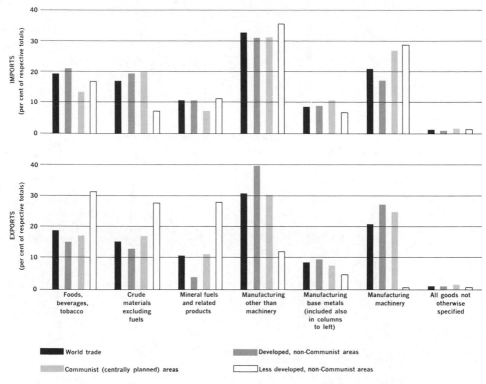

Fig. 2.4. *The Gross Structure of World Trade and of Major Trading Areas in 1960, in per cent by value.*

the world average, and that involving fuels is slightly above the world average. Non-Communist, developed economies import primary commodities at rates above the world average, yet import more manufactured goods than primary commodities. The Communist group is substantially beneath the world average in receipt of food and fuels but is a major importer of machinery.[4]

Graphic Summary

Figures 2.5-2.16 constitute a graphic summary of the volume, direction, and composition of international trade, viewed at the one-digit detail. The conclusions of preceding paragraphs can be verified at a higher level of insight through a study of these graphs.

[4] For an excellent study of trends between 1900 and 1959 in the volume, composition, and pattern of world trade see Alfred Maizels, *Industrial Growth and World Trade* (New York: Cambridge University Press, 1963).

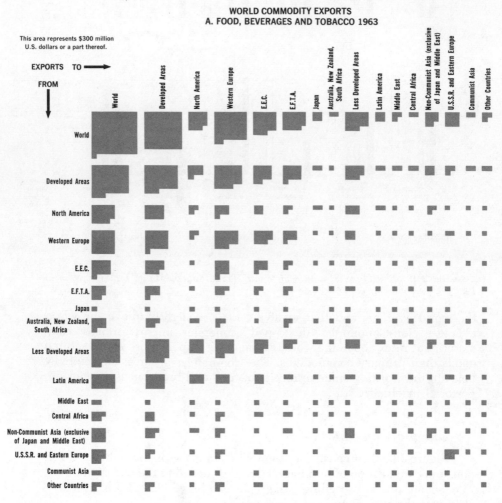

Fig. 2.5.

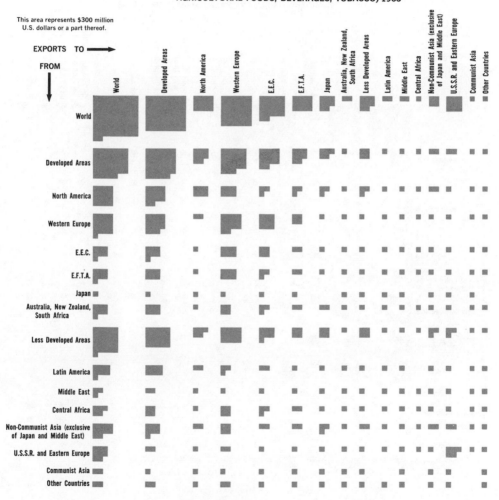

Fig. 2.6.

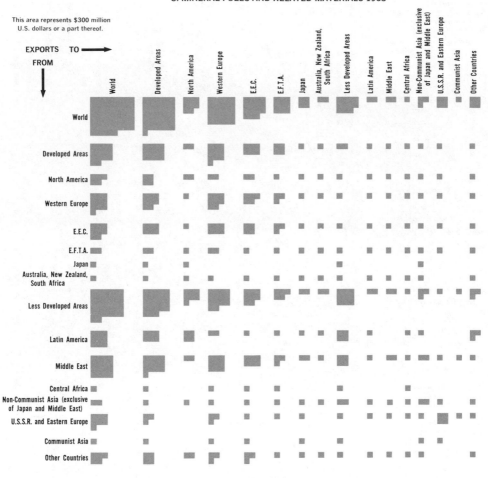

WORLD COMMODITY EXPORTS
C. MINERAL FUELS AND RELATED MATERIALS 1963

Fig. 2.7.

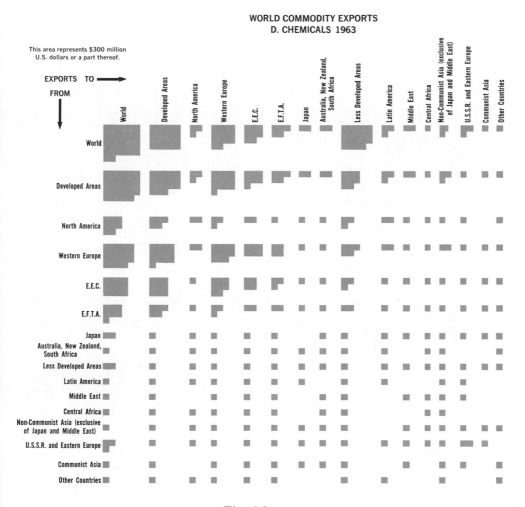

Fig. 2.8.

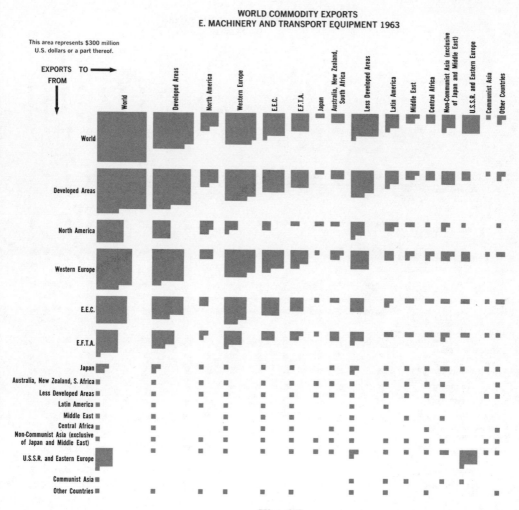

Fig. 2.9.

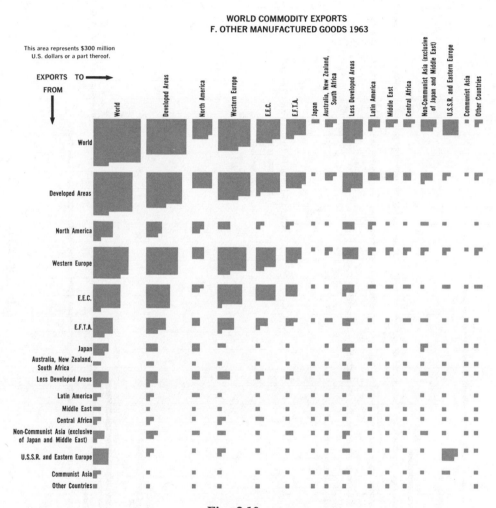

Fig. 2.10.

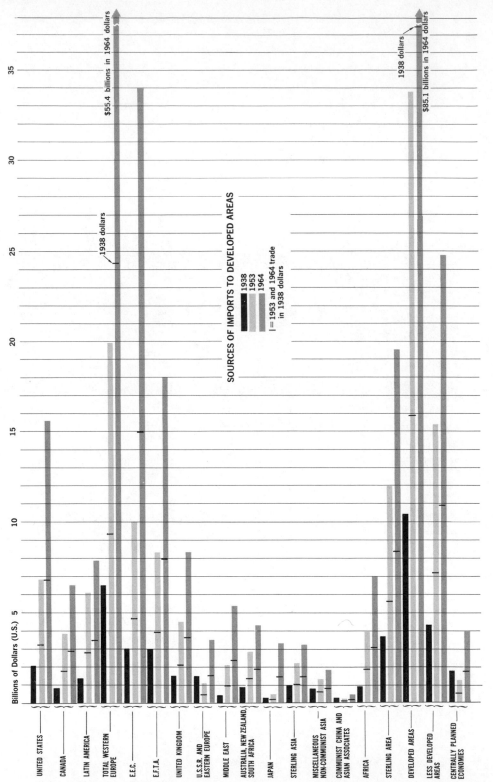

Fig. 2.11.

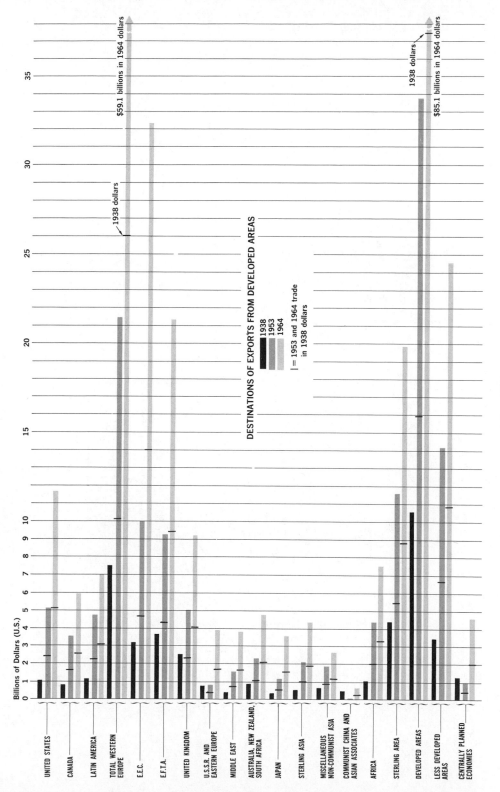

Fig. 2.12.

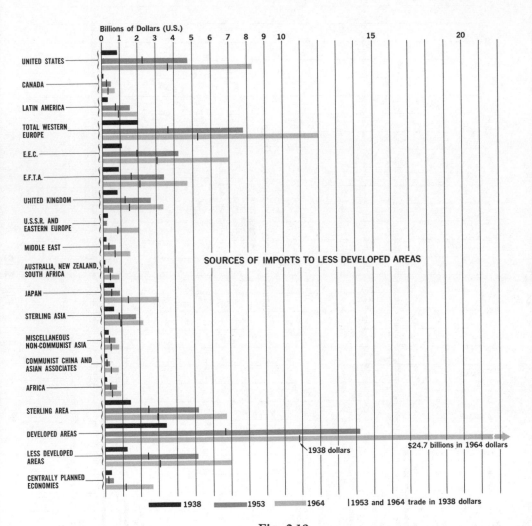

Fig. 2.13.

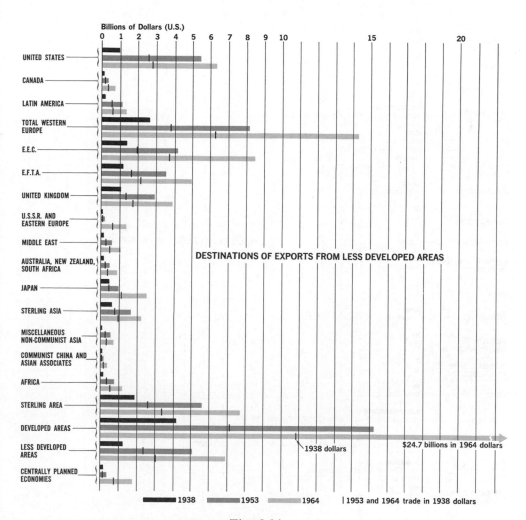

Fig. 2.14.

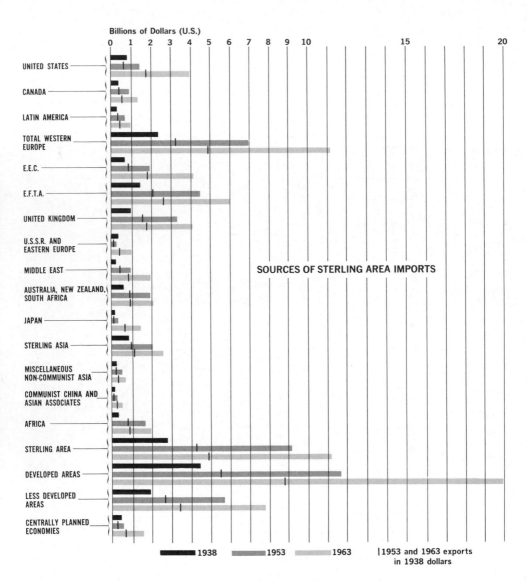

Fig. 2.15.

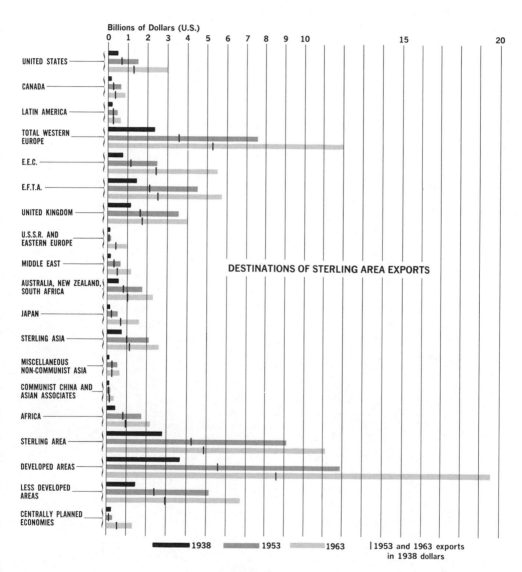

Fig. 2.16.

CHAPTER 3
trade of non-communist, economically advanced countries

The economically advanced countries have emerged from previous chapters as established nuclei of world trade that export increasing amounts of manufactured products, that are continuing to dominate the trade of non-Communist, less developed countries, but that are being challenged by the growing commerce of Communist, or centrally planned, economies. This chapter is an evaluation of the pattern, composition and trends with respect to trade of the economically advanced, non-Communist economies. Specific nations to be considered are:

The Atlantic Community
    The United States
    Canada
    Full members of the European Economic Community (EEC)
    Full members of the European Free Trade Association (EFTA) [1]
    Ireland
    Iceland
    Finland
Countries outside the Atlantic Community
    Japan
    Australia
    New Zealand
    South Africa
    Argentina
    Chile
    Uruguay
    Venezuela
    Israel

[1] Portugal, although not considered economically advanced at this time, is a full member of EFTA and is included in the EFTA assessment.

As a group, these countries are responsible for nearly two-thirds of all imports and over two-thirds of all exports, measured by value. The United States, the EEC, and the EFTA account for over one-half of the value of all imports and exports.

The Atlantic Community

The Atlantic Community, here considered to be comprised of all non-Communist, technically advanced nations in Europe and North America, includes the two major continental nuclei of all world commerce. The Community originates and terminates most of the very heavy intracontinental international traffic within Europe and, to a lesser degree, within North America. Furthermore, each nucleus is in an anchor position with respect to the very active North Atlantic shipping route and is a focal point for other oceanic shipping lanes.

THE UNITED STATES AND CANADA.   These two countries accounted in 1964 for nearly 15 per cent of all imports and over 20 per cent of all exports, with the United States accounting for approximately 11 per cent and 15 per cent, respectively (Table 2.1). International trade is important to both countries, but especially so to Canada, where exports amount to 15 per cent of gross national product as compared with 4 per cent in the United States.[2]

The United States.   Trading patterns for the United States during three selected years beginning in 1938 are shown in Figs. 3.1 and 3.2 and in Table 3.1. In rate of growth compared with the world average, US trade has fluctuated; its position in 1953 was much better than in 1938, but its rate of growth between 1953 and 1964 was slightly below the world average. (Note percentage of world exports accounted for by the US in these years in Table 3.1.) This is a trade emphasizing western Europe, Latin America, Canada, and Japan yet looking to aggregate commerce from the less developed areas for approximately one-third of both exports and imports in 1964. Trends over the 1938-1964 period have favored economically advanced economies, notably the EEC, EFTA, Canada, and Japan. Although the immediate effects of World War II are masked by the particular years selected in the graphs, one can discern a striking increase in the tempo of trade between the United States and Canada, and between the United States and Latin America, in the 1938-1953 period, whereas expansion of United States foreign trade between 1953 and 1964 has pointed up the resurging economies of western Europe and Japan. Despite this relative shift in trading partners, there has been a rise in absolute trade between the United States and most other technically advanced countries (Figs. 3.1 and 3.2).

The trade balance of the United States is highly favorable, with $26.23 billion in merchandise being forwarded and $18.12 billion received in 1964.

---

[2] However, exports amount to a much higher per cent of US production of *movable goods*, reaching nearly 9 per cent of US GNP in the early 1960's.

Table 3.1. Trends in Trade Between the United States and Selected Areas

(In per cent of respective totals)

Trading Partners	Imports 1938	Imports 1953	Imports 1964	Exports 1938	Exports 1953	Exports 1964
US–Canada	13.5	23.5	22.6	15.0	18.8	17.8
Canada–US	65.7	75.4	70.0	32.9	59.5	53.4
US–Western Europe	27.7	20.3	27.9	38.9	18.1	30.3
Western Europe–US	10.3	9.2	10.3	6.3	7.5	7.1
US–EEC	9.7	9.6	15.7	16.2	9.3	17.2
EEC–US	9.3	10.0	10.7	4.7	7.0	6.7
US–EFTA	14.9	8.5	10.1	21.2	6.4	9.7
EFTA–US	12.0	7.5	9.3	7.6	7.6	7.7
US–UK	10.9	4.2	5.5	16.8	3.7	5.7
UK–US	13.3	7.1	11.0	9.5	6.2	8.3
US–Latin America	24.4	33.8	18.8	16.2	18.7	13.9
Latin America–US	35.9	48.7	40.4	30.1	47.3	32.6
US–Japan	5.9	2.2	10.3	7.8	4.3	7.2
Japan–US	24.2	31.0	29.5	11.3	18.5	28.0
US–Sterling Asia	8.5	4.1	4.4 *	2.3	2.1	6.3 *
Sterling Asia–US	5.5	8.3	19.3 *	11.3	10.5	12.5 *
US–Miscellaneous Asia **	8.0	5.3	3.5 *	3.1	4.7	4.7 *
Miscellaneous Asia–US	12.1	30.0	29.8 *	15.9	29.9	22.3 *
US–Middle East	0.7	2.1	2.5	1.0	2.1	3.7
Middle East–US	5.5	14.9	18.0	3.0	7.9	6.1
US–Australia, New Zealand, South Africa	2.1	2.3	4.1 *	5.2	2.4	3.4 *
Australia, New Zealand, South Africa–US	15.7	13.2	16.7 *	5.0	7.4	13.7 *

* 1963
** Asia other than Sterling Asia, Japan, Communist countries and the Middle East.
Source: Calculated from *Yearbook of International Trade Statistics 1963*, and *Monthly Bulletin of Statistics*, June, 1965, United Nations.

Canada is the leading individual nation among trading partners of the United States. Commerce between the two countries rose steadily from the early 1930's until the mid-1950's and subsequently declined relatively while continuing to rise absolutely (Figs. 3.1 and 3.2; Table 3.1).

This is a two-way movement that approaches equilibrium. In 1964, the United States sent goods to Canada valued at $4.66 billion and received merchandise valued at $4.1 billion. However, because of the differing sizes of the two economies, the United States is by far Canada's leading trading partner while depending on Canada for only about 20 per cent of US total foreign commerce.

The composition of this trade differs with direction. Goods moving from the United States to Canada are largely manufactured products, of which over one-half is capital equipment and the remainder industrial supplies. Among detailed categories, the leading single item is automobile parts and accessories, which account for nearly one-eighth of all US exports to Canada. Various categories of machinery and electrical apparatus also are important, as are chemicals. The reverse flow emphasizes industrial supplies and materials, of which well over one-fourth is pulp and paper semimanufactures, especially newsprint. Semifinished and finished machinery and petroleum (including products) are outstanding among commodities of secondary importance.

Western Europe as a trading bloc accounted for approximately 30 per cent of all United States imports and exports in 1964, with the European Economic Community and the European Free Trade Association jointly responsible for some 27 per cent of US imports and exports. Considered as a unit, western Europe thus is the leading trading partner of the United States, and its importance is rising.

The EEC is particularly responsible for this rise. In 1938, the countries now comprising the EEC accounted for a smaller portion of US foreign trade than did the United Kingdom alone (Table 3.1). By 1964, the level of trade between the US and EEC was higher than that with any other US trading partner except Canada. Significantly, the EEC looms larger in the total trade of the US than does the US in total trade of the EEC (Table 3.1). This was true in 1938 (although at the time the EEC as such did not exist), and in 1964. In 1953, when much of Europe was completing postwar rebuilding, the two trading partners were almost equally dependent upon the other's commerce, with the EEC actually relying more heavily upon the United States for its imports than did the US upon the EEC (Table 3.1). In over-all trend, the United States has come to depend upon the EEC during the 25-year period under observation for a much larger share of its imports but has only recently returned to its 1938 dependence concerning exports. The recent expansion of this trade is particularly dramatic when seen in absolute terms (Figs. 3.1 and 3.2).

In actual amount, commerce between these two trading partners favors the United States, which in 1964 sent to the EEC merchandise valued at $4.53 billion while receiving goods from the EEC worth $2.85 billion. This imbalance is not new; it has existed throughout the 1938-1964 period, with occasional exceptions.

If Belgium and Luxembourg are considered a single economic unit, as indeed they are for all practical purposes, one can say that all members of the EEC enter actively into trade with the United States. West Germany is the leader with respect to both US imports and exports, with the others varying in relative positions from year to year. No one country is outstandingly dominant or inactive.

In large measure this is an exchange of semimanufactures and of finished goods. As in US exports to Canada, machinery and electrical apparatus are outstanding among single commodities in eastbound cargoes across the Atlantic, cargoes which also include chemicals and chemical products in various stages of manufacture, textile fibers, and semiprocessed metals to be smelted and refined in Europe. Among leading west-east commodities of agricultural origin are grains and vegetable products. The reverse flow is dominated by automobiles and parts, machinery, and processed metals and textiles.

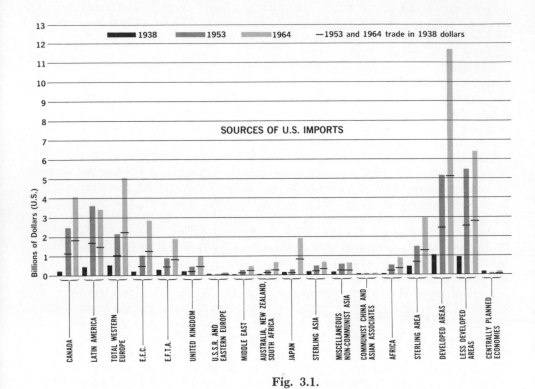

Fig. 3.1.

The European Free Trade Association has varied in significance as a trading partner of the United States. In 1938, the countries now comprising the EFTA supplied nearly 15 per cent of US imports and accepted over 21 per cent of US exports (Table 3.1). In 1964, the EFTA share of US imports and exports was approximately 10 per cent. Between 1953 and 1964, however, EFTA had increased its trade with the United States. Whether the changing trade relationships between the two trading partners represents an increase or decrease thus varies with the periods of appraisal and the years chosen for comparison. However, increases during the 1953-1964 period have not as yet nullified relative declines in the 1938-1964 period, except for US-EFTA exports, which rose from 7.5 per cent of the US total in 1938 to 7.7 per cent in 1964.

EFTA depends less on the United States as a trading partner than does the US upon EFTA. Table 3.1 shows that this condition obtained for all three selected years except 1953, at which time EFTA was the more dependent of the two for exports only.

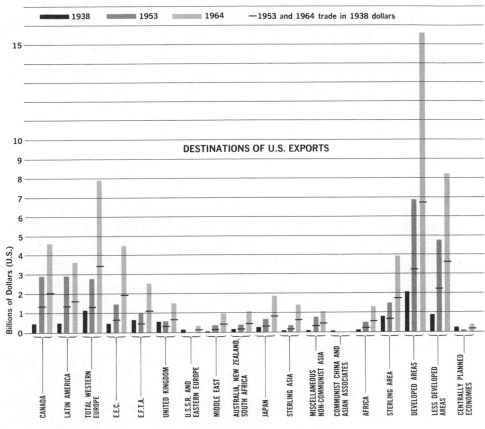

Fig. 3.2.

The balance of trade favors the US over the whole of EFTA but the UK over the US. In 1964, the US sent merchandise valued at $2.55 billion to EFTA while receiving goods worth $1.83 billion and forwarded $0.99 billion worth of cargo to the UK while accepting commodities valued at $1.51 billion.

Although the United Kingdom is the major trading nation in EFTA, trade between Britain and the US expanded more slowly in the 1953-1964 period than did trade between the US and EFTA. Table 3.1 shows that imports to the US from EFTA rose from 8.5 per cent of the US total in 1953 to 10.1 per cent in 1964, while trade between the US and the UK increased from 4.2 per cent to 5.5 per cent in the same years. Exports from the US to EFTA amounted to 6.4 per cent of the US total in 1953 and 9.7 per cent in 1964, whereas comparable shipments to the UK alone were 3.7 and 5.7 per cent respectively. Britain thus appears to be in relative decline, although that decline is slight, among EFTA members in competing for trade with the US. This trend becomes clear in a comparison of relative dependence on trading partners. We have seen that the US depends more heavily upon EFTA with respect to both imports and exports than does EFTA upon the US. However, Britain's situation is the opposite in this respect. Britain relied upon the US in 1964 for 11.0 per cent of its imports (compared with a US reliance upon the UK for only 5.5 per cent of its imports), and for 8.3 per cent of its exports (compared with the US reliance upon the UK for only 5.7 per cent of its exports).

Composition of US-EFTA trade is analogous to that between the US and EEC. Such differences as exist are principally in foodstuffs, which are slightly more important, and industrial supplies, which are slightly less so, than in the US-EEC trade. In the reverse flow, beverages, especially whisky, are more important in EFTA-US movement than in EEC-US trade, whereas other consumer goods are in shorter supply in EFTA-US cargoes than in EEC-US shipping.

Latin America as a trading bloc has been a significant but fluctuating factor in US trade during the entire 1938-1964 period. Ties between the two areas were strongest during and after World War II, when contact between Latin America and countries outside the western hemisphere was weakened, as is suggested in Figs. 3.1 and 3.2 and Table 3.1. The United States consistently has been less dependent upon Latin America as a trading partner than has Latin America been upon the US.

Over-all exchange is closely balanced. In 1964, the United States sent goods to Latin America valued at $3.66 billion and received from Latin America commodities worth $1.87 billion.

In composition, US-Latin American trade is basically an exchange of manufactured and semimanufactured commodities for mineral and agricultural resources. Nearly one-half of all US exports to Latin America involves machinery and vehicles, with industrial machinery and automobiles and parts leading the list. Grains, chemicals and chemical products, and semiprocessed metals also are important. Over one-fourth of the reverse flow involves petroleum and its products, and another one-fourth is made up of coffee. Sugar, bauxite, alumina, and iron ore are outstanding among commodities of lesser significance.

The most interesting aspect of US-Japanese trading relationships is the growing dependence by Japan upon the United States, especially for Japanese exports. Table 3.1 and Figs. 3.1 and 3.2 show this trend clearly. In 1964, Japan sold 28 per cent of all her exports to the US, compared with 18.5 per cent in 1953 and 11.3 per cent in 1938. Japan's role in US exports, in contrast, is not yet so prominent as in 1938. (However, 1938 was a year of large importation by Japan from the US prior to World War II.) This increase in flow of materials from Japan to the United States is also reflected in the rising portion of all US imports that are received from Japan—10.3 per cent in 1964 compared with 2.2 per cent in 1953 and 5.9 per cent in 1938. United States exports to Japan, on the other hand, are not so high in relation to total US exports as in 1938, although they constitute a higher percentage of all Japanese imports than in 1938.

In amount, exchange between the two countries approaches a balance. Goods moving westward across the Pacific were valued at $1.9 billion in 1964, whereas eastbound cargoes were worth $1.87 billion.

Composition of trade between the US and Japan is diverse, with no single commodity or group of commodities outstanding in either direction of movement. Industrial machinery, vegetable products (chiefly vegetable oils) grain, chemicals, and unprocessed and semiprocessed minerals are among the main items forwarded from the United States to Japan, with the leading group, industrial machinery, accounting for slightly less than 17 per cent of the total. Imports to the US from Japan comprise textile fibers and manufactures, metals and manufactures (especially iron and steel products), machinery and apparatus (notably radios), and wood manufactures. The leading category in this list, textile fibers and manufactures, was valued in 1964 at slightly under 19 per cent of all shipments in that year from Japan to the United States.

Individual countries or groups of countries discussed above are responsible for approximately 77 per cent of all US imports and about 66 per cent of all exports. The remaining trading partners of the United States are shown in Figs. 3.1 and 3.2. These are: Australia, New Zealand, and South Africa; the Middle East; sterling Asia; non-Communist Asia other than the sterling countries; Central Africa (i.e., Africa other than South Africa and the African section of the Middle East, with the Middle East here considered to include Tunisia, Algeria and Morocco). All share in this trade, in declining rank as listed. Trade between the US and any respective partner is not heavily imbalanced. Trade between the United States and Communist countries is very small, although it has risen in the past few years.

Foreign trade of the United States thus is both a forwarding and receiving of manufactured goods, agricultural produce, and industrial supplies. More finished goods are sent by the United States than are received; more industrial supplies are received than sent; and the value of incoming and outgoing foods, beverages, and tobacco is about equal.

Canada.   Canada's role in world trade, like that of the United States, expanded between 1938 and 1953 but did not keep pace with world expansion between 1953 and 1964. As is shown in Figs. 3.3 and 3.4 and in Table 3.2, Canada's trade is closely focused upon the United States, in a movement previously analyzed. EFTA and EEC also are important Canadian trading partners. EFTA is the more important of the two blocs, although both Canadian exports and imports to EFTA have declined in the three selected years. Most Canadian trade with EFTA is in fact with the United Kingdom, but this too is in relative decline. On the other hand, Canadian trade with EEC, while much smaller, is expanding, especially in imports from EEC.

The world's three major trading areas account for nearly 85 per cent of Canadian imports and about 75 per cent of the country's exports. Because of the size of each respective economy (considering EEC and EFTA as possessing individual economies), Canada depends much more heavily upon each trading partner than does that partner upon Canada. Except for specialty goods or markets for which alternatives are not readily available, therefore, Canadian trade could be dispensed with rather easily by any of the three trading partners. In view of the fact that Canadian exports amount to about 15 per cent of the country's gross na-

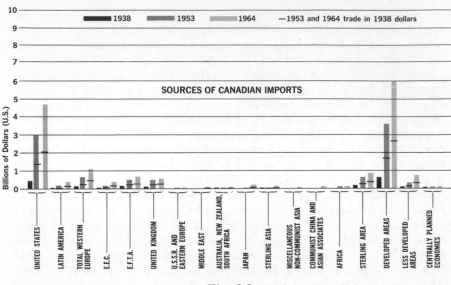

Fig. 3.3.

tional product, Canada's role in world trade emerges as vital to its domestic economy yet expendable from the viewpoint of leading trading partners.

Canadian trade relationships with the country's smaller trading partners vary with the case and year under observation. The country is raising its level of imports from Latin America but has reached at least a temporary plateau in exports to that area. Even so, Canada relies the more heavily of the two upon trade with the other. Commerce with Japan is rising, while that with Australia, New Zealand, and South Africa (the three considered as a single unit) is declining. Trade with selected Communist countries has remained low except in times of grain shortage in Communist China and the Soviet Union, when exports to those places rose sharply. Imports from the Soviet Union and Eastern Europe also rose in 1964 in comparison with 1953.

In gross pattern, Canada's foreign trade has been chiefly with non-Communist, economically developed countries, which have been responsible since 1938 for some 90 per cent of Canada's exports and imports, with the exception of grain shipments to the Soviet Union and mainland China in 1964. However, trade with the sterling area has dropped during the 1938-1964 period, with most of the lost commerce being replaced by the rising trade with the United States.

We have seen that the balance of trade between Canada and the United States favors the latter, but only slightly ($4.66 billion in US 1964 exports to Canada compared with $4.1 billion in Canadian exports to the United States). Canadian trade with EFTA is highly unbalanced in Canada's favor ($1.26 billion in 1964 Canadian exports to EFTA; $0.635 billion in EFTA exports to Canada), and that with EEC also favors Canada ($0.525 billion from Canada to EEC in 1964 compared with $0.37 billion from EEC to Canada). Canada also enjoys a favorable balance of trade with lesser trading partners except Latin America, where the scale is tipped

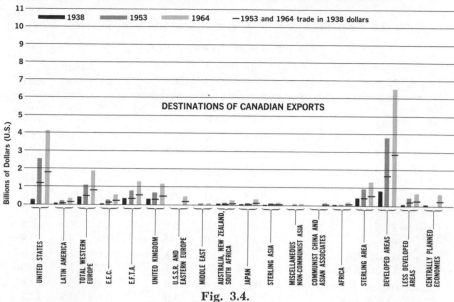

Fig. 3.4.

slightly in favor of the latter. As a generalization, we find that Canada trades favorably in the Eastern Hemisphere to settle its accounts in the Western Hemisphere. All in all, Canada enjoys a favorable balance of trade, exporting goods valued at $7.68 billion in 1964 while receiving merchandise worth $6.66 billion.

Canadian trade is made up largely of imported manufactures and an exported mixture of manufactures, raw materials, and semimanufactures. Some 81 per cent of all imports to Canada in 1960 were partially or fully manufactured, 12 per cent were raw materials, and 7 per cent were partly manufactured. In contrast, 41 per cent of all exports were fully manufactured, 31 per cent partly manufactured, and 28 per cent raw materials. The 15 leading import commodities account for about one-half the value of all incoming products. These are led by non-farm machinery and parts, automobile parts excluding engines, electrical apparatus, crude and partly refined petroleum, and aircraft and parts. Except for coal, all of these 15 are at least partially manufactured at time of entry. However, some raw mineral and agricultural products are to be seen farther down the import list. In exports, the 15 leading commodities amount to about two-thirds of the total. The first five commodities are newsprint, paper, wheat, lumber and timber, wood pulp, and nickel and products. The remaining items involve both raw materials and semifinished goods in nearly equal proportions, as is indicated in the percentages above.

WESTERN EUROPE

The European Economic Community. This is the most active trading unit in the world.[3] Even when considered apart from internal commerce, EEC forwarded merchandise valued at $24.16 billion in 1964

[3] However, it should be remembered that trade between individual members of EEC is as yet considered international commerce, whereas trade between states of the United States or provinces of Canada is considered internal commerce.

Table 3.2.   Trends in Trade Between Canada and Selected Areas

(In per cent of respective totals)

Trading Partners	Imports			Exports		
	1938	1953	1964	1938	1953	1964
Canada–US	65.7	75.4	70.0	32.9	59.5	53.4
US–Canada	13.5	23.5	22.6	15.0	18.8	17.8
Canada–Western Europe	21.4	15.4	15.5	49.7	25.3	23.9
Western Europe–Canada	3.7	3.5	2.4	1.6	2.1	1.4
Canada–EFTA	17.1	12.3	9.5	42.8	18.1	16.4
EFTA–Canada	6.8	5.7	4.6	2.9	4.0	2.7
Canada–UK	16.4	11.3	7.8	40.5	16.0	14.6
UK–Canada	9.0	8.2	8.1	4.7	6.1	4.4
Canada–EEC	3.7	2.9	5.5	6.3	6.3	6.8
EEC–Canada	1.0	1.8	1.2	0.6	0.8	0.9
Canada–Latin America	2.6	3.3	4.8	2.1	4.7	4.0
Latin America–Canada	1.3	3.3	3.4	1.0	1.7	3.0
Canada–Japan	0.6	0.4	2.5	2.4	2.8	4.0
Japan–Canada	2.1	5.5	4.8	0.4	1.2	2.5
Canada–USSR & Eastern Europe	0.8	0.1	0.4	0.7	—	5.7
USSR & Eastern Europe–Canada				0.3	0.05	0.1
USSR–Canada	0.7	—	3.9			
Eastern Europe–Canada	0.5	—	1.4			
Canada–Australia, New Zealand & South Africa	2.0	0.9	1.4 *	7.4	2.4	2.8 *
Australia, New Zealand, South Africa–Canada	6.3	3.5	3.8 *	1.6	1.1	1.7 *

* 1963

Source: As for Table 3.1. Breakdown for USSR and Eastern Europe is due to data arrangement in original source.

compared with US exports of $26.23 billion; and EEC accepted goods worth $23.82 billion compared with US imports of $18.12 billion. Internal traffic of EEC excluded, the group thus is second to the US in exports but more than compensates for this by a very high level of imports and emerges as the leader in total commerce.

The importance of international trade to the European Common Market is indicated by the fact that all exports (including internal EEC trade) amount to about 15 per cent of the EEC aggregate gross domestic product. The outgoing materials are essentially equal in value to incoming goods, so that a trade balance obtains.

European Common Market trade is first and foremost with western Europe—indeed, in the final analysis, with itself. In 1964, 61.7 per cent of EEC imports and 69.6 per cent of EEC exports involved western Europe. The pronounced relative growth of this trade is shown in Figs. 3.7 and 3.8 and in Table 3.3. The consistent rise in western Europe as a trading partner with EEC is clear, not only with respect to EEC ship-

Table 3.3. Trends in Trade Between EEC and Other Countries of Western Europe

(In per cent of respective totals)

Trading Partners	Imports			Exports		
	1938	1953	1964	1938	1953	1964
EEC—Western Europe (including EEC)	47.2	51.6	61.7	57.8	57.7	69.6
Western Europe—EEC	21.8	27.5	38.6	27.0	26.1	36.8
EEC—EEC	22.6	31.5	43.6	27.5	31.3	43.2
EEC—EFTA	19.0	16.5	14.9	23.6	20.4	20.8
EFTA—EEC	19.0	22.4	32.1	24.3	20.0	26.7
EEC—UK	5.8	6.4	5.6	10.7	6.2	5.3
UK—EEC	12.0	11.1	16.6	12.8	13.1	19.8

Source: Same as in Table 3.1.

ments to western Europe, but also in the reverse flow. That EEC is its own best customer is attested by the rising share of internal traffic as a percentage of all EEC commerce, with the 1964 percentage for imports nearly twice that of 1938 and the rise in exports almost as spectacular. When one remembers that the total commerce of the area now known as EEC has more than tripled since 1938, even when measured in constant dollars, the importance of the above percentages is re-emphasized. That western Europe also is increasingly dependent upon EEC is shown in Table 3.3.

European Common Market imports from EFTA have declined relatively in the 1953-1964 period, while exports have remained at about the 1953 level. In neither category did percentages reach their 1938 levels. EFTA, in contrast, has increased its import dependence upon EEC in each reporting year; its export dependence is above the 1938 level. Meanwhile, internal trade of the European Common Market has risen rapidly in comparison with internal commerce of EFTA (Tables 3.3 and 3.5).

The United Kingdom accounted in 1964 for over one-third of all EEC imports from EFTA and accepted over one-fourth of all European Common Market exports to EFTA. However, the role of the UK appears to have declined somewhat in the 1953-1964 period: the UK forwarded only 5.6 per cent of all EEC imports in 1964 compared with 6.4 per cent in 1953, and accepted from the European Common Market only 5.3 per cent of EEC's total exports in 1964 compared with 6.2 per cent in 1953. These figures would suggest that the role of the UK in EEC commerce is not only declining slightly in itself but also with respect to EFTA's role in EEC commerce. Meanwhile, the European Common Market is rising sharply as a factor in UK commerce, accounting for 16.6 per cent of all UK imports in 1964 compared with 11.1 per cent in 1953, and 19.8 per cent of all 1964 exports from the UK compared with 13.1 per cent in 1953.

Countries of western Europe other than the two major trading blocs have declined relatively as EEC trading partners, aggregately accounting

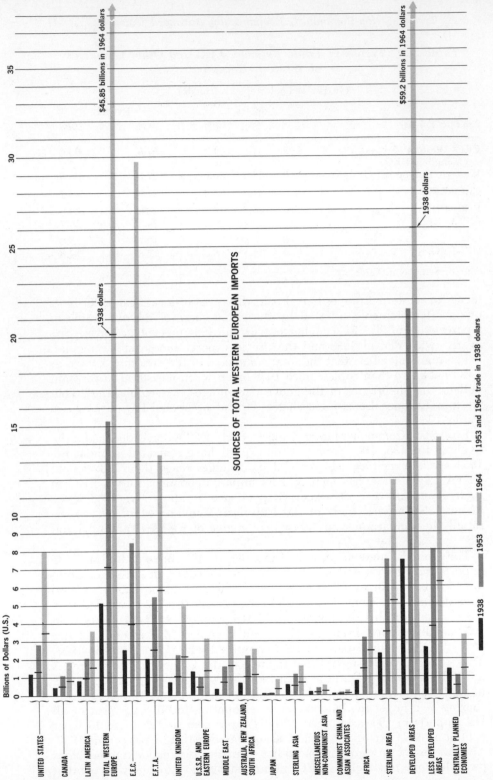

Billions of Dollars (U.S.)

$45.85 billions in 1964 dollars

1938 dollars

$59.2 billions in 1964 dollars

1938 dollars

SOURCES OF TOTAL WESTERN EUROPEAN IMPORTS

1953 and 1964 trade in 1938 dollars

1964

1953

1938

UNITED STATES
CANADA
LATIN AMERICA
TOTAL WESTERN EUROPE
E.E.C.
E.F.T.A.
UNITED KINGDOM
U.S.S.R. AND EASTERN EUROPE
MIDDLE EAST
AUSTRALIA, NEW ZEALAND, SOUTH AFRICA
JAPAN
STERLING ASIA
MISCELLANEOUS NON-COMMUNIST ASIA
COMMUNIST CHINA AND ASIAN ASSOCIATES
AFRICA
STERLING AREA
DEVELOPED AREAS
LESS DEVELOPED AREAS
CENTRALLY PLANNED ECONOMIES

Fig. 3.5.

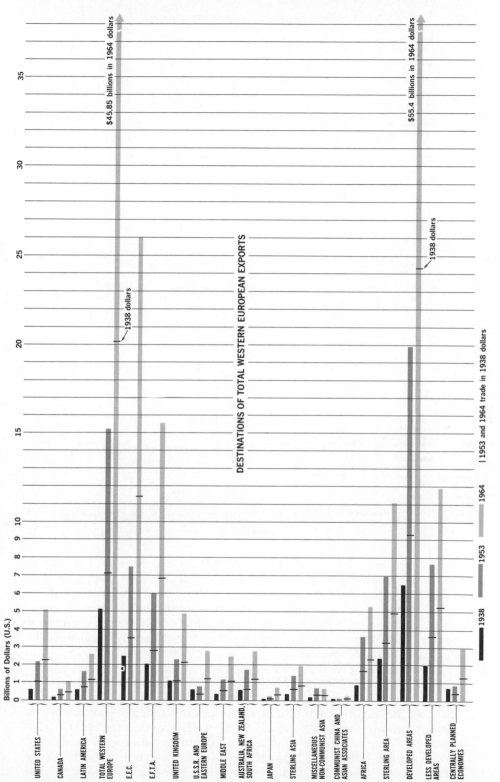

DESTINATIONS OF TOTAL WESTERN EUROPEAN EXPORTS

Fig. 3.6.

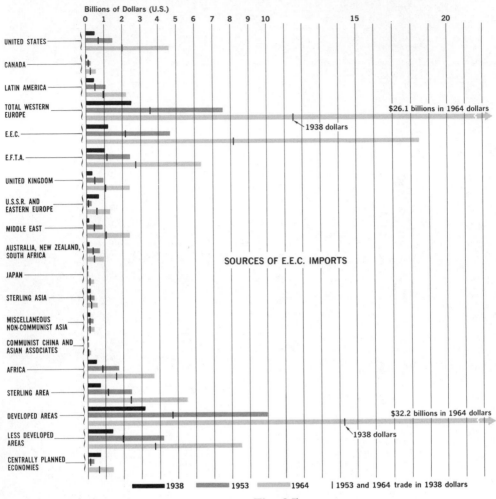

Fig. 3.7.

for 3.2 per cent of EEC imports in 1964 compared with 5.5 per cent in 1938, and accepting 5.7 per cent of EEC exports in 1964 compared with 6.6 per cent in 1938. (For a graphic indication, see Figs. 3.5 and 3.6.)

The increase in EEC trade in western Europe thus largely is an increase in internal EEC commerce, with both EFTA and unaffiliated countries of western Europe either remaining relatively unchanged or declining in importance.

Manufactured products dominate trade between EEC and western Europe (including EEC). Although Europe traditionally is regarded as an importer of raw materials and fuels and an exporter of finished products, we find nearly one-fourth of all European Common Market imports (value measurement) to be made up of machinery and transport equipment and over one-fourth of other manufactures (chemicals excepted). Well over one-fifth of EEC imports involves crude materials, and another fifth is foods, beverages, and tobacco. Only one-tenth includes mineral

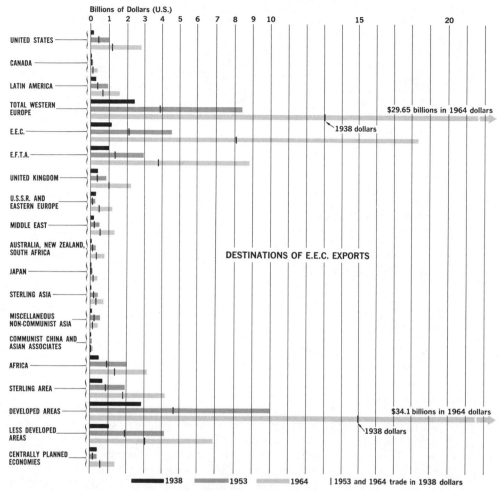

Fig. 3.8.

fuels, and over one-fifteenth is made up of chemicals and chemical products. Nearly one-third of all EEC exports are metals and machinery, and
slightly over one-third involves other manufactures (again, without chemicals). Chemicals and chemical products amount to nearly one-tenth of
EEC exports; foods, beverages, and tobacco to slightly over one-tenth;
mineral fuels to nearly one-tenth; and crude materials the small remainder.
Internal EEC trade, included in the above summaries, is not markedly
different in composition from the over-all pattern.

The balance of EEC external trade favors EEC over other areas in
western Europe: in 1964, EEC forwarded $11.23 billion of merchandise
to other areas of western Europe and received $7.65 billion in imports
from those areas. The balance with EFTA is slightly more favorable than
with unaffiliated countries: again in 1964, EEC sent $8.84 billion to
EFTA, while receiving $6.3 billion worth of goods in return.

Beyond Europe, the European Economic Community does not have

Table 3.4. Trends in Trade Between EEC and Selected Areas

(In per cent of respective totals)

Trading Partners	Imports			Exports		
	1938	1953	1964	1938	1953	1964
EEC–Latin America	8.2	7.2	5.2	7.7	6.5	3.8
Latin America–EEC	24.3	15.9	17.8	25.4	13.8	20.9
EEC–Middle East	2.8	6.1	5.5	4.9	3.5	3.2
Middle East–EEC	37.1	23.1	24.9	28.0	31.6	31.1
EEC–Japan	0.5	0.3	0.9	0.9	0.7	0.9
Japan–EEC	4.0	4.6	6.1	2.4	3.9	5.5
EEC–Australia, New Zealand, South Africa	2.7	4.8	2.2 *	1.8	2.0	1.7 *
Australia, New Zealand, South Africa–EEC	7.8	10.4	13.7 *	16.3	21.0	16.4 *
EEC–USSR & Eastern Europe	12.6	1.9	3.0	7.9	1.9	2.8
USSR & Eastern Europe–EEC				34.2	4.0	6.9
USSR–EEC	25.0	3.2	5.1			
Eastern Europe–EEC	35.7	5.7	8.0			
EEC–Communist China & Asian Associates	0.9	0.5	0.3	1.1	0.3	0.3
Communist China & Asian Associates–EEC	8.0	3.5	7.6	11.9	6.2	7.8

* 1963

Source: Same as in Table 3.1.

very active trading partners from its own point of view. The United States supplies some 10.7 per cent of EEC imports and accepts 6.7 per cent of EEC exports in a movement previously described (Table 3.1). Canada sends some 1.2 per cent of EEC imports and accepts 0.9 per cent of EEC exports (Table 3.2). Other trading partners are shown in Table 3.4.

Latin America, the Middle East, and the Soviet Union and eastern Europe are the principal trading partners of this group. Significantly, trading dependency in each case favors the EEC, in most instances by a wide margin. In 1964, 17.8 per cent of Latin American imports and 20.9 per cent of that area's exports concerned EEC, which relied upon Latin America for only 5.2 per cent of EEC imports and 3.8 per cent of EEC exports. Table 3.4 indicates that analogous conditions of imbalance obtain with respect to other minor trading partners of EEC. This is true of EEC trade with Communist as well as non-Communist countries.

In composition, trade between EEC and minor trading partners largely involves petroleum and products from the Middle East; petroleum and products plus selected agricultural raw materials from Latin America; agricultural and semiprocessed raw materials and mineral products from Australia, New Zealand, and South Africa; petroleum and products, wood, coal, wheat, various additional agricultural raw materials, some chemicals and fertilizers, and selected raw mineral products from the Communist countries. Exports to all areas emphasize machinery and semi-processed but diverse additional manufactures and semi-manufactures.

In summary, EEC is the most active trading unit in the world. It trades largely with itself and with other western European nations. Its over-all trade is in balance; but such a balance does not characterize individual trading relationships, which tend to be unfavorable in western Europe and favorable beyond Europe. Despite large and expanding markets within individual member countries, EEC exports merchandise valued at about 15 per cent of its aggregate gross domestic product. However, when exports to other EEC nations are removed, the figure drops to 11 per cent. Current trends indicate an even higher dependence upon western Europe, and a corresponding decrease in dependency beyond Europe, than is now the case. Because so many trading partners outside Europe, both developed and underdeveloped, are heavily committed to trade with EEC, such trends could be detrimental to these outlying countries. However, because the type of exports from these areas cannot be entirely duplicated by European products or substitutes, an irreducible minimum amount of trade beyond Europe can be expected to continue.

The exchange between EEC and its trading partners largely involves specialized types of manufactures plus certain specialized raw materials where manufacturing nations are trading partners and shipment of raw materials and energy sources to EEC from underdeveloped economies which receive machinery and other manufactured goods in return. Trade in manufactures between such technically advanced units as EEC and the United States now is so specialized that one must look to the fine meshes of classification—third or fourth digit details—to find commodities in which each area still specializes in production.[4] Significantly, much of the movement of machinery from the United States to EEC involves capital equipment to produce merchandise EEC now is importing, so that one may expect this specialization of exported product to become even more refined as each producing unit "tools up" to maximum advantage in production.

The European Free Trade Area. The EFTA is comprised of seven full members—six on the continent of Europe plus the United Kingdom. The six are Norway, Sweden, Denmark, Austria, Switzerland, and Portugal. The trade of the European Free Trade Association is dominated by commerce of the United Kingdom to a degree not duplicated in EEC by any of its members; in 1964, the UK received and forwarded approximately one-half of all EFTA imports and exports (Figs. 3.9-3.12). Approximately 20 per cent of EFTA trade that year (slightly more regarding exports) was internal, while over 40 per cent of all EEC trade fell into this category. Total trade is unbalanced away from EFTA, which in 1964 sent $23.6 billion into world markets and received $27.5 billion. Considered by total trade, the European Free Trade Association is ex-

---

[4] Some cross flows also are due to the "geography of the firm"; individual trading concerns have their own specific "contacts" at home and abroad and may order goods for a customer from a foreign "contact" rather than a domestic source, or vice versa, despite nearer supply sources of the commodity.

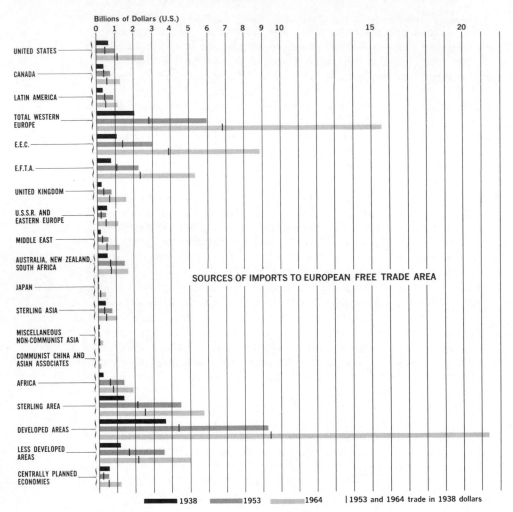

Fig. 3.9.

ceeded in world commerce only by EEC (1964: $84.8 billion for EEC; $51.11 billion for EFTA; $44.35 billion for US). However, when internal shipments are excluded, the total value of EFTA commerce is less than that of either EEC or the US (1964: $66.39 billion for EEC; $44.35 billion for US; $40.51 billion for EFTA).

As with EEC, western Europe is very important in the commerce of EFTA, (shown in Table 3.5 and Figs. 3.9 and 3.10).

The European Free Trade Association thus relies upon western Europe, including internal EFTA traffic, for over one-half of all imports and exports. The dependence has increased between 1938 and 1964 with respect to both imports and exports, but especially the former. This increase has been due mainly to growth in trade between EFTA and EEC and only secondarily to growth of commerce within EFTA. Countries in western Europe other than the two major trading blocs have varied in aggregate role

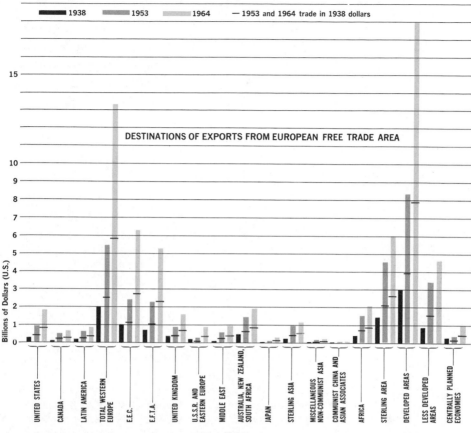

Fig. 3.10.

but on the whole have declined between 1938 and 1964. EFTA's importance to trading partners, on the other hand, has varied with specific partners. The whole of western Europe has remained rather consistently dependent upon countries now in EFTA for the 1938-1964 period. However, EEC has become less dependent upon EFTA and EFTA more dependent upon itself. The balance of trade between EFTA and the remainder of western Europe favors the latter slightly. All major classifications of goods are traded, with machinery and transportation equipment leading the list and miscellaneous manufactures very important.

Although both the European Free Trade Association and the European Common Market rely heavily upon western Europe for international trade, EFTA looks beyond western Europe to a greater degree than does EEC (Tables 3.3 and 3.5). The significant role of the US in EFTA trade has been noted (Table 3.1, ff.) as has the role of Canada (Table 3.2 ff.). Other trading partners are shown in Table 3.6. In addition to partners shown in the table, about 5 per cent of all EFTA exports and imports involve Asia other than Japan, and an additional 5 per cent are with Africa other than the Middle East and South Africa. All in all, EFTA trade with areas beyond Europe is well distributed among those

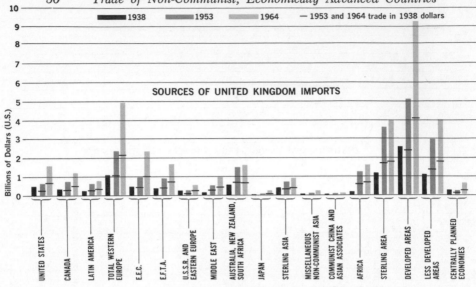

Fig. 3.11.

areas, as is indicated in Table 3.6. In every case, the trading partner is more heavily dependent upon EFTA than is EFTA on the partner, and the difference usually is rather large. If, therefore, the current trend continues toward increased trade on a relative as well as an absolute basis between EFTA and Western Europe, some of EFTA's trading partners will experience problems of readjustment when they are forced to find new markets and sources of supplies.

Meanwhile, the total balance of the European Free Trade Association trade to all parts of the world is unfavorable, although not substantially so. The imbalance is particularly heavy in fuels but can be seen also in foods and beverages and crude materials other than agricultural. In manufactured goods, EFTA enjoys a favorable balance that, however, does not fully offset the unfavorable situation in the above-mentioned categories.

Other economically advanced countries in Europe.   Finland, Ireland, and Iceland are economically advanced nations of western Europe that are not closely affiliated with a trading bloc, although Finland is an associate member of EFTA.[5] Their total volume of commerce amounts to about 3 per cent of all western European trade.[6]

Of the three, Finland commands by far the most trade. Exports and imports of the country are essentially in balance. As is true with so many modern economies, machinery and transport equipment are the principal commodities imported. Pulp, paper, paperboard, and lumber are clearly

[5] Associate membership in EFTA as applied to Finland pertains especially to certain aspects of administration. Concerning tariffs, Finland has until Dec. 31, 1967 to eliminate import duties from other EFTA members. For full members of EFTA, the final date for elimination of all import duties on goods from other members was Dec. 31, 1966.

[6] Western Europe is here considered to include EEC, EFTA, Iceland, Ireland, Finland, Greece, Spain, Turkey, and Yugoslavia, as grouped in the United Nations *Yearbook of International Trade Statistics.*

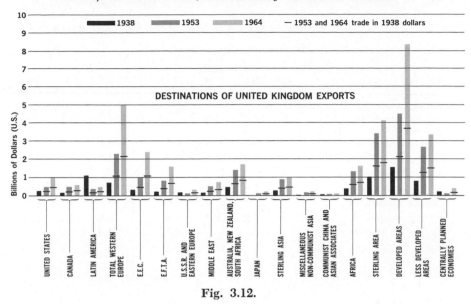

Fig. 3.12.

dominant in the relatively small number of export commodities. Trade is largely with EFTA, EEC, the USSR, and the United States.

Ireland's trade is unfavorably out of balance. Machinery and transport equipment lead in the country's substantial imports, with other manufactures a close second. More than one-half of the country's exports are agricultural products, with live cattle and fresh meat leading the lists. Well over one-third of all commerce is with the United Kingdom, and most of the remainder is with other countries of western Europe, with the United States, or with Canada.

EFTA, EEC, the USSR and the United States all are major trading partners with Iceland, in whose trade imports also exceed exports by a considerable margin. Imports are manufactured goods, especially machinery and transport equipment, while over two-thirds of all exports are fish products.

Table 3.5. Trends in Trade Between EFTA and Other Countries of Western Europe

(In per cent of respective totals)

Trading Partners	Imports			Exports		
	1938	1953	1964	1938	1953	1964
EFTA–Western Europe	37.9	44.8	56.6	48.8	45.2	56.5
Western Europe–EFTA	17.5	17.7	17.3	22.3	20.8	22.0
EFTA–EEC	19.0	22.4	32.1	24.3	20.0	26.7
EEC–EFTA	19.0	16.5	14.9	23.6	20.4	20.8
EFTA–EFTA	14.1	17.1	19.3	18.4	19.0	22.4

Source: Same as in Table 3.1.

Table 3.6.   Trends in EFTA Trade With Selected Areas

(In per cent of respective totals)

Trading Partners	Imports 1938	1953	1964	Exports 1938	1953	1964
EFTA—Australia, New Zealand, South Africa	9.8	11.0	5.5 *	12.0	11.8	8.0 *
Australia, New Zealand, South Africa—EFTA	49.0	50.1	36.9 *	60.1	44.0	26.8 *
EFTA—Latin America	6.4	6.7	4.0	5.6	5.1	3.5
Latin America—EFTA	17.0	10.1	9.2	20.5	11.7	10.5
EFTA—Middle East	2.8	4.2	4.1	2.9	4.7	4.1
Middle East—EFTA	20.7	25.1	17.6	29.0	20.1	15.2
EFTA—Japan	0.8	0.4	1.4	0.8	0.7	1.2
Japan—EFTA	3.2	3.7	4.5	4.0	4.3	5.9
EFTA—USSR and Eastern Europe	9.8	3.4	4.0	5.2	2.3	2.7
USSR and Eastern Europe—EFTA				27.3	6.8	6.0
USSR—EFTA	23.2	3.0	4.2			
Eastern Europe—EFTA	19.5	5.6	5.4			

* 1963
Source: Same as in Table 3.1.

Countries Outside the Atlantic Community

Economically advanced countries outside the Atlantic Community account for about nine per cent of all world trade—somewhat less than does the United Kingdom. Specific countries in this group are Japan, Australia, New Zealand, South Africa, Venezuela, Argentina, Chile, Uruguay, and Israel.

Japan.   Japan is by far the leader in this group, being responsible for over 40 per cent of the group's total trade and between 3 and 4 per cent of all world trade. Japanese foreign trade, slightly favorable as to balance, is increasing rapidly. Primary trading partners and trends are indicated in Table 3.7 and in Figs. 3.13-3.14. (However, see footnote, Table 3.7.) Japanese trade, long oriented to Asia, has been partially readjusted since World War II and the subsequent Communist assertion in Asia. Thus an Asia (other than Communist China and the Middle East) that supplied 43.8 per cent of Japanese imports in 1938 sent only 16.6 per cent in 1964. The same area received 42.3 per cent of Japan's exports in 1938 and only 26.6 per cent in 1964. (These data are all the more remarkable when we remember that Korea, Taiwan, and other sections of Asia were under Japanese control in 1938, and hence not "foreign.") Asia's loss has been the gain of other areas, especially the United States, as a receiving market for Japanese goods. Western Europe does not figure very prominently in Japanese foreign commerce, although its role is enlarging. EEC is slightly more active as a trading partner than EFTA. Trade also is increasing between Japan on the one hand and Australia, New Zealand, and South Africa on the other. This is true particularly of exports to Japan. Ties between Japan and the Middle East are strengthening, again with emphasis on imports to Japan. Latin America's role is important, although fluctuating. Canada as yet occupies a relatively minor position as a trading partner, but it accepts more Japanese exports than in earlier years. Trade with Communist countries is comparatively small but rising. Mainland China's role, greatly reduced in the early 1950's, has grown in recent years.

Japanese foreign trade is well balanced in total movement but very skewed within specific categories. Foodstuffs and beverages, crude non-agricultural materials, and fuels are all imported in larger quantities than they are exported. However, manufactured goods, especially the miscellaneous group, are exported in very large quantities, making the balance of trade in this category highly favorable to Japan.

Other countries.   The remaining eight technically advanced countries, which together account for about 7 per cent of the world's trade, are primarily exporters of agricultural and other crude materials and importers of manufactured goods. Six are especially so: Australia, New Zealand, South Africa, Venezuela, Argentina, and Uruguay. Chile and Israel are the exceptions. In a sense, however, Chile is not an exception, because the country's primary export, copper from domestic mines, is concentrated or refined before export and thus technically is a manufactured product rather than a crude material. Israel's case is quite unusual in that the country's export as well as import lists are dominated by manufactures. But, as will be explained below, Israel's ratio of imports to export in manufactured goods is very high, so that the country joins certain other technically advanced economies in this group as a prime importer of manufactured goods.

With the exceptions noted, this group of nations is in a trading position similar to those of many less developed economies in that the terms of trade are trending against crude materials, especially agricultural products, in the world markets. Stated differently, countries exporting such crude materials are paying more and more for their purchased manufactured goods than they are obtaining for their exports. Other factors not considered, their outflows of currency thus are increasingly exceeding their inflows.

Six of the eight countries enjoy a trade that is balanced or nearly so, while Israel and Uruguay are experiencing unfavorable imbalances. For Israel, imports are exceeding exports at ratios sometimes greater than 2:1; and this figure applies not only to crude materials and fuels, but also to the manufactured goods that dominate outgoing cargoes. Public and private foreign assistance is relied upon to overcome the resulting deficits in payments. Uruguay's situation is not so extreme, but the country lacks adequate resources to adjust balance of payments deficits accompanying the imbalances of trade and currently is attempting to adjust this difference.

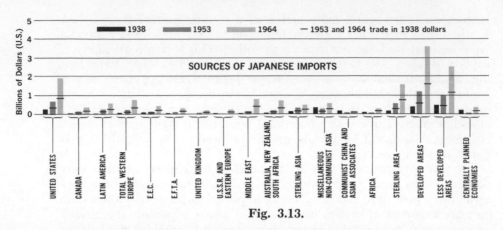

Fig. 3.13.

All eight countries are in somewhat unusual circumstances in the world market place in that, individually or as a group, they do not command a sizable amount of trade. Like the less developed countries to be discussed in the next chapter, these countries act almost as uncommitted agents, seeking the best market conditions at a given time. Australia and New Zealand still benefit from membership in the sterling area and the Commonwealth. However, as has been shown in Chapter 2 (Table 2.1), trade in the sterling area is in relative decline, and no new bloc or group has arisen to replace it in tying these outlying areas to a major nodal market.

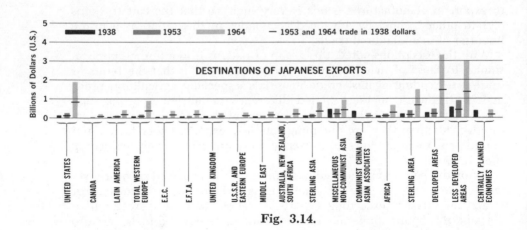

Fig. 3.14.

Table 3.7. Trends in Trade Between Japan and Trading Partners

(In per cent of respective totals)

Trading Partners	Imports			Exports		
	1938	1953	1964	1938	1953	1964
Japan—Asia *	43.8	26.1	16.6	42.3	42.8	26.6
Asia *—Japan	22.8	6.9	15.3	16.4	9.0	12.2
Japan—US	24.2	31.0	29.5	11.3	18.5	28.0
US—Japan	5.9	2.2	10.3	7.8	4.3	7.2
Japan—Western Europe	7.5	9.4	11.0	6.7	9.4	12.8
Western Europe—Japan	0.6	0.3	1.1	0.8	0.7	1.0
Japan—EEC	4.0	4.6	6.1	2.4	3.9	5.5
EEC—Japan	0.5	0.3	0.9	0.9	0.7	0.9
Japan—EFTA	3.2	3.7	4.5	4.0	4.3	5.9
EFTA—Japan	0.8	0.4	1.4	0.8	0.7	1.2
Japan—Australia, New Zealand, South Africa	2.4	4.8	10.7	3.0	3.1	5.9
Australia, New Zealand, South Africa—Japan	5.8	1.4	6.9	2.6	3.1	12.8
Japan—Latin America	2.4	11.3	8.0	1.2	8.2	5.9
Latin America—Japan	1.0	1.7	4.4	1.4	3.2	4.9
Japan—Middle East	1.4	4.8	11.4	2.0	3.7	4.3
Middle East—Japan	3.9	2.1	5.3	2.6	3.7	9.8
Japan—USSR & Eastern Europe	1.4	0.3	3.0	0.09	—	3.2
USSR & Eastern Europe—Japan				0.7	0.08	1.1
USSR—Japan	0.3	—	2.4			
Eastern Europe—Japan	—	—	0.3			
Japan—Canada	2.1	5.5	4.8	8.4	1.2	2.5
Canada—Japan	0.6	0.4	2.5	2.4	2.8	4.0
Japan—Communist China & Asian Associates	14.6	1.2	1.8	29.7	0.3	2.5
Communist China and Asian Associates—Japan	52.8	0.2	10.7	34.5	2.3	6.6

* Asia other than Middle East and Communist (centrally planned) countries. Data for 1938 do not regard Korea, Taiwan, and other Asian areas then under Japanese control as foreign. The 1938 figures for Japan-Asia trade thus are lower than are 1953 and 1964 figures.

Source: Same as in Table 3.1.

CHAPTER 4 *trade of the less developed and the centrally planned countries*

We have seen in the preceding chapter that the world's economically advanced nations are responsible for about two-thirds of all international trade, that their share is rising, and that they are exchanging increasingly with other developed areas. In this chapter we shall examine the trade of less developed economies, which account for about one-fifth of all international trade, and of the Communist, or centrally planned economies, which originate and terminate the remaining one-eighth.

Trade of the Less Developed Countries

Table 4.1 shows selected groupings of less developed economies and the share of trade accounted for by each grouping.

ASIA.   The non-Communist, less developed countries of Asia, considered as a unit, constitute the most active trading group among the less developed economies. In this chapter, these countries are classified into two categories: those adhering to the sterling area and those outside that area. As can be seen in Table 4.1, the commerce of sterling Asia is more than twice as large as that of miscellaneous Asian countries.

Sterling Asia.   The leading trading countries of both groups are shown in Table 4.2, arranged in a declining rank by value of exports. In sterling Asia, India is easily the leader, followed by those long-standing re-export centers, Singapore and Hong Kong. Malaya's specialty exports enable that country to achieve a third ranking position above Hong Kong in the export column, although its total trade is less than that of Hong Kong. Pakistan's fifth position is due mainly to imports. All other countries in this group are minor trading units.

The changing direction of sterling Asia's trade is indicated in Tables 4.3 and 4.4 and in Figs. 4.1 and 4.2. The trade is somewhat unusual in

Table 4.1. International Trade Groupings of Less Developed Economies

(In per cent of total trade of all less developed economies)

Trading Grouping	Imports	Exports
Asia	36.5	31.5
(Sterling Asia)	(24.8)	(21.8)
(Miscellaneous Asia *)	(11.7)	(9.7)
Middle East **	17.8	24.5
Latin America ***	20.0	18.9
All Other ****	25.7	25.1

* Excludes the Middle East, Sterling Asia, Communist Asia, and Japan. (For countries included, see Table 4.2.)

** In Africa, excludes Tunisia and countries to the west of Tunisia. (For specific countries included, see Table 4.7.)

*** Excludes Argentina, Venezuela, Uruguay, and Chile, here considered economically advanced.

**** Includes Tunisia, Algeria, Morocco, all of Central Africa (between Middle East and South Africa), plus Netherlands Antilles, Jamaica, Trinidad and Tobago, and numerous small economies.

Source: Calculated from Table A, United Nations *Yearbook of International Trade, 1963.*

that whereas only three countries are predominant, several countries are so active in a secondary way that their individual as well as aggregate trade is important.

Among individual countries, the United States is the leading trading

Table 4.2. Leading Trading Groups and Countries in Asia

	Sterling Asia	
	Per cent of Sterling Asia Trade	
Country	Imports	Exports
India	28.7	28.1
Singapore	19.2	19.4
Malaya	11.3	15.1
Hong Kong	17.8	14.9
Pakistan	12.2	7.1
Ceylon	4.3	6.2
Burma	3.2	4.6
Other *	3.3	4.6

	Miscellaneous Asia	
	Per cent of Miscellaneous Asia Trade	
Country	Imports	Exports
Philippines	19.1	28.5
Indonesia	15.7	27.3
Thailand	18.4	18.5
Nationalist China (Taiwan)	11.2	13.0
Korea	17.3	3.4
South Viet-Nam	8.8	3.0
Other **	9.5	6.3

* Sarawak, Sabah, Brunei
** Ryukyu Islands, Cambodia, Laos

Source: As for Table 4.1.

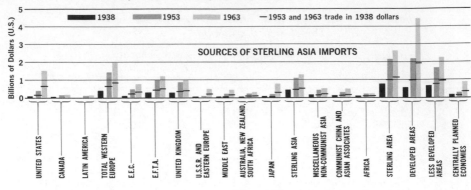

Fig. 4.1.

partner of sterling Asia, accounting in 1963 for 19.3 per cent of all of that area's imports and 12.5 per cent of exports. Trends in this trade since 1938 are upward from the viewpoint of the Asian countries, particularly

Table 4.3.   Trade Between Sterling Asia and Selected Non-Communist Areas

(In per cent of respective totals)

| | Imports | | | Exports | | |
Trading Partners	1938	1953	1963	1938	1953	1963
Sterling Asia—US	5.5	8.3	19.3	11.3	10.5	12.5
US—Sterling Asia	8.5	4.1	4.4	2.3	2.1	6.3
Sterling Asia—UK	21.2	20.5	13.1	23.6	16.5	15.0
UK—Sterling Asia	9.7	8.4	7.3	11.1	11.5	8.6
Sterling Asia—Japan	5.5	3.4	9.6	5.6	7.3	8.1
Japan—Sterling Asia	9.1	14.1	8.4	6.3	10.6	13.1
Sterling Asia—Western Europe	28.7	34.8	25.9	35.8	28.0	28.0
Western Europe—Sterling Asia	4.9	3.8	2.4	3.9	4.8	3.1
Sterling Asia—EEC	5.5	10.9	9.9	11.3	9.3	9.3
EEC—Sterling Asia	3.3	2.6	1.4	1.7	3.0	2.0
Sterling Asia—EFTA	22.8	23.4	15.6	24.2	17.7	16.6
EFTA—Sterling Asia	7.1	5.5	4.0	7.0	7.8	5.3
Sterling Asia—Sterling Asia	32.3	25.3	16.5	25.8	24.2	21.3
Sterling Asia—Miscellaneous Asia	12.2	9.1	6.3	4.7	9.3	6.3
Miscellaneous Asia—Sterling Asia	9.5	16.0	10.2	14.5	19.3	18.1
Sterling Asia—Middle East	2.4	3.6	5.2	1.9	3.1	4.2
Middle East—Sterling Asia	5.2	5.8	5.0	5.8	5.1	5.9
Sterling Asia—Australia, New Zealand, South Africa	1.7	4.5	3.2	3.0	4.7	4.8
Australia, New Zealand, South Africa—Sterling Asia	4.7	6.9	5.8	2.5	5.3	4.8

Source: As for Table 3.1.

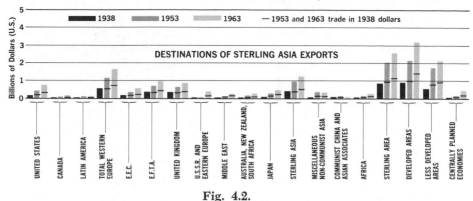

Fig. 4.2.

regarding imports to those countries. From the viewpoint of the United States, this trade has remained rather consistent since 1953 regarding imports but has risen sharply in exports. In brief, the major change in this sector of trade has been a marked rise in movement of commodities from the United States to sterling Asia (Table 4.3). This rise, in turn, has involved foodstuffs and beverages to a marked degree and has reflected measures of long-term and emergency assistance, particularly to the two largest countries of the area, India and Pakistan.

Important but weakening ties between the United Kingdom and sterling Asia also are to be seen in Table 4.3. The decline is especially conspicuous from the viewpoint of the latter, which has veered from the United Kingdom by more than seven percentage points with respect to imports and has declined slightly in exports. Dependence by the United Kingdom upon sterling Asia also is waning. The trade largely is an exchange of manufactured goods, notably machinery and transportation equipment, for agricultural foodstuffs and other crude materials.

If the trade of sterling Asia with the United Kingdom is declining relatively, that with Japan is rising. The major trend is an increase in the flow of goods, primarily manufactures, from Japan. The reverse movement is less important—indeed, of declining importance to Japan, although of slightly rising importance to its Asian partners.

Groups of countries play differing roles in the trade of sterling Asia. Western Europe is extremely active as a trading partner. Of the larger western European subgroups, it is not surprising that EFTA, with its UK-Commonwealth-sterling Area ties, is the most dynamic trading bloc. Other parts of Asia also are active traders, including sterling Asia itself. However, trade between both of these two blocs of non-Communist Asia has declined. Imports to sterling Asia from other Asian members of the sterling area have dropped by nearly 16 percentage points since 1938, while exports have declined by some four percentage points (Table 4.3). Imports to sterling Asia from miscellaneous non-Communist Asian countries also have declined relatively since 1938 from the viewpoint of sterling Asia, while exports have risen erratically. The net trend in trade among and within these two blocs, from the viewpoint of sterling Asia, thus is one of relative decline.

Other non-Communist trading partners of consequence include the Middle East and Australia, New Zealand, and South Africa. Trade with each of these has remained relatively stable since 1953, with the Middle East showing the most persistent, though small, gains.

Relative trends in trade between sterling Asia and the centrally planned economies are shown in Table 4.4 and Figs. 4.1 and 4.2. Except for ex-

Table 4.4. Trade Between Sterling Asia and Centrally Planned Countries

(In per cent of respective totals)

	Imports			Exports		
Trading Partners	1938	1953	1963	1938	1953	1963
Sterling Asia—USSR & Eastern Europe	2.8	0.5	2.4	0.8	0.8	6.8
USSR & Eastern Europe—Sterling Asia				1.8	0.3	5.5
USSR—Sterling Asia	0.3	0.4	3.6			
Eastern Europe—Sterling Asia	1.5	0.6	1.6			
Sterling Asia—Communist China & Asian Associates	6.7	5.4	5.8	5.0	3.8	1.2
Communist China & Asian Associates—Sterling Asia	12.8	11.9	5.0	20.2	19.0	25.6

Source: As for Table 3.1. Breakdown for USSR & Eastern Europe is due to nature of data arrangement in original source.

ports from sterling Asia to Communist China and other Communist nations in Asia, there has been a rise in trade between the two groups. Commerce between sterling Asia and the Soviet Union and eastern Europe has risen very sharply.

Miscellaneous Asia.   That part of non-Communist Asia not included in the Middle East or in the sterling area cannot be considered a trading bloc. It is, as indicated by its name, a cluster of political units, most of them politically independent and relatively small, situated along the southern and eastern rim of the continent in either fringe mainland or island locations. As summarized in Table 4.2, the Republic of the Philippines is the most active trading unit in the group, followed closely by Thailand and Indonesia (with Indonesia leading Thailand in exports but not in total trade) and less closely by Nationalist China (Taiwan), Korea, North Viet-Nam, and others. As seen in Table 4.5 and Figs 4.3 and 4.4, the United States and Japan are outstanding among individual nations as trading partners, while non-Communist trading blocs in Europe and Asia also are important. Significantly, trade with the United States, western Europe, and even sterling Asia is declining from the viewpoint of these Asian countries. On the other hand, commerce within this group, and between the group and Japan, is rising sharply.

Table 4.6 shows that trade between miscellaneous Asian countries and the centrally planned bloc is rising, although more slowly than trade

Table 4.5. Trade Between Miscellaneous * Asian Countries and Selected Non-Communist Areas

(In per cent of respective totals)

Trading Partners	Imports			Exports		
	1938	1953	1963	1938	1953	1963
Miscellaneous Asia—US	12.1	30.0	29.8	15.9	29.9	22.3
US—Miscellaneous Asia	8.0	5.3	3.5	3.1	4.7	4.7
Miscellaneous Asia—Japan	50.9	16.9	24.8	32.2	13.7	21.2
Japan—Miscellaneous Asia	34.8	12.0	9.9	36.0	32.3	16.3
Miscellaneous Asia—Western Europe	19.7	28.0	17.7	19.6	21.9	20.8
Western Europe—Miscellaneous Asia	1.8	1.3	0.8	1.7	2.4	1.0
Miscellaneous Asia—EEC	14.6	21.4	11.0	15.4	18.0	13.5
EEC—Miscellaneous Asia	3.1	2.3	0.9	2.6	3.5	1.1
Miscellaneous Asia—EFTA	5.0	6.4	5.7	4.0	3.7	6.7
EFTA—Miscellaneous Asia	0.8	0.5	0.7	0.9	1.3	0.9
Miscellaneous Asia—Sterling Asia	9.5	16.0	10.2	14.5	19.3	18.1
Sterling Asia—Miscellaneous Asia	12.2	9.1	6.3	4.7	9.3	6.3
Miscellaneous Asia—Miscellaneous Asia	1.8	2.7	6.1	1.3	3.4	8.5

* For countries comprising Miscellaneous Asia, see Table 4.2.
Source: As for Table 3.1.

Table 4.6. Trade Between Miscellaneous * Asian Countries and Centrally Planned Group

(In per cent of respective totals)

Trading Partners	Imports			Exports		
	1938	1953	1963	1938	1953	1963
Miscellaneous Asia—USSR & Eastern Europe	1.6	0.6	0.9	0.6	0.7	3.5
USSR & Eastern Europe—Miscellaneous Asia				0.7	0.2	4.0
USSR—Miscellaneous Asia	1.4	0.3	1.0			
Eastern Europe—Miscellaneous Asia	0.2	0.1	0.3			
Miscellaneous Asia—Communist China & Asian Associates	2.5	0.4	1.5	1.7	0.05	1.1
Communist China & Asian Associates—Miscellaneous Asia	2.9	0.07	2.0	4.8	1.0	3.3

* For component countries see Table 4.2.
Source: As for Table 3.1.

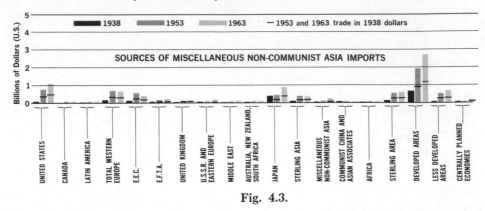

Fig. 4.3.

between sterling Asia and the centrally planned group. Increases in exports are more apparent than those in imports affecting the miscellaneous Asian group. Trade with China and other Asian nations in the centrally planned bloc as yet has not reached its 1938 relative level.

The total trade of the less developed countries of Asia is unfavorable at a ratio of approximately 11:8. Trade of each of the two major subdivisions is unfavorable at about the same ratio, although sterling Asia's position is nearer equilibrium than is that of other parts of Asia. As to composition, Asian exports and imports are only slightly unfavorable concerning foods, beverages, and tobacco; decidedly favorable in crude materials (other than fuels) of agricultural and mineral origin; unfavorable in mineral fuels and related materials; definitely unfavorable in chemicals, machinery, and transportation equipment; but surprisingly even, though slightly unfavorable, in miscellaneous manufactured products.

THE MIDDLE EAST.   Although the prominent position of the Middle East among less developed trading nations is due appreciably to exports of petroleum and its products, one cannot ignore the sizable volume of imports into that area (Table 4.1 and Figs. 4.5 and 4.6). Nevertheless,

Table 4.7. Leading Trading Countries in the Middle East

Country	Per cent of Middle East Trade	
	Imports	*Exports*
Kuwait	6.6	18.7
Saudi Arabia	6.5	17.7
Iran	10.6	15.7
Iraq	6.5	14.1
Egypt (UAR)	18.6	8.8
Israel	13.6	5.9
Libya	4.9	5.7
Sudan	5.8	.3.8
Aden	5.5	3.3
Syria	4.8	3.2
Other *	16.6	3.1

* Chiefly Cyprus, Jordan, Lebanon, Ethiopia.

Source: Calculated from *Yearbook of International Trade Statistics, 1963,* and International Monetary Fund, *International Trade Statistics, 1965.*

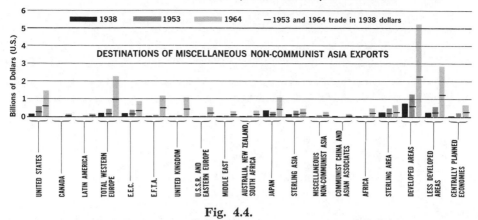

Fig. 4.4.

as is seen in Table 4.7, the leading trading countries are somehow associated with petroleum.

Trends in Middle Eastern trade, with emphasis on trading partners, are to be seen in Tables 4.8 and 4.9. Western Europe continues to play a dominant role in both directions of movement, although that role is declining—again, with respect to both directions of movement. The decline has been especially heavy in EEC trade between 1938 and 1953 but somewhat stable since 1953. EFTA, on the other hand, has continued to decline in relative importance. Japan is a major and expanding outlet for exports, ranking in total trade behind the United States and the Middle East itself. Sterling Asia is at least maintaining a relative position, with

Table 4.8. Trade Between the Middle East and Selected Non-Communist Areas

(In per cent of respective totals)

Trading Partners	Imports			Exports		
	1938	1953	1964	1938	1953	1964
Middle East—Western Europe	58.6	51.6	45.1	58.9	55.1	50.7
Western Europe—Middle East	2.7	5.1	5.0	3.7	4.0	3.5
Middle East—EEC	37.1	23.1	24.9	38.0	31.6	31.1
EEC—Middle East	2.8	6.1	5.5	4.9	3.5	3.2
Middle East—EFTA	20.7	25.1	17.6	29.0	20.1	15.2
EFTA—Middle East	2.8	4.3	4.1	2.9	4.7	4.1
Middle East—Japan	4.0	2.1	5.3	2.6	3.7	9.8
Japan—Middle East	1.4	4.9	11.5	2.1	3.8	4.3
Middle East—Middle East	12.9	15.8	11.4	14.0	12.5	8.2
Middle East—United States	5.5	14.9	18.0	3.0	7.9	6.1
United States—Middle East	0.7	2.1	2.5	1.0	2.1	3.7
Middle East—Sterling Asia	5.2	5.8	5.0	5.8	5.1	5.9
Sterling Asia—Middle East	2.4	3.6	5.2	1.9	3.1	4.2

Source: As in Table 3.1.

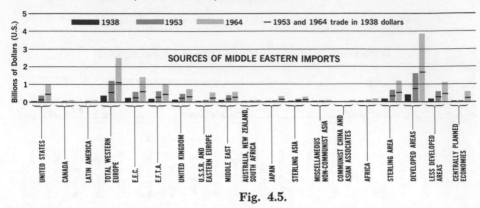

Fig. 4.5.

its slight decline in imports compensated for by a rise in exports since 1953. Trade with centrally planned economies also is rising, notably imports from the Soviet Union and eastern Europe (Table 4.9).

*Table 4.9.   Trade Between the Middle East and the
Centrally Planned Countries*

(In per cent of respective totals)

Trading Partners	Imports			Exports		
	1938	1953	1964	1938	1953	1964
Middle East—USSR & Eastern Europe	8.6	3.8	9.2	5.6	1.9	4.5
USSR & Eastern Europe— Middle East				2.5	1.2	2.7
USSR—Middle East	5.3	1.0	1.9			
Eastern Europe—Middle East	1.9	0.8	1.8			
Middle East—Communist China & Asian Associates	0.2	0.04	1.0	0.2	0.4	0.8
Communist China & Asian Associates—Middle East	0.2	0.7	3.7	0.2	0.08	3.1

Source: As in Table 3.1.

In brief, then, the export trade of the Middle East goes decreasingly to the economically advanced nations of Europe and the western hemisphere and increasingly to Japan, to non-Communist, less developed countries other than the Middle East, and to the centrally planned group. The import trade also is declining with respect to western Europe, although rising with the United States. However, it also is rising with Japan and with the centrally planned economies.

Middle Eastern trade is slightly unfavorable in balance. As with so many less developed areas, this condition is due largely to heavy imports of manufactured goods, which are not compensated for by sales of petroleum and other materials of mineral and agricultural origin.

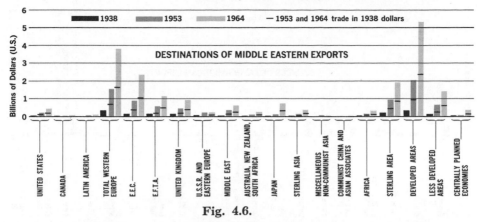

Fig. 4.6.

LATIN AMERICA.   The less developed countries of Latin America (i.e., Latin America exclusive of Argentina, Chile, Venezuela, and Uruguay) are third in rank among less developed non-Communist countries when considered as a unit (Table 4.1).[1] The primary trading nations of all Latin America, including economically advanced and less developed countries, are shown in Table 4.10. Although twenty nations supply the bulk of Latin American trade, nine are responsible for most of that commerce.

Table 4.10.   Leading Trading Countries in Latin America

	Per cent of Latin American Trade in 1963	
Country	*Imports*	*Exports*
Venezuela °	10.0	27.0
Brazil	17.4	14.5
Argentina °	11.5	14.0
Mexico	14.5	10.0
Cuba	10.1	5.6
Chile °	7.4	5.6
Peru	6.5	5.6
Colombia	5.9	4.6
Uruguay °	2.1	1.7
Other °°	14.6	11.4

° Classified in this study as economically advanced.
°° Bolivia, Costa Rica, Dominican Republic, Ecuador, El Salvador, Guatemala, Haiti, Honduras, Nicaragua, Panama, Paraguay.
Source: As for Table 4.1.

The nature of Latin American trade is indicated in Figs. 4.7-4.8, and in Tables 4.11 and 4.12. This commerce is oriented primarily to the United States and to western Europe and, within western Europe, to EEC. Actually, the dominance of the United States is more apparent in Caribbean America (with Cuba a major exception at the time of this writing) and that of western Europe more conspicuous farther to the

[1] Cuba also may qualify as an economically advanced nation, but insufficient data are now being released for its classification.

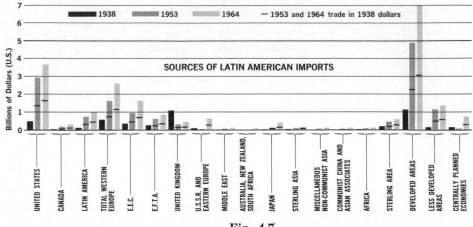

Fig. 4.7.

south (although Chile here is somewhat of an exception). With increased competition from western Europe since the 1950's, the trading position of the United States has declined relatively in Latin America, as can be seen in a comparison of conditions in 1953 with those in 1964 (Table 4.11). Significantly, the gain has gone primarily to EEC, while EFTA actually has declined in a relative sense.

Two trading blocs formed within Latin America in the 1960's have not yet had sufficient time to register an impact on Latin American trade. In 1960 there was created a Central American Common Market made up of El Salvador, Guatemala, Honduras, and Nicaragua and joined by Costa Rica in 1962. CACM currently accounts for some 6 per cent of Latin American imports and 5 per cent of the area's exports. In 1961 the Latin

Table 4.11. *Trade Between Latin America and Selected Non-Communist Areas*

(In per cent of respective totals)

Trading Partners	Imports			Exports		
	1938	*1953*	*1964*	*1938*	*1953*	*1964*
Latin America–US	35.9	48.7	40.4	30.1	47.3	32.6
US–Latin America	24.4	33.8	18.8	16.2	18.7	13.9
Latin America–Western Europe	42.4	26.9	28.6	47.4	27.1	34.1
Western Europe–Latin America	7.0	6.7	4.6	6.3	5.6	3.7
Latin America–EEC	24.3	15.9	17.8	25.4	13.8	20.9
EEC–Latin America	8.2	7.2	5.2	7.7	6.5	3.8
Latin America–EFTA	17.0	10.0	9.2	20.5	11.7	10.5
EFTA–Latin America	6.4	6.7	4.0	5.6	5.1	3.5
Latin America–Latin America	7.6	12.1	10.8	6.1	9.5	9.4
Latin America–Japan	1.0	1.7	4.4	1.4	3.2	5.0
Japan–Latin America	2.4	11.3	8.1	1.3	8.3	6.0

Source: As for Table 3.1.

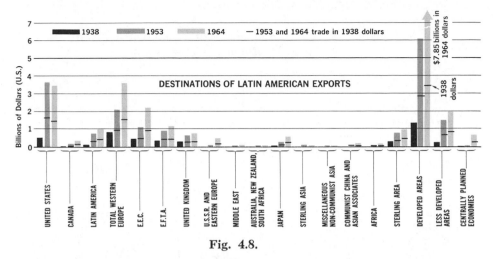

Fig. 4.8.

American Free Trade Association came into being. This group now includes Argentina, Brazil, Chile, Colombia, Ecuador, Mexico, Paraguay, Peru, and Uruguay. It commands over 67 per cent of Latin American imports and over 57 per cent of exports. Like their respective namesakes in Europe, the first is a common market and the second a free trade association; it is expected that the first may merge into a single trading bloc with a common customs border, whereas the second will offer preferential treatment to other members without actually raising a customs barrier around the entire LAFTA membership. Perhaps the time has come for some stimulation such as may be provided by these two associations; between 1953 and 1964, intra-Latin American trade declined relatively, though slightly, with respect to both imports and exports (Table 4.11).

All in all, Latin America maintains a favorable balance of trade that varies in composition. Foodstuffs and beverages make up over 40 per cent of all exports, fuels over 25 per cent, crude raw materials nearly 20 per cent, and miscellaneous manufactured goods nearly 10 per cent. As is apparent in Figs. 2.6 to 2.10, North America and western Europe are the prime receivers of these commodities. Very few chemicals and very little transportation equipment is shipped from Latin America. Imports to that region are dominated by manufactures—machinery and transportation equipment (over 33 per cent of all incoming materials), miscellaneous manufactures (over 25 per cent), and chemicals (over 10 per cent). Again, North America and western Europe are the major trading partners. All other trading countries or blocs are comparatively minor; the four blocs already mentioned—The United States and Canada, EEC, EFTA, and Latin America—account for over three-fourths of all Latin American foreign trade. Nevertheless, we find Latin America looking increasingly to Japan among non-Communist trading partners, as is shown in Table 4.11. The composition of this trade is not unlike that between Latin America and its major trading partners.

Trade between Latin America and the centrally planned economies is shown in Table 4.12 and Figs. 4.7 and 4.8. Latin American exports to both the Soviet Union and eastern Europe have risen since 1953, with eastern

Table 4.12. Trade Between Latin America and the Centrally Planned Countries

(In per cent of respective totals)

Trading Partners	Imports			Exports		
	1938	1953	1964	1938	1953	1964
Latin America—USSR & Eastern Europe	7.2	0.5	6.8	1.6	0.4	4.2
USSR & Eastern Europe— Latin America				5.1	0.4	3.4
USSR—Latin America	0.3	0.4	2.7			
Eastern Europe—Latin America	3.2	0.7	2.3			
Latin America—Communist China & Asian Associates	0.1	0.03	1.0	0.05	0.01	1.5
Communist China & Asian Associates—Latin America	0.2	0.07	10.1	0.2	0.2	5.0

Source: As for Table 3.1. The threefold breakdown for trade with the USSR and Eastern Europe is due to the nature of data arrangement in the original source.

Europe's receipts growing to the greater degree. Imports from the Soviet Union and eastern Europe, here considered as a single bloc, also rose dramatically between 1953 and 1964, although in the latter year they did not yet equal their relative importance as of 1938. Trade with Communist China has risen modestly from the Latin American viewpoint but rather sharply from the viewpoint of the Communist Chinese and their associates in Asia. In 1964, over 10 per cent of all Chinese imports and 5 per cent of her exports involved Latin America. The Cuban revolution and its aftermath are reflected in this rising pace of trade.

AFRICA.   In the preceding pages we have accounted for three-fourths of the international trade of all less developed, non-Communist economies (Table 4.1). Countries originating and terminating the remaining one-fourth are situated for the most part in central and northwestern Africa and on small islands of the Caribbean Sea (again, Table 4.1). Precise data matrixes comparable to those already presented for other parts of the world are not available for this miscellaneous group, but data are available for the whole of the continent of Africa. Use of such data means including again the following countries already discussed under other headings: Libya, Egypt, The Sudan, Ethiopia, French Somaliland, South Africa. These countries account for somewhat more than 30 per cent of all of Africa's trade, and their inclusion a second time affects the overall patterns which emerge. Nevertheless, with our reservations appropriately stated, we shall proceed to examine the trade of the African continent. The importance, yet relative decline, of western Europe in African international trade is indicated in Table 4.13. Both EEC and EFTA have been and are active in this trade, with the former retaining its position rather effectively, especially with respect to shipments from Africa to Europe. EFTA, in contrast, has declined—notably between 1953 and

Table 4.13. Trade Between Africa and Selected Non-Communist Areas

(In per cent of respective totals)

Trading Partners	Imports			Exports		
	1938	1953	1963	1938	1953	1963
Africa—Western Europe	68.2	68.0	60.5	77.7	69.3	67.7
Western Europe—Africa	6.8	10.5	7.4	9.5	12.4	8.0
Africa—EEC	36.0	38.3	35.9	50.0	38.0	43.2
EEC—Africa	9.5	12.1	8.6	10.7	13.7	8.0
Africa—EFTA	31.0	28.8	22.9	27.2	29.8	22.3
EFTA—Africa	5.1	10.4	6.9	9.6	12.6	8.8
Africa—US	8.9	9.5	11.7	3.7	10.5	9.3
US—Africa	1.7	4.6	4.2	3.7	3.2	4.3
Africa—Africa	4.6	8.2	6.3	5.9	9.2	7.1
Africa—Japan	2.9	2.5	5.6	1.3	1.1	2.9
Japan—Africa	1.3	2.3	4.0	3.4	10.2	8.6
Africa—Sterling Asia	2.9	3.2	3.2	3.5	3.3	2.2
Sterling Asia—Africa	2.7	3.9	2.2	2.4	4.1	4.7
Africa—Middle East	3.5	2.8	3.7	2.8	2.0	2.0
Middle East—Africa	4.8	4.2	3.1	8.4	5.3	4.7

Source: As for Table 3.1.

1963—in both directions of movement. The United States has supplied a slightly rising share of African imports, while accepting a portion of African exports that rose sharply between 1938 and 1953 but declined slightly in the subsequent decade. Intra-African shipments also rose between 1938 and 1953 but declined between 1953 and 1963. Japanese trading in Africa obviously grew in the period under observation, while relationships between Africa and other parts of non-Communist Asia remained stable at a low level of activity.

Exchanges between Africa and the Soviet Union and eastern Europe have risen somewhat. Trade with Communist China and other centrally planned economies of Asia has not risen very significantly from the viewpoint of Africa, but Africa obviously became increasingly important to the Asian group of centrally planned economies.

TRENDS. We have mentioned previously that the trend in volume of trade of less developed economies has been a rise that is less than the world average. We have shown also that the less developed countries are continuing to export crude materials and to import manufactures, notably machinery and transport equipment, while becoming increasingly self-reliant in certain manufactured textiles, processed foods, and consumer goods. Trends in the direction of trade are shown in Figs. 2.3-2.16. Even when allowance is made for inflation, trade with developed areas rose sharply between 1938 and 1964, while that with other less developed areas rose only modestly. Among specific trading partners, the United States experienced an especially sharp rise between 1938 and 1953, but western Europe and Japan have gained the most between 1953 and 1964.

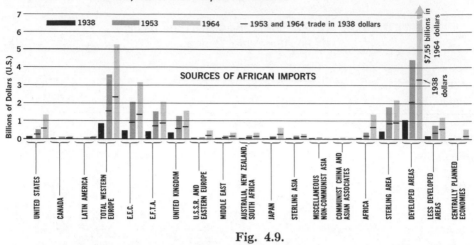

Fig. 4.9.

Trade of the Centrally Planned Countries [2]

The one-eighth of the world's trade originated and terminated within centrally planned economies can be subdivided handily into that of the Soviet Union and eastern Europe, and that of Communist China and its Asian neighbors. For convenience, we shall call the first of these the "European bloc" and the second the "Asian bloc". The European bloc includes the Soviet Union, Poland, the German Democratic Republic, Czechoslovakia, Hungary, Rumania, Bulgaria, Yugoslavia, and Albania (although trading relationships between the last of these and the remainder are somewhat strained). The Asian bloc consists of Communist China, North Korea, the Mongolian People's Republic, and the Democratic Republic of Vietnam. At the time of this writing, the volume of trade of the European bloc exceeded that of the Asian bloc by a ratio of nearly ten to one.

The Soviet Union and Eastern Europe.   Between four-fifths and two-thirds of the trade of the European bloc moves within the bloc itself. The Soviet Union accounts for about 40 per cent of this trade, with Czechoslovakia, the German Democratic Republic, Poland, and Hungary the leading trading nations at the secondary level. This exchange within the centrally planned countries of eastern Europe is appreciably an exchange within all categories and not merely a movement of crude materials in one direction and finished products in the other. The foreign trade of the Soviet Union, for example, involves a heavy outward movement of minerals, including fuels, as well as some agricultural products and a variety of manufactured goods. Interestingly, the largest single item of export is a classification not generally in use: equipment for complete industrial plants.[3] Imports also involve all major trading categories, with

[2] Although much more information about the centrally planned countries is available now than was true a decade ago, it is still difficult to obtain enough data for a thorough examination. Especially for the centrally planned economies of Asia, the data which are available tend to come from records of trading partners rather than from the countries themselves.

[3] United Nations, *Yearbook of International Trade Statistics, 1963*, p. 720.

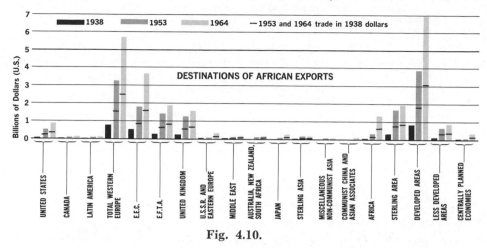

Fig. 4.10.

miscellaneous mineral products and manufactured clothing, machinery, and transportation equipment at the top of the import lists.

Trends in trade between the eastern European centrally planned group and other trading areas are shown in Table 4.15 and Figs 4.11 and 4.12. The heavy dependence by this group upon western Europe in the 1930's is clearly shown, as is the mutation effect of World War II and its aftermath and a slight rise in trade with western Europe during the past decade. Of the two major trading blocs in western Europe, EEC has not regained its 1938 position quite so effectively as has EFTA. Sterling Asia and Latin America are more active trading partners than before World War II. Communist China and other Asian centrally planned economies had developed a very active trade with the eastern European bloc by 1953, but the well-known rift between the two blocs, especially between the Soviet Union and China, is reflected in the sharp drop in the 1963 figures as

Table 4.14. **Trade Between Africa and the Centrally Planned Countries**

(In per cent of respective totals)

Trading Partners	Imports			Exports		
	1938	1953	1963	1938	1953	1963
Africa—USSR & Eastern Europe	3.0	1.2	4.9	1.9	1.2	4.6
USSR & Eastern Europe—Africa				2.5	0.9	2.4
USSR—Africa	—	1.0	2.3			
Eastern Europe—Africa	2.5	0.9	2.0			
Africa—Communist China & Asian Associates	0.5	0.2	0.5	0.09	0.2	0.9
Communist China & Asian Associates—Africa	0.2	0.7	4.8	1.4	1.0	2.7

Source: As for Table 3.1.

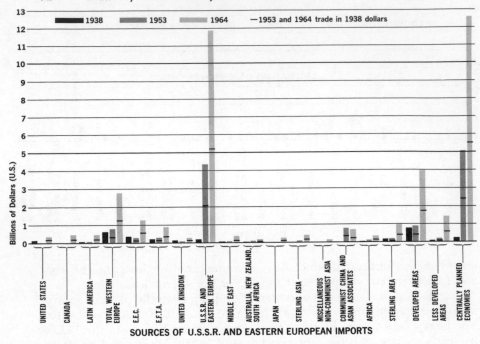

SOURCES OF U.S.S.R. AND EASTERN EUROPEAN IMPORTS

Fig. 4.11.

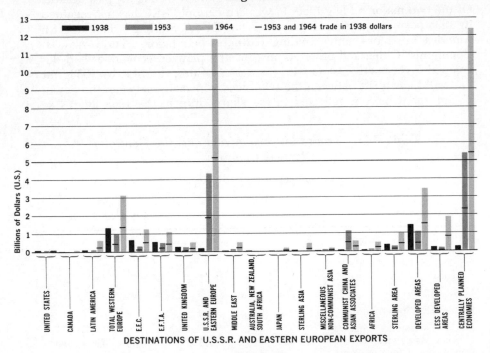

DESTINATIONS OF U.S.S.R. AND EASTERN EUROPEAN EXPORTS

Fig. 4.12.

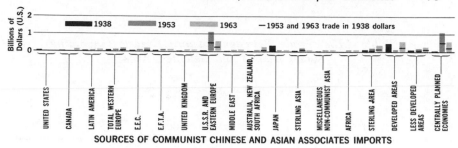

Fig. 4.13.

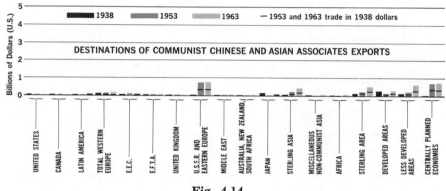

Fig. 4.14.

compared with 1953. Meanwhile, trade with the Middle East has risen since 1953 but on the whole is at a lower relative level than in 1938. This is due in no small part to the discovery of large reserves of petroleum within the Soviet Union.

Asian countries.   The trade between the centrally planned Asian bloc and other parts of the world is shown in Table 4.16 and Figs. 4.13 and 4.14. The continued importance in 1963 of the eastern European bloc is apparent in the table, despite the decline since 1953. It is also significant that the eastern bloc is more vital to the Asian bloc as indicated by relative percentages of the trade of each going to the other—but this thought must be weighed against the volume of trade in each bloc. Also significant is trade with sterling Asia—in appreciable degree, with Hong Kong. Again, the dependence by Communist China upon sterling Asia is much more pronounced than is the reverse situation with respect to the exports of each bloc, although a comparison of imports favors the centrally planned economies slightly. Western Europe is of comparatively minor but growing importance to the Asian centrally planned economies, with EEC exceeding EFTA by only a narrow margin. Trade with Japan and Latin America is rising rapidly, and that with the Middle East and Asian countries outside the sterling bloc is rising also. A pattern of increasing trade ties with the eastern hemisphere, notably other Asian countries, is clearly in the making.

Table 4.15. *Trade Between Eastern Europe (Including Soviet Union) and Selected Areas*

(In per cent of respective totals)

Trading Partners	Imports			Exports		
	1938	1953	1964	1938	1953	1964
USSR & Eastern Europe—Western Europe				68.4	14.4	17.3
Western Europe—USSR & Eastern Europe	11.6	3.2	4.0	6.5	2.7	3.9
USSR—Western Europe	50.0	12.5	13.6			
Western Europe—USSR				1.5	1.1	1.4
Eastern Europe—Western Europe	59.7	13.1	16.7			
Western Europe—Eastern Europe				5.0	1.6	2.5
USSR & Eastern Europe—EEC				34.2	4.0	6.9
EEC—USSR & Eastern Europe	12.6	1.9	3.0	7.9	1.9	2.9
USSR—EEC	25.0	3.2	5.1			
EEC—USSR				1.6	0.5	0.9
Eastern Europe—EEC	35.7	5.7	8.0			
EEC—Eastern Europe				6.3	1.4	2.0
USSR & Eastern Europe—EFTA				27.3	6.8	6.0
EFTA—USSR & Eastern Europe	9.8	3.4	4.0	5.2	2.3	3.7
USSR—EFTA	23.2	3.0	4.2			
EFTA—USSR				1.6	0.6	1.3
Eastern Europe—EFTA	19.5	5.6	5.4			
EFTA—Eastern Europe				3.6	1.7	2.4
USSR & Eastern Europe—Sterling Asia				1.8	0.3	5.5 °
Sterling Asia—USSR & Eastern Europe	2.8	0.5	2.4 °	0.76	0.8	6.6 °
USSR—Sterling Asia	0.3	0.4	3.6 °			
Sterling Asia—USSR				0.06	0.2	4.2 °
Eastern Europe—Sterling Asia	1.5	0.6	1.6 °			
Sterling Asia—Eastern Europe				0.7	0.6	2.6 °
USSR & Eastern Europe—Latin America				5.1	0.4	3.4
Latin America—USSR & Eastern Europe	7.2	0.5	6.8	1.55	0.4	3.9
USSR—Latin America	0.3	0.4	2.7			
Latin America—USSR				0.05	0.1	1.9

Table 4.15. Continued

(In per cent of respective totals)

Trading partners	Imports			Exports		
	1938	1953	1964	1938	1953	1964
Eastern Europe—Latin America	3.2	0.7	2.3			
Latin America—Eastern Europe				1.5	0.3	2.3
USSR & Eastern Europe— Communist China & Asian Associates				2.5	15.9	3.0
Communist China & Asian Associates—USSR & Eastern Europe	8.0	80.6	34.2	3.0	64.1	37.2
USSR—Communist China & Asian Associates	4.3	22.0	6.7			
Communist China & Asian Associates—USSR				2.8	48.2	27.8
Eastern Europe—Communist China & Asian Associaes	0.1	5.0	1.6			
Communist China & Asian Associates—Eastern Europe				0.2	15.9	9.4
USSR & Eastern Europe— Middle East				2.5	1.2	2.7
Middle East—USSR & Eastern Europe	8.6	3.8	9.2	5.6	1.9	4.5
USSR—Middle East	5.3	1.0	1.9			
Middle East—USSR				2.8	0.9	1.9
Eastern Europe—Middle East	1.9	0.8	1.8			
Middle East—Eastern Europe				2.8	1.0	2.6

* 1963

Source: As for Table 3.1. Three sets of figures within each category necessitated by grouping of data in original source.

Table 4.16. Trade Between Communist China (Including Asian Associates) and Selected Areas

(In per cent of respective totals)

Trading Partners	Imports			Exports		
	1938	1953	1963	1938	1953	1963
China & Asian Associates—USSR & Eastern Europe	8.0	80.6	34.2	3.0	64.1	37.2
USSR & Eastern Europe—China & Asian Associates				2.5	15.9	3.0
China & Asian Associates—USSR				2.8	48.2	27.8
USSR—China & Asian Associates	4.3	22.0	6.7			
China & Asian Associates—Eastern Europe				0.2	15.9	9.4
Eastern Europe—China & Asian Associates	0.1	5.0	1.6			
China & Asian Associates—Sterling Asia	12.8	11.9	5.0	20.2	19.9	25.6
Sterling Asia—China & Asian Associates	6.7	5.4	5.8	5.0	3.8	1.2
China & Asian Associates—Western Europe	13.6	6.0	13.0	21.4	10.6	13.9
Western Europe—China & Asian Associates	0.8	0.4	0.3	0.9	0.3	0.3
China & Asian Associates—EEC	8.0	3.5	7.6	11.9	6.2	7.8
EEC—China & Asian Associates	0.9	0.5	0.3	1.1	0.3	0.3
China & Asian Associates—EFTA	5.3	2.1	5.2	9.8	4.2	5.5
EFTA—China & Asian Associates	0.7	0.3	0.4	0.8	0.2	0.3
China & Asian Associates—Japan	52.8	0.3	10.7	34.5	2.4	6.7
Japan—China & Asian Associates	14.6	1.2	1.9	29.7	0.3	2.5
China & Asian Associates—Latin America	0.2	0.1	10.1	0.2	0.2	5.0
Latin America—China & Asian Associates	0.1	0.03	1.0	0.05	0.01	1.5
China & Asian Associates—Miscellaneous Asia	2.9	0.07	2.0	4.8	1.0	3.3
Miscellaneous Asia—China & Asian Associates	2.5	0.4	1.5	1.7	0.05	1.1
China & Asian Associates—Middle East	0.2	0.7	3.7	0.2	0.08	3.1
Middle East—China & Asian Associates	0.2	0.04	1.0	0.2	0.4	0.8

Source: As for Table 3.1.

CHAPTER 5   *the trade of individual countries—*
an analysis of certain trade characteristics

Having examined in broad outline the world trade of three general categories of countries—non-Communist, developed; non-Communist, less developed; and Communist—we now narrow our focus to the trade of individual countries. Employing various measurement techniques, we shall examine some of the differences among countries in the degree to which they participate in trade and in the content of that trade. The principal objective of this portion of the study will be to isolate those characteristics which distinguish the trade of countries in one category from those in another and to note whether or not such traits have undergone any change in recent years.

Several methods of calculation will be presented, and, as an aid to comparative analysis, the results will be expressed in graphic form. One combination of techniques will be used to measure participation in international trade as a proportion of national income, which will then be related to levels of economic development. Another set of calculations will be employed to detect differences in the extent to which the various countries have shared in the general increase in levels of per capita trade. Finally, we shall introduce a coefficient of specialization of exports and relate this to level of national income and degree of participation in international trade.

Although the calculations are based upon data from the most reliable sources available, especially the current publications of the United Nations,[1] the usual problems of employing international statistics occur. The lack of standardization in statistical reporting is one such difficulty, which, despite some progress in recent years, has still not been fully overcome.

---

[1] Statistical Office, *Demographic Yearbook, 1963* (New York, 1965).
————, *Yearbook of National Account Statistics, 1964* (New York, 1965).
————, *Yearbook of International Trade Statistics, 1963* (New York, 1965).

The four-digit Standard International Trade Classification code (SITC) of the United Nations is not as yet employed by several leading Communist states and certain Latin American countries, thereby limiting the number whose trade can be compared in detail. Several countries also fail to report certain types of valuable data. This is particularly true of national income statistics, such information being generally unavailable for the Communist bloc. Some measures to be used here also depend upon population statistics, which are missing in some instances and are undependable in others. There are numerous other deficiencies and inconsistencies in international data, most of which have been discussed in the literature.[2]

Despite these data limitations, which will require somewhat unequal treatment of the major categories of countries, we shall expect a number of distinctive features, broadly characterizing the trade of each bloc, to be disclosed by the techniques used in the following sections.

Trade and National Income

One useful indicator of participation in international trade is the size of a country's trade in relation to its national income. By means of this comparison it is possible to gauge the importance to the national economy of the country's trade with the rest of the world. As a measure of national income we shall employ *gross domestic product at factor cost* (hereafter referred to as GDP), obtained from the Statistical Office of the United Nations.[3] Dividing a country's exports by its GDP, and multiplying by 100 to remove the decimal, gives us an index we shall term the "export coefficient":

$$\frac{\text{exports}}{\text{GDP}} \times 100.$$

For example, Canada, whose 1963 exports were US $6,457 million and whose GDP in that year was US $35,419 million, had an export coefficient of 18.2, derived as follows:

$$\frac{6,457}{35,419} \times 100 = 18.2.$$

This might be interpreted as suggesting that approximately 18 per cent of Canada's national production enters the export market. The use of

---

[2] See, for example, Andreas Grotewald, "What Geographers Require of International Trade Statistics," *Annals of the Association of American Geographers,* Vol. 53, No. 2 (June, 1963), 247-252.

[3] *Yearbook of National Accounts Statistics, 1964* (New York, 1965). On page *xi* *gross domestic product at factor cost* is defined as "the value at factor cost of the product, before deduction of provisions for the consumption of fixed capital, attributable to factor services rendered to resident producers of the given country." It differs from *gross national product* in that it excludes net factor incomes received from abroad as well as the excess of indirect taxes over subsidies. GDP was considered more appropriate than GNP for the present purposes since only merchandise trade is included in the calculations performed here, all other international income being excluded. (See Glossary, page 181, for United Nations definitions of the various concepts of product and the distinctions between them.)

merchandise exports has the effect of excluding the results of other types of foreign earnings.[4]

Table 5.1 lists the 1953 and 1963 export coefficients of those countries for which the United Nations has computed the GDP. Note that the Communist countries are missing from the table. In explaining the absence of this information, statisticians of the United Nations have pointed out that the concept of production as a function of the state, which is the generally accepted view in the centrally planned economies, differs from that current in the non-Communist world, particularly as it is reflected in accounting procedures, and thus provides little basis for comparison.[5]

For purposes of analysis, the export coefficients for 1963 are presented graphically in Fig. 5.1, where they have been plotted on the Y-axis, with the X-axis representing per capita GDP. The latter often serves as a measure of relative economic development and it is for this reason that we have employed it here.[6] Fig. 5.1, then, is intended to permit an examination of a possible relationship between economic development and level of international trade. To facilitate this analysis, we have divided the diagram into sectors by means of three lines drawn parallel to the X-axis. One of these has been placed at an export coefficient value of 23.0, which is the approximate mean of the coefficients, and the others have been constructed at 11.5 and 46.0, which are respectively one-half the mean and twice the mean. This gives four categories of trade participation: low (coefficient from 0 to 11.4), moderately low (11.5 to 23.0), moderately high (23.1 to 46.0), and high (above 46). In similar fashion three vertical lines have been drawn parallel to the Y-axis at per capita GDP values of $280, $559, and $1,118, representing one-half the mean, the approximate mean, and twice the mean respectively. Four classes of countries according to economic development result from this arrangement. The two categories lying below the mean we shall regard as less developed, those having a per capita GDP of $280 or less being at a low level of development and those between $281 and $559 being moderately less developed. The two groups above the mean are the moderately developed countries (per capita GDP of $560 to $1,118) and the highly devel-

[4] If there is an express desire to include such "hidden exports," other measures of trade may be employed. One way is to use the sum of both exports and imports as the numerator of the fraction, which would result in a relatively higher coefficient for a country such as Norway having a high proportion of income of this type. For an example of this "trade coefficient," see W. S. and E. S. Woytinsky, *World Commerce and Governments* (New York: The Twentieth Century Fund, 1955), p. 67. Another method is to average each country's exports and imports, that is, to divide total trade by two, and use the resulting figure as the numerator. An illustration of this is to be found in Charles P. Kindleberger, *Foreign Trade and the National Economy*, Studies in Comparative Economics No. 2 (New Haven: Yale University Press, 1962), pp. 9-11.

[5] *The Growth of World Industry, 1938-1961: National Tables* (New York, Statistical Offices of the United Nations, Department of Economic and Social Affairs, 1963), p. *viii*. In the absence of the profit motive, Communist officials presumably are able to assign items of expense and income in a more or less arbitrary fashion, possibly guided in their accounting decisions by political and other non-economic considerations.

[6] *Cf.* Norton Ginsburg, *Atlas of Economic Development* (Chicago: The University of Chicago Press, 1961), pp. 18-19.

Table 5.1. Export Coefficients, 1953 and 1963

Country	Export Coefficient 1953	1963	Country	Export Coefficient 1953	1963
Africa South of Sahara			*Europe*		
Congo (Leopoldville)	40.6	—	*EFTA*		
Ghana	—	17.8	Austria	19.0	19.9
Ivory Coast	—	36.7	Denmark	25.9	27.4
Kenya	—	19.5	Norway	19.1	20.9
Madagascar	26.6	16.3	Portugal	14.5	15.2
Mauritius	49.2	42.1	Sweden	21.1	23.4
Niger	—	8.5	Switzerland	23.5	22.6
Nigeria	—	16.4	United Kingdom	17.3	15.6
Rhodesia & Malawi	—	40.0	*Other Europe*		
South Africa	17.6	15.4	Finland	20.1	21.9
Tanganyika	—	27.6	Greece	8.9	7.8
Uganda	—	31.0	Iceland	—	34.4
North Africa & Middle East			Ireland	26.4	28.6
Algeria	23.5	—	Malta	9.5	12.7
Cyprus	25.6	19.3	Spain	—	6.0
Ethiopia	—	10.3	*Anglo-America*		
Iraq	43.4	42.2	Canada	18.7	18.2
Israel	10.1	14.8	United States	4.7	4.3
Jordan	—	5.6	*Middle America*		
Lebanon	7.3	—	Barbados	58.5	47.1
Morocco	—	20.7	Costa Rica	28.9	21.3
Sudan	—	19.6	Cuba	34.5	—
Syria	19.2	20.0	Dominican Republic	29.3	25.0
Tunisia	24.3	15.1	El Salvador	—	23.1
Turkey	10.9	5.3	Guatemala	14.5	14.0
UAR: Egypt	19.5	—	Honduras	24.5	21.1
South & East Asia			Jamaica	24.1	29.0
Burma	22.6	18.2	Mexico	8.9	6.5
Cambodia	15.2	13.5	Panama	9.3	12.3
Ceylon	34.9	26.1	Trinidad & Tobago	67.0	63.5
China: Taiwan	14.4	18.5	*South America*		
Malaya	—	49.2	Bolivia	—	13.6
Hong Kong	—	79.7	British Guiana	46.2	59.6
India	4.9	4.8	Ecuador	16.7	19.3
Japan	7.5	9.6	Peru	—	19.8
Pakistan	7.0	5.6	Surinam	—	42.6
Thailand	19.5	16.2	Venezuela	35.5	38.1
Viet-Nam, Republic of	—	5.4	*Oceania*		
Europe			Australia	22.6	16.7
EEC			Fiji	—	50.0
Belgium-Luxembourg	29.0	38.0	New Zealand	30.7	22.2
France	10.9	12.0			
Germany, Federal Republic of	15.6	18.6			
Italy	9.0	12.9			
Netherlands	38.7	38.4			

Sources: United Nations, *Yearbook of International Trade Statistics, 1963* (New York, 1965).

United Nations, *Yearbook of National Account Statistics, 1964* (New York, 1965).

oped countries (per capita GDP above $1,118).[7] Sixteen sectors result from the arrangement, each with its particular position on the two scales. For example, countries falling within the sector occupying the lower right-hand corner might be categorized as highly developed but having a relatively low rate of participation in international trade.

Although it is not feasible at this time to present a full discussion of the positions of individual countries in this diagram, some general observations concerning the broad blocs of developed and less developed countries are appropriate. We note first that, among the countries appearing in this diagram, the less developed categories include all of South and East Asia except Japan, all of North Africa and the Middle East except Israel, all of Africa south of the Sahara and all of Latin America except Venezuela and Trinidad. All the exceptions are classified as moderately developed, none being in the highly developed category. Within the developed group are all the European countries except Portugal, Greece, Malta, and Spain. In addition to those in Europe, other developed countries are Australia, New Zealand, Canada, and the United States, all classified as highly developed.

How these categories of technical advancement, as measured by per capita GDP, relate to participation in world trade is indicated on the Y-axis of Fig. 5.1. Twelve countries appear in the lowest class, one of these (the United States) falling within the highly developed group and another belonging to the moderately developed category. The other ten in this lowest range are all less developed. Most of the remaining less developed countries are clustered in the two intermediate levels of trade participation. Several highly specialized producers for the world market are scattered throughout the upper part of the high range in both the underdeveloped and moderately developed sectors, Malaya and Trinidad being prominent examples. The highly developed countries form two main clusters. In the lower part of the intermediate ranges of export coefficients are the majority of the countries of western and northern Europe plus Canada, Australia, and New Zealand. The moderately high range contains a somewhat more scattered group of the smaller developed countries of Europe.

This distribution suggests several general observations. Among the highly developed countries, the export coefficient tends to bear an inverse relationship to population size, as a comparison of the United States and Canada suggests. A similar relationship is indicated for the export coefficient and size of area, France and Belgium being examples. Among the underdeveloped countries, the two factors of area and population appear somewhat less obvious, although these elements are clearly present, as illustrated by the case of India, which has the lowest coefficient in its group. Possibly a more influential factor in underdeveloped areas is the character of natural resource utilization. Underdeveloped countries having high trade coefficients are typified by specialized oil producers (Iraq),

[7] Since a number of countries are missing from the United Nations data upon which the calculations are based, this method of classification is obviously arbitrary. However, the divisions which have been drawn here appear to conform with common usage and provide convenient reference points for the discussion which follows.

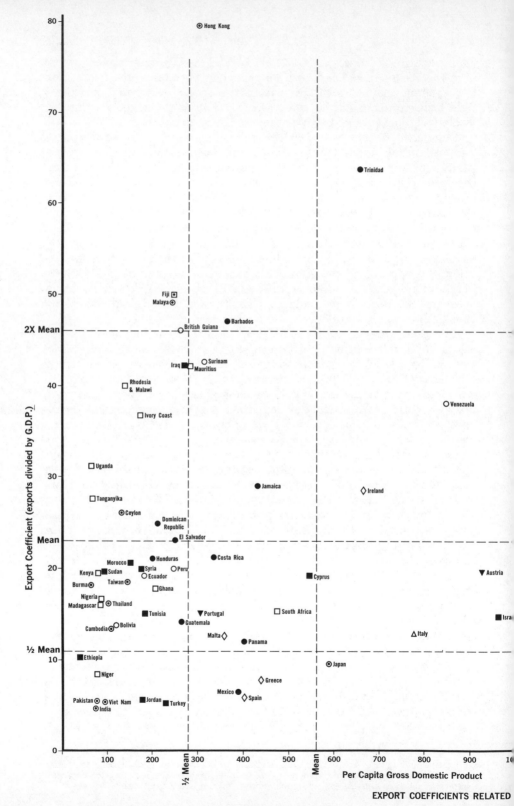

Fig. 5.1.

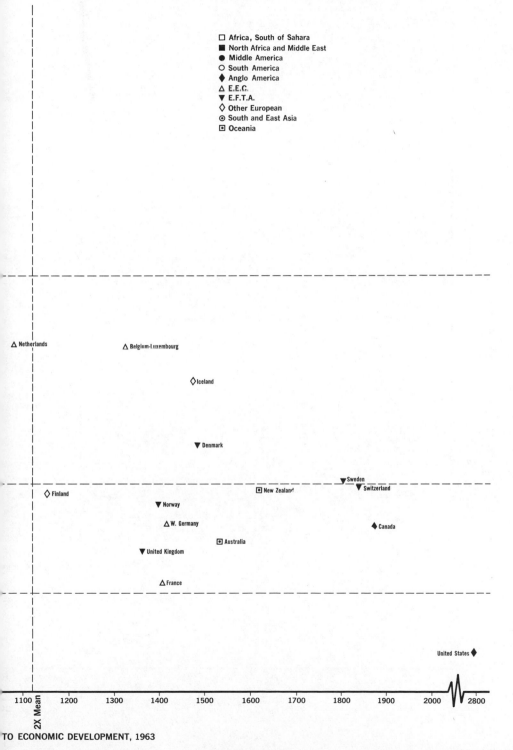

□ Africa, South of Sahara
■ North Africa and Middle East
● Middle America
○ South America
♦ Anglo America
△ E.E.C.
▼ E.F.T.A.
◇ Other European
⊙ South and East Asia
⊡ Oceania

△ Netherlands   △ Belgium-Luxembourg

                          ◇ Iceland

                    ▼ Denmark

                                              ▼ Sweden
                                    ⊡ New Zealand   ▼ Switzerland
◇ Finland
                  ▼ Norway
                  △ W. Germany   ♦ Canada
                          ⊡ Australia
        ▼ United Kingdom

              △ France

                                                United States ♦

1100   1200   1300   1400   1500   1600   1700   1800   1900   2000   2800

2X Mean

TO ECONOMIC DEVELOPMENT, 1963

Fig. **5.1** (*Continued*).

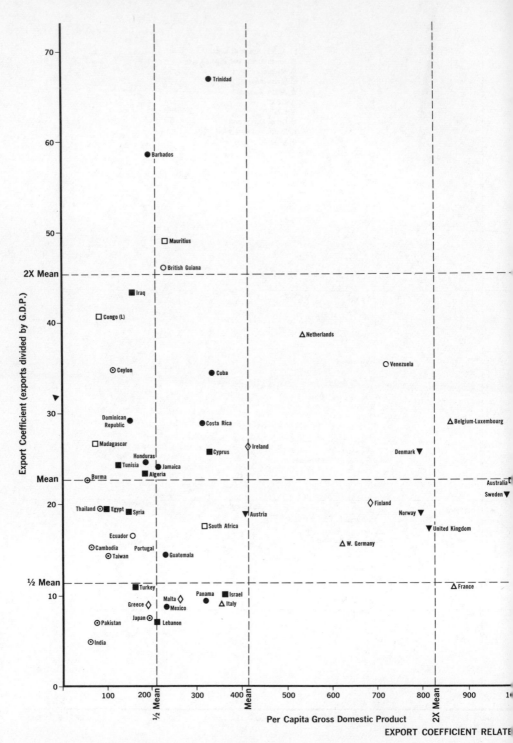

Fig. 5.2.

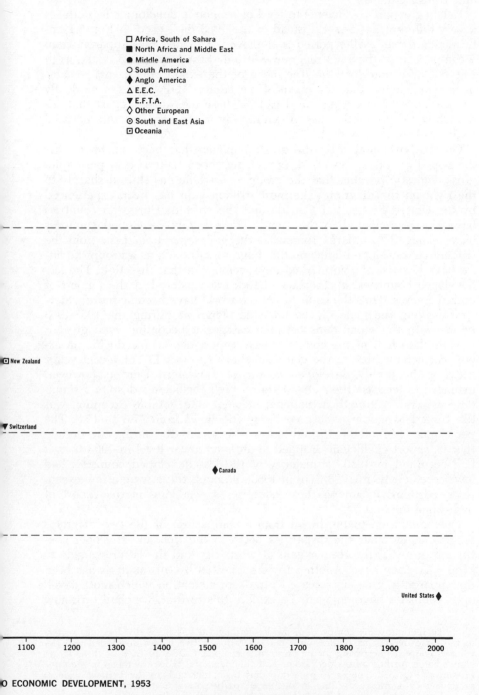

□ Africa, South of Sahara
■ North Africa and Middle East
● Middle America
○ South America
◆ Anglo America
△ E.E.C.
▼ E.F.T.A.
◇ Other European
⊙ South and East Asia
⊡ Oceania

⊡ New Zealand

▼ Switzerland

◆ Canada

United States ◆

| 1100 | 1200 | 1300 | 1400 | 1500 | 1600 | 1700 | 1800 | 1900 | 2000 |

O ECONOMIC DEVELOPMENT, 1953

Fig. 5.2 *(Continued)*.

sugar exporters (Barbados), and other raw material suppliers (Malaya and British Guiana).

Relating export coefficients to level of economic development produces a very different pattern if, instead of the 1963 data used in Fig. 5.1, information for an earlier period is employed. This becomes apparent from a comparison of the 1963 diagram with one based upon 1953 data, as in Fig. 5.2.[8] We note first that the mean of the export coefficients remains little changed but that the mean of per capita GDP has risen markedly from $412 to $559 during the decade.[9] These measures suggest that, although world production has grown rapidly in recent years, international trade has kept pace with it.

On the horizontal scale the greatest change has been shown by the developed countries. So rapid, in fact, has been their rise in per capita gross domestic product that the group as a whole has shifted sharply to the right on the diagram. The most striking gain has been experienced by the United States, but Canada and the western European countries have also participated in this trend. These highly developed countries have managed to enlarge somewhat the gap separating them from the moderately developed lands on the diagram, although as a group the latter have likewise shown marked improvement in that direction. The less developed countries, on the other hand, are clustered at the far left of both diagrams. Thus the countries of the world have become more widely spread along the scale of economic development during the 1953-1963 period with the separations between categories becoming even greater.

More than half of the countries have experienced some decline in export coefficients, due to the generally sharp rise in GDP of recent years. Most of the highly developed countries of western Europe, however, managed to increase their already fairly high coefficients despite a simultaneously rapid growth in national income. One notable exception was the United Kingdom, whose coefficient declined from 17.3 to 15.6. The per capita GDP of the United States rose so rapidly during the decade that its export coefficient dropped to an even lower level in 1963 than it had occupied in 1953. A majority of the less developed countries had lower coefficients in 1963 than in 1953, although there were a few exceptions, particularly among those countries specializing in the export of high-value minerals.

One conclusion to be drawn from a comparison of the two diagrams seems unavoidable: the disparities between the rich and the poor continue to grow as the former gain in prosperity and the latter struggle to keep what they have. Another trend suggested by this analysis has been the apparently greater increase in trade participation which most developed countries have enjoyed. To explore this further, we shall turn now

[8] To facilitate this comparison, the latter diagram has been divided into sectors in the same manner as before, with the separation between less developed and developed countries occurring at the mean of per capita GDP and each of these larger groups being further subdivided at one-half the mean and twice the mean in the same fashion as Fig. 5.1. The same procedure has been followed on the vertical scale in producing categories according to degree of participation in trade.

[9] If account is taken of the declining value of the US dollar during the ten years, the amount by which the mean per capita GDP increased becomes $103 instead of $147. Nevertheless, the change remains substantial.

to an examination of comparative changes in per capita exports during the postwar period.

Per Capita Trade

Earlier it was noted that total world trade has increased substantially in recent years and that the rate of this growth has exceeded that of world population. All parts of the world have not participated equally in this trend, however, as Table 5.1 and our study of export coefficients have suggested. By graphic means we shall now examine the per capita trade of the three groups of countries—Communist; non-Communist, developed; and non-Communist, less developed. Only exports will be considered at this time, since these provide a better insight into national differences than do imports, for reasons to be discussed in the next section.

The United Nations statistics used in these calculations are for the years 1948, 1953, and 1963.[10] The year 1948 was chosen as a date when postwar trade had been resumed but wartime dislocations had not as yet been overcome. In 1953, following the close of the Korean conflict, world trade returned to more nearly normal conditions. The most recent year for which complete United Nations data were available was 1963. In the ensuing discussion, our main interest will be directed toward the 1953-1963 period, since it more closely reflects the trends of trade during a time of relative world peace. Included in these calculations are all those countries for which realistic and dependable trade and population figures are available through the entire post-World War II era. Altogether, 113 countries and colonies fulfill these requirements in varying degrees. Several Communist countries, notably the Soviet Union, fail to qualify because of a lack of data prior to about 1955, and a few small political entities having extreme per capita export values are omitted.[11]

Per capita exports of the 113 reporting units are listed in Table 5.2 and shown graphically in Fig. 5.3. In the figure every country is represented by three bars, one each for 1948, 1953, and 1963, making possible a ready appraisal of changes during those years. Although the countries are grouped by geographic regions for convenience in referring to this diagram, only general observations will be made at this point.

The per capita export data for 1948 indicate that on the whole the non-Communist countries which are now regarded as technically advanced were, even in that time of postwar recovery, exporting at a higher level than the other two categories of countries. Among the countries ranking highest in this group were the specialized producers of raw materials and foodstuffs for the export market, as represented by New Zealand, Australia, Iceland, and Canada, all of whom had escaped from the war with their economies virtually unimpaired. As the diagram shows, the

[10] Export figures are from the United Nations *Yearbook of International Trade Statistics, 1963,* Table A (New York, 1965), pp. 12-19, and population data are from the *Demographic Yearbook, 1963,* Table 4 (New York, 1964), pp. 148-161.

[11] French Somaliland, Aden, Brunei, Singapore, Faeros Islands, Bermuda, Netherlands Antilles, Virgin Islands (USA), and Guam, all of which have per capita exports so high that they would alter the results out of proportion to their importance, have been dropped from the list. Some of these are mainly transshipment points, such as French Somaliland and Aden; others, including the Netherlands Antilles, gain their export earnings almost entirely from imported raw materials.

Table 5.2. Per Capita Exports of 113 Countries, 1948, 1953, 1963

(In US dollars)

Country	1948	1953	1963	Country	1948	1953	1963
Africa South of Sahara				Israel	26.27	36.34	141.84
Angola	14.93	28.79	32.72	Jordan	8.33	4.41	9.85
Cameroun	12.96	19.41	25.87	Syria-Lebanon *	8.42	26.34	33.62
Chad-Central African Republic—Congo (B)				Libya	11.02	9.32	111.02
Gabon *	15.17	12.26	31.49	Morocco	20.55	28.11	30.32
Congo, Democratic Republic	22.51	32.75	35.36 B	Sudan	9.65	13.98	17.61
Dahomey	7.64	9.49	5.78	Tunisia	17.81	29.54	27.81
Gambia	34.88	27.68	28.48	Turkey	9.82	17.35	12.13
Ghana	48.75	50.02	37.19				
Guinea	4.44	10.29	16.38	*South and East Asia*			
Ivory Coast	20.23	39.42	62.76	Burma	13.41	12.35	11.45
Kenya-Uganda *	9.90	13.54	18.40	Cambodia-Laos-Viet-Nam *	2.99	3.05	4.91 A
Liberia	19.00	34.48	78.64	Ceylon	42.24	39.69	34.26
Madagascar	12.15	18.88	13.80	China (Taiwan)	2.56	15.49	28.39
Mauritius	99.55	112.19	118.40	Malaya	105.51	93.00	115.99
Mozambique	7.18	9.49	14.87	Hong Kong	224.44	213.33	243.31
Niger	2.77	4.39	6.42	India	3.98	2.99	3.57
Nigeria	10.37	11.30	14.27	Indonesia	5.35	10.57	6.96
Portuguese Guinea	10.06	11.34	15.26	Japan	3.25	14.70	56.85
Reunion	85.84	116.54	102.70	Korea, Republic of	0.95	1.87	3.19
Rhodesia-Malawi *	35.90	56.67	55.65	North Borneo	41.79	56.34	181.63
Senegal	40.13	49.95	33.04	Pakistan	6.71	5.40	4.23
Sierra Leone	11.83	16.50	37.10	Philippines	16.20	17.83	23.97
South Africa	46.59	62.25	81.23	Sarawak	145.72	234.80	151.44
Tanganyika	8.44	11.89	18.26	Thailand	12.52	16.52	16.26
Togo	10.44	15.37	11.52				
Zanzibar	30.19	78.01	40.63 A	*Europe*			
				EEC			
North Africa & Middle East				Belgium-Luxembourg *	190.98	248.95	503.43
Algeria	49.74	42.37	33.33 A	France	51.41	94.25	168.44
Cyprus	49.25	84.98	105.26	Germany, Federal Republic	16.89	96.43	263.70
				Italy	23.39	31.70	100.03
				Netherlands	104.49	205.18	414.64

Country			
Egypt	31.14	18.59	18.67
Ethiopia	1.96	3.74	4.16
Iraq	3.52	67.75	113.93
Norway	129.65	151.40	292.61
Portugal	20.82	25.40	46.24
Sweden	160.83	206.39	421.09
Switzerland	173.39	246.87	415.66
United Kingdom	125.87	140.59	212.11
Other Non-Communist Europe			
Finland	128.32	138.13	252.09
Greece	12.56	16.89	34.20
Iceland	445.26	284.77	508.11
Ireland	67.00	108.51	193.24
Malta	16.34	25.24	45.73
Spain	13.59	16.90	23.68
Communist Europe			
Czechoslovakia	61.03	77.54	176.47
Hungary	18.13	51.85	119.55
Poland	22.23	31.65	57.67
Yugoslavia	19.12	10.91	41.44
Anglo-America			
Canada	236.12	283.49	341.13
United States	85.22	97.72	121.28
Middle America			
Bahamas	26.32	46.51	76.34
British Honduras	95.24	67.57	130.00
Costa Rica	60.85	90.50	68.76
Cuba	137.43	114.87	75.39
Dominican Republic	41.56	44.49	52.19
El Salvador	24.85	43.33	56.60
Guadeloupe	101.52	112.11	127.95
Guatemala	25.36	32.70	37.36
EFTA			
Austria	28.48	77.30	184.77
Denmark	135.80	204.85	407.13
Haiti	9.64	11.78	9.22
Honduras	40.65	45.48	41.33
Martinique	106.98	85.47	118.81
Mexico	19.01	20.71	25.60
Nicaragua	18.98	39.48	64.89
Panama	32.98	29.71	49.28
Barbados	59.70	108.60	173.73
Jamaica	34.07	48.45	121.52
Trinidad and Tobago	183.33	221.24	387.02 A
South America			
Argentina	100.12	61.14	62.77
Bolivia	33.22	26.69	15.85
Brazil	23.65	27.59	18.15
British Guiana	77.50	104.58	137.12 A
Chile	56.20	63.69	65.92
Colombia	25.54	49.21	29.61
Ecuador	17.57	26.56	35.12
Paraguay	20.97	20.72	21.02
Peru	19.17	24.24	49.37
Surinam	70.00	118.42	118.84 A
Uruguay	76.76	106.80	64.55
Venezuela	221.94	255.08	322.94
Oceania			
Australia	214.04	224.50	255.50
New Zealand	270.59	321.93	358.55
Fiji	92.59	97.48	119.54
Papua	9.90	15.11	14.73
New Guinea	3.97	13.85	22.43
New Caledonia	116.67	349.21	425.00 A
French Polynesia	155.17	119.40	137.50 A

* These countries are here treated as a unit in accordance with United Nations reporting procedures for at least one of the years concerned. For the sake of comparability, the same combinations are retained for all three years in the calculations based upon the information contained in this table.

A 1962

B 1959

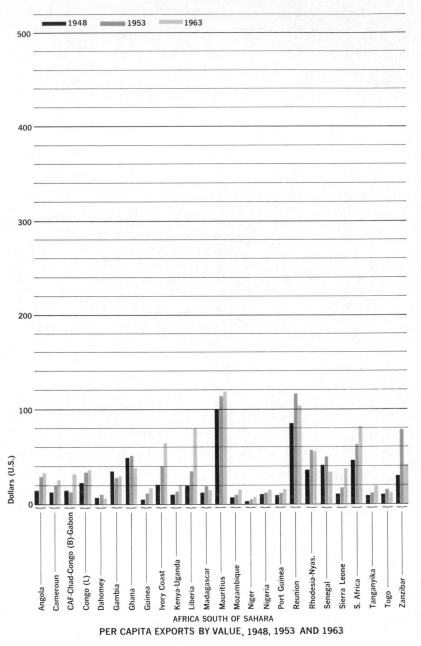

PER CAPITA EXPORTS BY VALUE, 1948, 1953 AND 1963

Fig. 5.3.

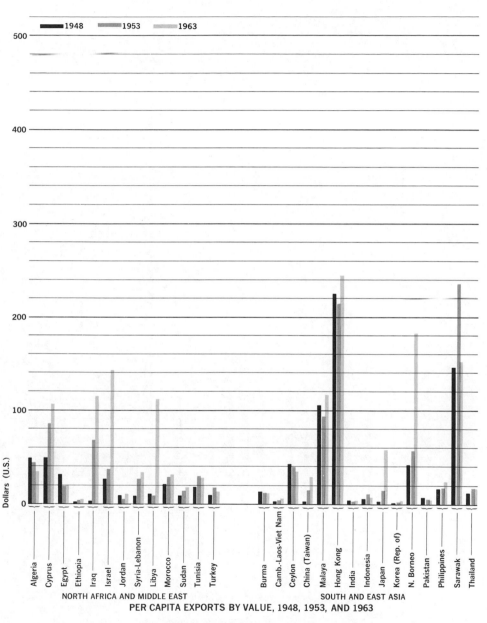

Fig. 5.3 *(Continued).*

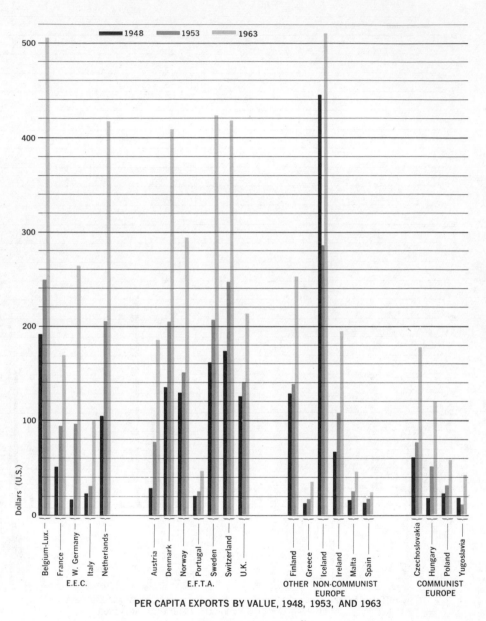

PER CAPITA EXPORTS BY VALUE, 1948, 1953, AND 1963

Fig. 5.3 *(Continued).*

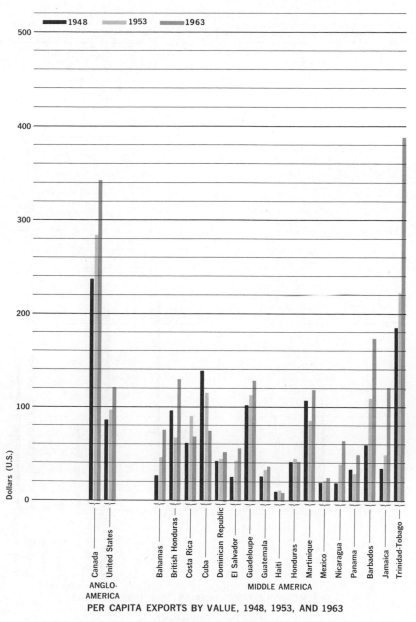

PER CAPITA EXPORTS BY VALUE, 1948, 1953, AND 1963

Fig. 5.3 *(Continued)*.

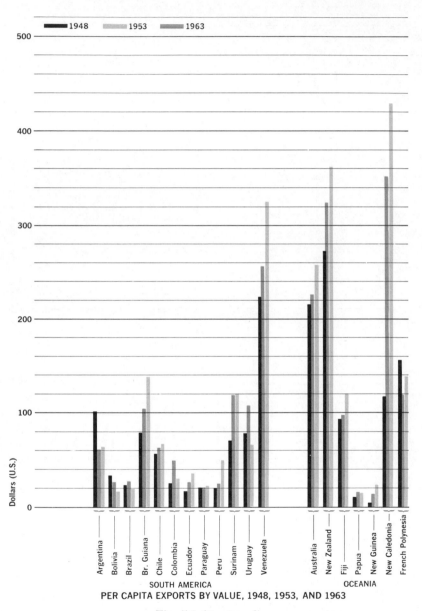

PER CAPITA EXPORTS BY VALUE, 1948, 1953, AND 1963

Fig. 5.3 *(Continued).*

war-battered countries of northern and western Europe had by this time rejuvenated sufficiently to regain some of their traditional leadership in world trade. Per capita exports of two central European countries which had taken part in the war, Austria and West Germany, were still very low.

As a group, the non-Communist, less developed countries also had comparatively small per capita exports in 1948, although within the category there were several political entities which ranked very high in this respect. Conspicuous among the latter were such specialized producers of valuable minerals as New Caledonia and such growers of tropical food crops as Mauritius. Only five Communist countries, four in Europe and one in the western hemisphere,[12] were represented in the United Nations data for 1948 and all but two of these ranked very low in per capita exports.

By the end of hostilities in Korea, most of the 113 countries had experienced increases in per capita exports. The 1953 data indicate modest gains in most underdeveloped countries, although there were some among this group whose trade, when measured on a per capita basis, had failed to improve or had even slipped backwards. Each of the four European Communist countries had shown slight improvement, while Cuba had declined somewhat. Among the non-Communist, technically advanced countries per capita trade figures for 1953 indicated mixed results. Although most showed some increase, the change was moderate in most parts of the world except western and northern Europe, where in all but a few cases the rise was substantial.

It is the period from 1953 to 1963, however, which provides us with the first clear indication of recent trends. During this ten-year interval the per capita exports of approximately two-thirds of the non-Communist, less developed countries increased slightly on the average, but the per capita trade of all the rest in this group declined. Although most of the change among these countries was slight, there were a few which rose or fell markedly. For example, sharp advances were shown by Libya and Jamaica, both of which commenced production of valuable minerals during those years. On the other hand, there were certain other producers of raw materials and food crops, such as Panama, whose per capita exports dropped precipitously. The four Communist countries of Europe experienced sharp increases, though all but Czechoslovakia had begun the period at a low base. Cuba's decline continued, however.

In absolute quantitative terms the most notable gains were recorded by non-Communist, developed countries. Nearly all the countries in this category participated in the advance, but the greatest progress was made by northern and western Europe. In part, this improvement reflects continued recovery from the effects of the war; however, it is probable that much of the change has resulted from the relaxing of barriers to intra-European trade. Evidence for this is to be found in the performances of members of the new trading blocs, the European Free Trade Association and the European Economic Community, especially the latter. In other

[12] For the purposes of this study, individual countries have been classified in accordance with their current status. Thus Cuba is included with the Communist bloc throughout.

parts of the world, non-Communist, developed countries such as Australia, New Zealand, Canada, and the United States rose by lesser amounts.

Although the foregoing discussion has disclosed certain broad trends and has pointed to some differences among countries, the expression of per capita exports as absolute values has limited the usefulness of this assessment. This method fails to take into account an important element of postwar change, namely the strong increase in the total value of world exports, because of which per capita exports have risen despite the world's population expansion. The mean value of the per capita exports of the 113 countries shown in Table 5.2 increased from $57.00 in 1948 to $71.18 in 1953 and to $103.69 in 1963. Another reason for noting this general increase is that the summary tables of the United Nations *Yearbook* express trade figures in *current* United States dollars, which means that part of the general rise in exports reflects an erosion in the value of this currency. Thus, although the tables provide fair comparability for any one year, they do not permit accurate comparison of one year's figures with those of the next.

One way in which we can at least partly adjust export figures for such general world changes is to express each of the per capita values in terms of its relationship to the world mean in the corresponding year. In other words, we can relate all 1948 values to the 1948 mean of the 113 countries, all 1953 values to the 1953 mean, and so forth. At this point it must be noted, however, that the distribution of per capita export data is so uneven that a simple arithmetic average has little meaning (see Fig. 5.4). Far more cases lie below the mean than above it, due to the effects of a few extremely high values, a situation fairly common for data in the social sciences. Our first step, then, must be to convert the figures into some form which will yield a more nearly normal distribution. This we accomplish by transforming the data into logarithms. Next we find the mean and standard deviation of the data for each of the three years and convert the individual values into standard deviation units.[13]

[13] The standard deviation is calculated by the formula,

$$s = \sqrt{\frac{\Sigma (X - \bar{X})^2}{N}}$$

where s = the standard deviation, X = per capita exports of each country, $\bar{X}$ = the mean, and N = the number of countries. Standard deviation units are obtained by dividing the standard deviation into the amount by which each country's per capita exports differ from the mean (all data at this point being in logarithmic form). For example, in 1948 the log of the United Kingdom's per capita exports was 2.09993, which was 0.62435 above the log mean of that year. Dividing this positive difference of 0.62435 by the standard deviation, 0.53573, we find that Britain's per capita exports exceeded the world mean in that year by 1.17 standard deviation units. This same procedure, when applied to 1953 and 1963 data, produces values of 1.10 and 1.12 standard deviation units respectively, indicating that, although Britain's per capita exports were well above those of the rest of the world in 1948, they have since scarcely managed to maintain that position.

In addition to removing the influence of the general world increase in per capita exports, this method has another effect which results from the nature of logarithms. Their use in this manner places emphasis upon *rates* of change, which means that a moderate gain from a small base will show a large logarithmic increase whereas the same absolute change from a large base will appear much less significant when presented in logarithmic form. It must be cautioned that this approach provides only a partial solution to the complex problem of changing monetary values. For example, we have not succeeded in eliminating the distortionary effects of changes in the structure of prices in the various countries.

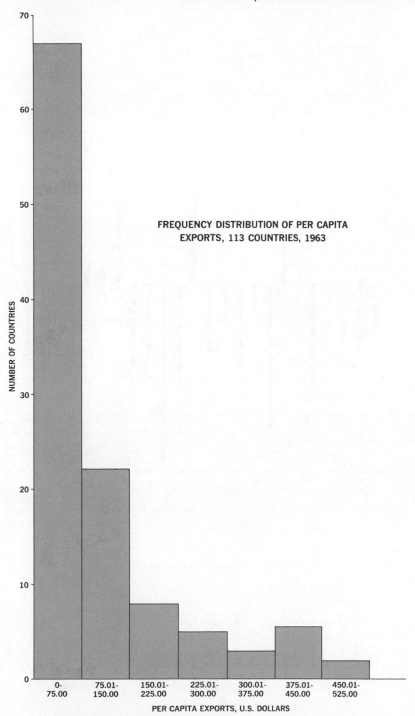

FREQUENCY DISTRIBUTION OF PER CAPITA
EXPORTS, 113 COUNTRIES, 1963

SOURCE: United Nations, Yearbook of International Trade Statistics, 1963 (New York, 1965).
United Nations, Demographic Yearbook, 1963 (New York, 1965).

Fig. 5.4.

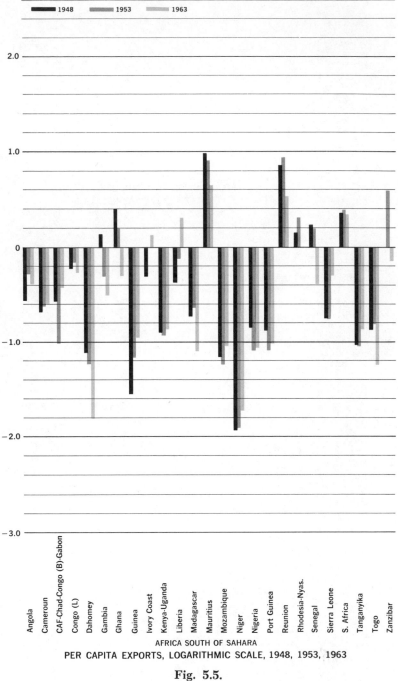

AFRICA SOUTH OF SAHARA
PER CAPITA EXPORTS, LOGARITHMIC SCALE, 1948, 1953, 1963

Fig. 5.5.

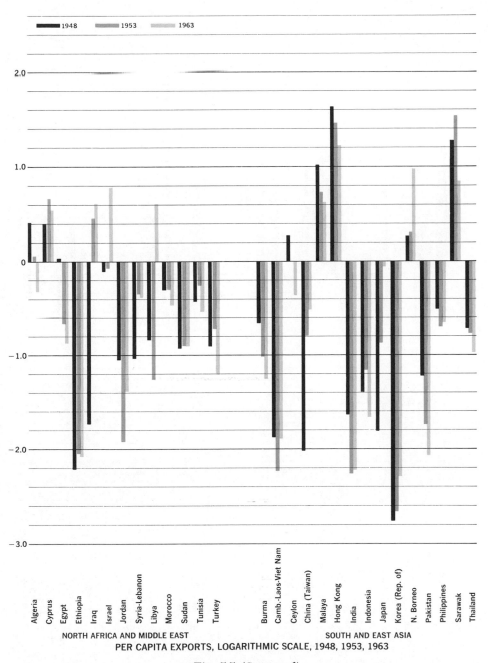

Fig. 5.5 *(Continued)*.

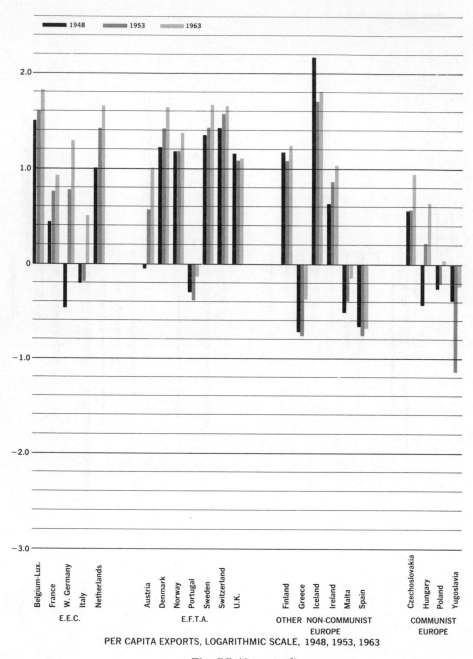

PER CAPITA EXPORTS, LOGARITHMIC SCALE, 1948, 1953, 1963

Fig. 5.5 *(Continued).*

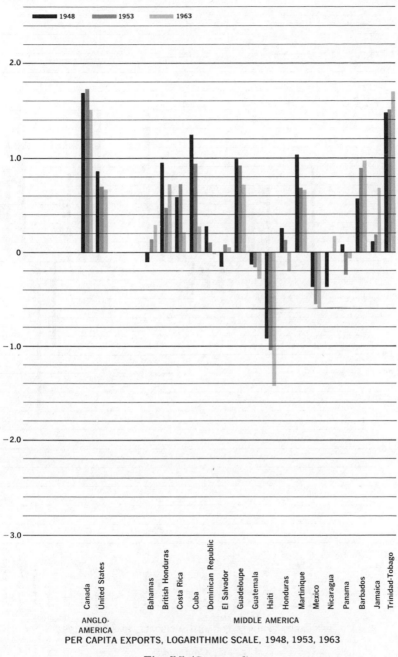

PER CAPITA EXPORTS, LOGARITHMIC SCALE, 1948, 1953, 1963

Fig. 5.5 *(Continued).*

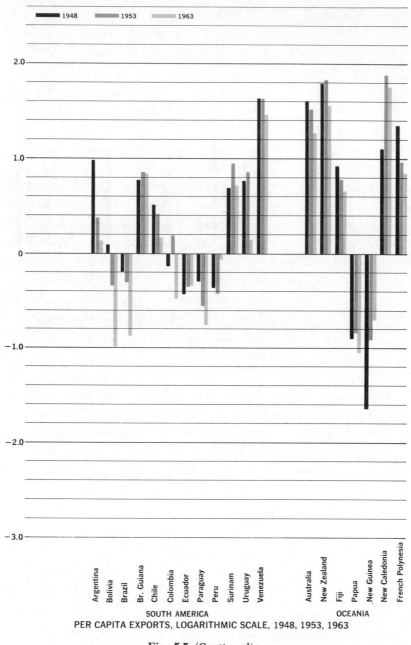

SOUTH AMERICA   OCEANIA
PER CAPITA EXPORTS, LOGARITHMIC SCALE, 1948, 1953, 1963

Fig. 5.5 (*Continued*).

Results of the calculations for the three years are shown in Fig. 5.5, which presents relative per capita exports of the 113 countries in a form similar to that used earlier with the absolute values appearing in Fig. 5.3. As before, each country is represented by three vertical bars, one each for 1948, 1953, and 1963. The same regional groupings of countries have also been maintained. This time, however, the log means of the three years have been superimposed upon a single horizontal line, with those bars portraying per capita exports greater than the world mean extending above the line and those less than the mean dropping below it. Having eliminated the major effects of the general world rise in exports and the decline in the value of the dollar, we are now ready to examine the per capita exports of individual countries and groups of countries in order to detect any changes which may have occurred during the fourteen-year period.

Although expressing the information in logarithmic form appears to exaggerate the low values and to minimize the high ones, positions of the various countries in relation to each other in any one year do not seem greatly altered by the conversion. The principal difference is to be found in a comparison of one year with another, as shown by an examination of the changes between the years 1948 and 1953. As previously mentioned, this period was a time of continued recovery from the dislocations of world trade caused by World War II but of some possible distortion of that trade, resulting from the Korean War. As we should expect, the changes are again most evident among the active participants in the war, especially those whose territory was directly affected. Thus, during this period the non-Communist, developed countries of northern and western Europe, most of which were already well above the world mean at the outset, experienced gains in per capita trade substantially in excess of the general world increase, especially certain of the present EEC countries. However, viewing the matter in this relative sense makes the increases less spectacular than was suggested by the absolute data in Fig. 5.3. The trade recovery by West Germany and Austria is nevertheless very prominent even in these relative terms. The highly developed countries of Anglo-America and Oceania were well above the mean throughout the period, but changes were slight. Canada's pronounced absolute increase appears minor when examined relatively; and the moderate absolute gain of the United States has been converted to a relative loss, at the point in time when that country's burden of aid to European reconstruction was diminishing. Australia and New Zealand remained in nearly the same positions in 1953 that they had occupied in 1948.

A prominent feature of Fig. 5.5 is the position of the less developed countries relative to the world mean. Although the Latin American countries are well represented on both sides of the mean during the 1948-1953 period, the great majority of African and Asian countries are below it and most are exceedingly low. Earlier we noted that the majority of non-Communist, less developed countries had registered slight absolute improvements in per capita exports. Most of these gains have disappeared in Fig. 5.5, where average world gains in per capita exports have been eliminated. Nearly three-fourths of these countries show declines or, in

a few cases, have barely maintained their previous positions. Most of the
losses occurred in Africa and Asia and, to a lesser degree, in Latin
America, where increases and decreases appear nearly balanced. Three
less developed countries of southern Europe were among those record-
ing decreases, as was a fourth Mediterranean country we have classified
as moderately developed. Notable exceptions among the less developed
countries were a few producers of valuable minerals, such as Iraq, whose
gains were well in excess of the world mean.

The four European Communist countries for which we have data produced mixed results, although the absolute figures had indicated modest
gains. Two remained virtually unchanged while the others increased
sharply. All but Czechoslovakia, however, were close to or below the
world mean. Cuba's absolute decline is even more noticeable when examined in this fashion.

In relative terms, then, the interval between 1948 and 1953 was a time
when the already large portion of world exports enjoyed by the countries
of northern and western Europe, and by a few particularly favored countries elsewhere, was being increased at the expense of less developed
parts of the world. Most of the non-Communist, developed countries outside of Europe scarcely managed to keep abreast of the general world increase in per capita exports and thus maintain their relatively good
positions.

The period from 1953 to 1963 was not only relatively free of international disturbances but was also characterized by greater economic stability, at least in the technically advanced parts of the world.[14] It was,
furthermore, a period of continued overall increase in international trade,
the mean per capita exports of the 113 countries having risen, in absolute
terms, from $71.18 in 1953 to $103.69 in 1963.[15] Nevertheless, as Fig. 5.5
shows, the increase was by no means equally shared by all countries nor,
for that matter, by the three major categories of countries we are employing here.

Of the political entities being considered in this portion of our study,
the non-Communist, developed countries comprise approximately one-
fifth, all of which were by 1963 exporting at a per capita rate greater than
the world average (see Fig. 5.5). Half of these experienced a moderate
to sharp rise, especially the EEC countries, Austria and Sweden in the
EFTA group, and Israel and Japan. Except for Italy, however, the EEC
countries do not evidence remarkable progress when presented in
this form rather than in absolute terms as previously. With one exception,
these countries were already far above the mean in 1953 and in most
cases the *rate* of change has subsequently declined, as the logarithmic
transformation discloses. It will be recalled from Fig. 5.3 that nearly all

---

[14] The value of the dollar steadied considerably during the latter part of this
ten-year interval. With the years from 1957 to 1959 = $1.00, the purchasing power
of this monetary unit, measured in terms of wholesale prices, had fallen sharply from
$1.138 in 1948 to $1.079 by 1953 and had further declined to $1.010 by 1957. In the
succeeding six years, however, it decreased only to $0.997. *Statistical Abstract of the
United States, 1965* (US Department of Commerce, Bureau of the Census, 1965),
Table 489, page 356.

[15] These figures do not allow for inflation of the US dollar, which would reduce
the 1953 mean to approximately $67.40 and that of 1963 to $90.84 in terms of 1948
dollars.

of the developed countries enjoyed absolute increase in per capita exports during these ten years; in relative terms, however, some failed to advance. Fig. 5.5 shows no significant change between 1953 and 1963 for seven countries in this category, thus indicating that their per capita exports were growing at or near the world average. Switzerland, the United Kingdom, Canada, and the United States are notable among these. Only five of the developed countries experienced relative decreases in per capita exports, and the change was minor for three of them. The five— Argentina, Chile, Uruguay, Australia, and New Zealand—are exporters principally of industrial raw materials and agricultural commodities.

All four of the Communist countries of Europe showed marked relative increases in per capita exports, although the Communist country of the western hemisphere, Cuba, continued to drop at an accelerated rate.

Comprising approximately three-quarters of the political entities included in this portion of our study, the non-Communist, less developed countries were mostly below the world mean in 1963—and many of them were far below it, as the diagram discloses. Fewer than one-third remained above the line in that year. During the decade relative increases in per capita exports were recorded by only one-fifth of this group, notably Iraq, Libya, Jamaica, and the countries of Mediterranean Europe. Another two-fifths showed little relative change, and the remainder fell sharply. It is of no little significance that, for nine-tenths of those underdeveloped countries losing substantially in per capita exports, population growth had equaled or exceeded any increase in exports, thus nullifying all gains in the latter.

To summarize the results of our study of per capita exports, we may say that, for the world as a whole, postwar gains have been substantial and nearly continuous but the majority of the world's nations have not participated in this quickened activity. Not more than a score of the 113 countries increased their per capita exports at a rate substantially above that of the mean of the group, and most of these were in Europe. Countries from all the main areas of that continent participated in the rise, including non-Communist, developed nations of the west and north, non-Communist, less developed lands of the Mediterranean, and Communist countries of the east.

Except for a few favored exporters of valuable products, non-Communist, less developed countries as a whole experienced only small absolute gains and lost ground in comparison with the world mean. As we noted, many of these depend upon only a few raw material exports, and it has been suggested that there is a possible connection between this fact and the failure of these countries to maintain their export earnings on a level with the rest of the world. Furthermore, at least two of the technically advanced countries seem to be similarly situated. The subject of export specialization, then, is one which merits closer examination.

Specialization of Exports

It has long been noted by students of international trade that most countries tend to import a greater variety of products than they export, since human needs and wants are numerous and are basically similar in different parts of the world, whereas resources are very unevenly distributed over the earth.[16] A country may produce only a few commodities in sufficient quantity to supply its own requirements and provide an exportable surplus, but it may have to import a wide range of goods to compensate for domestic deficiencies in supplying the varied needs of its people. Some specialization of exports is thus to be expected of most countries; there are obvious problems, however, associated with excessive dependence upon earnings from the export of a limited number of commodities which may be highly vulnerable to market fluctuations over which the producers have little or no control.

Characteristic as it is of much of the world's trade, export specialization varies widely in degree. To study the occurrence of specialization, however, it is essential that we measure it in some objective fashion in order to establish a basis for comparison. For this purpose we shall use the Lorenz Curve (illustrated by Fig. 5.6), which yields a specialization index having a possible range of values from 0 to 100. The cumulated values of commodity classes, expressed as percentages and joined by a line extending from the origin to the upper right-hand corner of the diagram, produce a curve which indicates by its shape the degree of specialization. For a country with exports equally divided among all major commodity categories, the cumulated values would produce a straight line and give a specialization index of 0. By contrast, a country with all of its exports in a single category would have a curve of maximum concavity and an index of 100. A detailed description of the method used in this study for determining the curvature of the line and deriving an index of specialization is to be found in Appendix A.

As a basis for measurement we shall use *value* of exports, broken into categories according to the Standard International Trade Classification (SITC), by which the trade of most countries is reported in the UN *Yearbook*.[17] In this study we shall employ only the first-digit level of this four-digit system, which gives us ten categories in all.[18] The first-digit commodity headings are listed in Table 5.3. Export data of 131 countries

[16] This basic assumption of classical economic theoreticians has been confirmed in a study by Michaely in which export coefficients and import coefficients were used to measure specialization of trade among a number of countries. Comparing the two groups of coefficients indicated exports to be the more highly specialized in a majority of cases. Michael Michaely, "Concentration of Exports and Imports: An International Comparison," *The Economic Journal*, Vol. 68 (December, 1958), 722-736.

[17] The SITC, adopted by the United Nations Economic and Social Council in 1950 and revised in 1960, is a four-digit code, with a fifth digit for a few categories. The first digit corresponds to ten major sections, which are subdivided into 56 divisions at the two-digit level. The third digit produces 177 groups and the fourth and fifth digits yield 1312 items. Statistical Office of the United Nations, *Yearbook of International Trade Statistics, 1963* (New York, 1965), p. 5.

[18] Others have considered two or more digits preferable for this purpose, arguing that a coarser grouping combines goods that are distinctly different (see Michael Michaely, *op. cit.*, p. 723). On the other hand, it has been found that a classification of greater fineness distinguishes between goods so similar as to be readily substitutable. Still more important, data from the second and subsequent digits are frequently missing from the export tables of many less developed countries, thus introducing problems of comparability. A final reason for confining this present study to the first-digit level of the SITC is that the technique employed is considered to be better suited to a small number of classes.

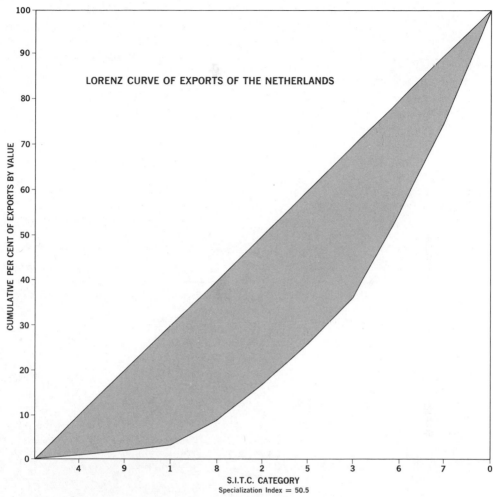

Fig. 5.6.

have been included in the UN *Yearbook* for 1963, with 115 [19] having reported by the SITC code. Regrettably, in the case of all Communist countries except Yugoslavia, export data are either lacking or have not been tabulated by the SITC code. This is true also of certain South American republics. With these important exceptions, the coverage is nearly complete.

[19] In the UN *Yearbook* certain colonial possessions in widely scattered parts of the world have been combined in a manner unsuited to this present analysis. Deducting these leaves a total of 107 countries and colonies for which indices might be calculated.

Table 5.3. United Nations Standard International Trade Classification * First-Digit Commodity Headings

SITC Code	Commodity
0	Food and live animals
1	Beverages and tobacco
2	Crude materials, inedible, except fuels
3	Mineral fuels, lubricants, related materials
4	Animal and vegetable oils and fats
5	Chemicals
6	Manufactured goods classified by material
7	Machinery and transport equipment
8	Miscellaneous manufactured articles
9	Commodities and transactions, n.e.s.

* Revised, 1960

Table 5.4. Indices of Export Specialization, 107 Countries, 1963

Country	S.I.*	Country	S.I.*
Africa South of the Sahara		Israel	78.2
Cameroon	83.6	Libya	99.7
Central Africa Republic	95.1	Morocco	80.1
Chad	94.8	Sudan	97.3
Congo (Brazzaville)	81.3	Tunisia	61.9
Congo, Democratic Republic	84.2	Turkey	76.0
Dahomey	86.7	UAR: Egypt	86.9 B
Gabon	88.6		
Gambia	99.6 A	*Anglo-America*	
Ghana	92.6	Canada	63.3
Ivory Coast	92.2	United States	52.1
Kenya	86.0		
Liberia	96.2	*Middle America*	
Madagascar	88.2	Barbados	96.0
Mali	88.5	British Honduras	92.3 A
Mauritania	86.5	Costa Rica	95.9
Mauritius	99.8	Cuba	92.2 C
Niger	90.7	Dominican Republic	94.1
Nigeria	77.3	El Salvador	82.4
Reunion	95.6	Guadeloupe	96.2
Rhodesia & Malawi	83.7	Guatemala	92.8
Senegal	77.0	Honduras	92.0
Sierra Leone	90.7	Jamaica	83.6
Somalia	97.8 A	Martinique	94.6
South Africa	70.6 A	Mexico	72.9
Tanzania: Tanganyika	89.2	Netherlands Antilles	99.2
Tanzania: Zanzibar	90.5 A	Nicaragua	86.8 A
Togo	85.4	Panama	90.2
Uganda	89.6	Trinidad & Tobago	94.1
Upper Volta	85.8		
		South America	
North Africa & Middle East		Argentina	85.4
		Brazil	87.8
Aden	76.5 B	Chile	89.6 A
Cyprus	84.5	Colombia	89.3
Ethiopia	92.2	Ecuador	98.6 B
		Surinam	92.9

Table 5.4. Continued

Country	S.I.*	Country	S.I.*
South & East Asia		*EFTA*	
Afghanistan	88.4	Austria	67.0
Brunei	98.2	Denmark	71.0
Burma	94.0 ᴬ	Norway	59.6
Ceylon	91.9	Portugal	59.7
China: Taiwan	80.1	Sweden	71.4
Hong Kong	73.8	Switzerland	65.3
India	73.0	United Kingdom	63.7
Indonesia	81.1	*Other Non-Communist Europe*	
Japan	73.7	Finland	79.9
Korea, Republic of	69.4	Greece	74.3
Malaysia: Malaya	83.5	Iceland	94.4
Malaysia: Sabah	89.1	Ireland	70.2
Malaysia: Sarawak	84.9	Malta	61.3
Malaysia: Singapore	50.8	Spain	48.6
Pakistan	86.8		
Philippines	85.8	*Communist Europe*	
Thailand	88.5	Yugoslavia	55.9
		Oceania	
		Australia	75.9
Europe		Cook Islands	90.2
EEC		Nive Island	88.1
Belgium-Luxembourg	65.3	Fiji	95.3
France	54.3	New Guinea	80.2
Germany, Federal Republic	71.3	New Zealand	86.3
Italy	58.3	Papua	98.8
Netherlands	50.5	Western Samoa	92.0

* Specialization Index (See Appendix A for method of calculation)
ᴬ 1962   ᴮ 1961   ᶜ 1960

Source of export data: United Nations, *Yearbook of International Trade Statistics, 1963* (New York, 1965)

Table 5.4 lists the specialization indices of 107 countries or colonies, the values ranging from 48.6 to 99.8. The frequency distribution of the indices, Fig. 5.7, shows a marked concentration of high values, indicating the large proportion of the world's nations dependent upon only a few major exports. The median, 86.5, is also very high. Only those countries whose indices are in the lowest quartile, from 48.6 to 73.8 inclusively, may be regarded as having a truly diversified export trade. Those with indices below 60 are typified by France (54.3), the United States (52.1), and The Netherlands (50.5). Fig. 5.6, in which Dutch exports have been plotted as a cumulative frequency curve, shows a typical example of the export characteristics of the countries at this lower end of the continuum. All ten of the first-digit SITC categories are well represented and describe a gradual progression from the lowest to the highest, as the figure shows. A distribution of this nature is possible only for a country having a good balance between exports of agricultural commodities and manufactured products, with much variety in both groups. Several manufacturing countries, for example, have higher indices due to the lack of agricultural exports in significant quantities, but no important manufacturing country has a specialization index outside the first quartile.

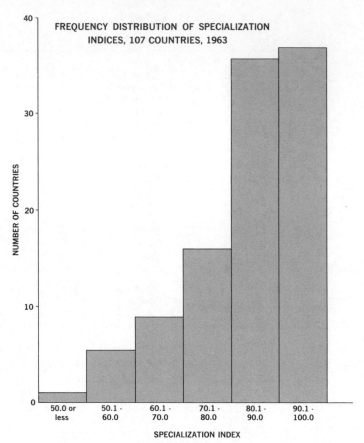

FREQUENCY DISTRIBUTION OF SPECIALIZATION
INDICES, 107 COUNTRIES, 1963

SOURCE: United Nations, Yearbook of International Trade Statistics, 1963 (New York, 1965).

Fig. 5.7.

Proceeding upward in the scale, we find the first clear evidence of concentration of exports as we enter the second quartile, which extends from 74.3 to 86.5. Table 5.5 lists the export specialties of all countries having indices in this range and above. As the table shows, Australia (75.9) depends upon two major SITC categories, consisting mainly of wool, meat, and cereals, for more than four-fifths of her export earnings, being spared a still higher index by the fairly even distribution of her remaining exports among the other classes. Countries within this range of index values—Nigeria, Jamaica, and the Philippines being other examples— are mainly exporters of industrial raw materials and agricultural products, although each has more than one specialty. It appears reasonable, then, to set the lower limit of this quartile, 74, as the dividing line between the diversified and the specialized exporting countries.

At the median (86.5) we find a decided specialization of exports. A large cluster of countries is to be found centered around this point, seven of them having indices ranging from 86.0 to 86.9. The countries in the

Table 5.5. *Principal Exports of Countries Having High Specialization Indices, 1963*
81 Countries and Colonies Ranked by Intensity of Specialization

	Specialization Index	Leading Export Category			Next Largest Export Category		
		SITC Code	Per Cent of Total	Principal Items	SITC Code	Per Cent of Total	Principal Items
1. Mauritius	99.8 A	0	99.4	sugar	2	0.6	copra
2. Libya	99.7	3	98.7	crude petroleum	2	1.1	oil seeds and nuts
3. Gambia	99.6 A	2	98.2	ground nuts	0	1.8	fish products
4. Netherlands Antilles	99.2	3	98.5	mineral fuels	2	0.6	fertilizer
5. Papua	98.8 B	2	96.6	rubber, copra	1	1.6	cacao beans
6. Ecuador	98.6 B	0	95.3	bananas, cacao, coffee	2	3.4	castor seed, wood
7. Brunei	98.2	3	96.7	crude oil	2	1.4	rubber
8. Somalia	97.8 A	0	90.4	live animals	2	9.5	hides
9. Sudan	97.3	2	89.2	cotton, oil seeds, gum	0	9.8	millet
10. Guadeloupe	96.2	0	88.0	sugar, bananas	1	8.1	rum
11. Liberia	96.2	2	89.6	rubber, iron ore	6	4.8	diamonds
12. Barbados	96.0	0	92.8	sugar	1	3.8	rum
13. Costa Rica	95.9	0	93.5	coffee, bananas	6	1.7	plywood
14. Reunion	95.6	0	86.3	sugar	5	9.0	essential oils
15. Fiji	95.3	0	84.8	sugar	4	10.9	coconut oil, copra
16. Central African Republic	95.1	2	83.1	cotton, oil seeds, diamonds	0	14.8	coffee
17. Chad	94.8	2	82.0	cotton	0	15.1	animals, meat
18. Martinique	94.6	0	79.5	bananas, pineapples	1	17.5	rum
19. Iceland	94.4	0	84.2	fish	4	9.8	fish oil
20. Dominican Republic	94.1 A	0	85.2	sugar, coffee, bananas	2	6.6	bauxite
21. Trinidad and Tobago	94.1	3	84.2	petroleum	0	11.2	sugar
22. Burma	94.0 A	0	76.8	rice	2	20.1	wood, cotton, rubber
23. Surinam	92.9	2	79.1	bauxite	0	12.0	rice
24. Guatemala	92.8	0	79.5	coffee, bananas	2	14.6	cotton
25. Ghana	92.6	0	74.2	cacao	2	22.6	wood products, diamonds
26. British Honduras	92.3 A	0	68.4	sugar, fruit	2	28.3	wood, chicle

Table 5.5. *Continued*

	Specialization Index	SITC Code	Leading Export Category Per Cent of Total	Principal Items	SITC Code	Next Largest Export Category Per Cent of Total	Principal Items
27. Cuba	92.2 c	0	82.4	sugar	1	10.5	tobacco
28. Ethiopia	92.2	0	67.5	coffee, fruit	2	31.2	hides, oil seeds & nuts
29. Ivory Coast	92.2	0	72.1	coffee, cacao, bananas	2	24.6	wood
30. Honduras	92.0	0	73.5	bananas, coffee	2	21.6	wood
31. Western Samoa	92.0	0	64.9	cacao, bananas	2	34.1	copra
32. Ceylon	91.9	0	72.5	tea, coconut, spices	2	20.4	rubber, copra, fibers
33. Sierra Leone	90.7	6	63.6	diamonds	2	31.1	cacao, coffee
34. Niger	90.7	2	69.7	ground nuts	0	23.6	cattle
35. Tanzania: Zanzibar	90.5 A	0	70.8	cloves	2	17.9	copra
36. Panama	90.2	0	57.8	bananas	3	41.3	petroleum products
37. Cook Islands	90.2	0	64.1	fruits	8	27.6	clothing
38. Uganda	89.6	0	61.1	coffee	2	31.5	cotton
39. Chile	89.6 A	6	67.8	copper	2	23.3	ores, nitrates, wool
40. Colombia	89.3	0	72.9	coffee, bananas, sugar	3	18.3	petroleum
41. Tanzania: Tanganyika	89.2	2	65.0	oil, seeds, hides	0	25.1	cashews
42. Malaysia: Sabah	89.1	2	75.8	sawlogs	1	15.8	tobacco
43. Gabon	88.6	2	69.9	wood, ores	3	14.5	petroleum
44. Mali	88.5	2	56.9	ground nuts	0	39.0	fish
45. Thailand	88.5	0	56.1	rice, maize	2	40.0	rubber, jute, tin
46. Afghanistan	88.4	2	63.7	furs, hides	0	23.7	fruits
47. Madagascar	88.2	0	68.1	coffee, spices	2	21.0	sisal
48. Nive Island	88.1	2	51.6	copra	0	43.1	fruits
49. Brazil	87.8	0	68.9	coffee, cacao, sugar	2	22.9	fibers, ores
50. UAR: Egypt	86.9 B	2	69.4	cotton	0	12.6	rice
51. Nicaragua	86.8 A	2	50.2	coffee	0	42.8	cotton
52. Pakistan	86.8	2	62.1	textile fibers	6	22.5	yarns
53. Dahomey	86.7	2	69.2	oil seeds	4	14.9	palm oil
54. Mauritania	86.5	7	62.1	machinery & vehicles (re-exports)	0	25.4	fish

Table 5.5. Continued

	Specialization Index	Leading Export Category			Next Largest Export Category		
		SITC Code	Per Cent of Total	Principal Items	SITC Code	Per Cent of Total	Principal Items
55. New Zealand	86.3	0	49.1	meat, dairy products	2	45.7	wool, hides
56. Kenya	86.0	0	56.7	coffee, tea	2	32.8	sisal
57. Philippines	85.8	2	58.9	copra, wood, ores	0	28.1	coconuts, pineapple
58. Upper Volta	85.8	0	64.4	animals, meat	2	23.4	oil seeds
59. Argentina	85.4	0	65.9	cereals, meat	2	21.1	wool
60. Togo	85.4	2	47.7	oil seeds and nuts	0	45.6	coffee, cacao
61. Malaysia: Sarawak	84.9	2	45.0	rubber, wood	3	40.7	petroleum products
62. Congo, Democratic Republic of	84.8	6	62.7	copper, diamonds	2	16.6	rubber, ores
63. Cyprus	84.5	0	49.0	citrus	2	40.3	ores
64. Rhodesia-Malawi	83.7	6	61.0	copper	1	21.8	tobacco
65. Jamaica	83.6	0	46.7	coffee, tea	2	43.0	sisal
66. Cameroon	83.6	0	56.6	coffee, cacao	6	20.2	aluminum metal
67. Malaysia: Malaya	83.5	2	61.7	rubber, ores	6	25.2	tin
68. El Salvador	82.4	0	58.4	coffee	2	25.9	cotton
69. Congo (Brazzaville)	81.3	6	48.6	diamonds	2	39.1	wood, oil seeds
70. Indonesia	81.1	2	42.9	rubber, tin	3	38.9	petroleum
71. New Guinea	80.2	0	40.5	copra, ground nuts	2	36.0	cacao, coffee
72. China: Taiwan	80.1	0	54.7	sugar, fruit, rice	6	27.2	textiles
73. Morocco	80.1	2	46.4	phosphates, ores	0	38.7	citrus
74. Finland	79.9	6	41.0	paper, wood products	2	39.3	wood
75. Israel	78.2	6	52.3	cut diamonds, textiles	0	29.5	fruits
76. Nigeria	77.3	2	52.4	oil seeds and nuts	0	20.0	cacao
77. Senegal	77.0	2	38.8	oil seeds and nuts	4	35.3	ground nut oil
78. Aden	76.5 B	3	62.5	mineral fuels *	0	13.4	coffee, cereals *
79. Turkey	76.0	0	38.5	fruits and nuts	2	33.9	cotton, wool
80. Australia	75.9	2	41.8	wool	0	39.0	cereals, meat
81. Greece	74.3	1	42.2	wine, tobacco	0	24.0	fruits

A 1962   B 1961   C 1960
* Mainly re-exports

113

group between the median and the third quartile point (92.2) receive well over nine-tenths of their export earnings from three SITC categories, all consisting of raw materials and foodstuffs.

In the upper quartile, from 92.2 to 100, specialization becomes almost complete. At the lower end of this range are countries, such as Ghana, which receive nine-tenths of their foreign exchange income from only two export classes, one of these normally predominating. Twelve countries having specialization indices from 96.0 to 99.8 form a tight cluster at the top. Figure 5.8 shows the cumulative frequency distribution of the exports of Mauritius, the most specialized of all 107 countries, deriving virtually its entire income from the sale of sugar. This example is typical of the group.

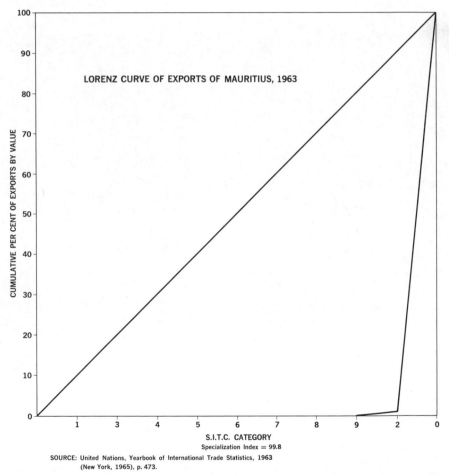

LORENZ CURVE OF EXPORTS OF MAURITIUS, 1963

S.I.T.C. CATEGORY

Specialization Index = 99.8

SOURCE: United Nations, Yearbook of International Trade Statistics, 1963
(New York, 1965), p. 473.

Fig. 5.8.

Implicit in the foregoing discussion is the existence of a close correlation between export specialization and economic development. The examples we cited from the lower end of the scale are virtually all highly developed economically; those at the upper extreme are less developed countries and colonies. This relationship is portrayed graphically in Figure 5.9, in which the specialization index is plotted against per capita gross domestic product, the latter serving as a measure of relative economic development. To each of the major world regions, as delineated for the purposes of this study, we have assigned a distinctive symbol corresponding to that used in similar diagrams earlier in this chapter (see Figs. 5.1 and 5.2). The divisions between developed and less developed countries (per capita GDP of $559), between the less developed and the moderately less developed ($2.80), and between the moderately developed and the highly developed countries ($1,118), also remain unchanged from the earlier diagrams. The two middle ranges are more sparsely populated in this diagram than in the earlier figures based upon per capita gross domestic product, however, because of the lack of data for most of the Communist and certain of the Latin American countries. Countries having diversified exports are separated from specialized exporters along the first quartile line, equal to an index of 74, as explained earlier.

Inspection of the diagram tends to confirm the presence of a relationship between specialization of exports and economic development. Many countries of Africa and Asia are knotted together in the upper left-hand corner, where they have been relegated by their combination of high specialization indices and low per capita GDP. The few Latin American countries which appear here tend to be somewhat higher in the scale of development; however, some are high also in specialization of exports and thus represent deviations from the general pattern. The moderately developed countries of Europe, and even the less developed ones, especially Greece, Spain and Portugal, tend to be diversified in their exports, reflecting the place of both agricultural products and fabricated goods in their sales abroad. The highly developed European countries are generally diversified in their exports, although Iceland and Finland provide notable exceptions. A Middle Eastern country, Israel, appears to belong with the European cluster, although its exports are somewhat more specialized than the others in that group. Australia and New Zealand also rank with western Europe in development but have higher specialization indices. Canada and the United States are far to the right on the development scale and low in the specialization range. Indeed, the United States stands alone in the lower right-hand corner of the diagram. On the whole, then, the highly developed countries are highly diversified, with only the five exceptions mentioned.

Although specialization of exports has been a feature of international trade from early times and was regarded by classical economists as a logical outcome of unrestrained trade among nations, it appears possible that such specialization is more widely prevalent in today's more complex world than is generally appreciated. Our analysis has shown that at least three-fourths of the 107 countries for which there are adequate data have exports that are concentrated within a few, often related classes. At the upper end of the scale of specialization indices we have found a large group of countries depending upon only one or two SITC categories for virtually all of their foreign exchange earnings. At the opposite end of the continuum we have noted a much smaller number of countries whose diversified exports include both manufactured prod-

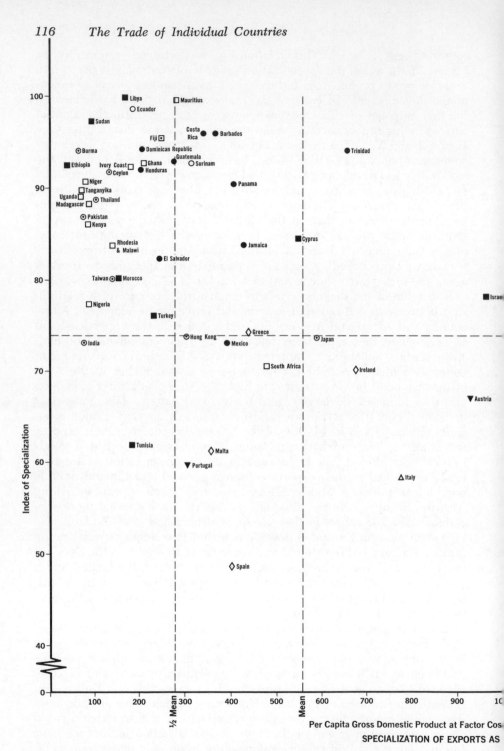

Fig. 5.9.

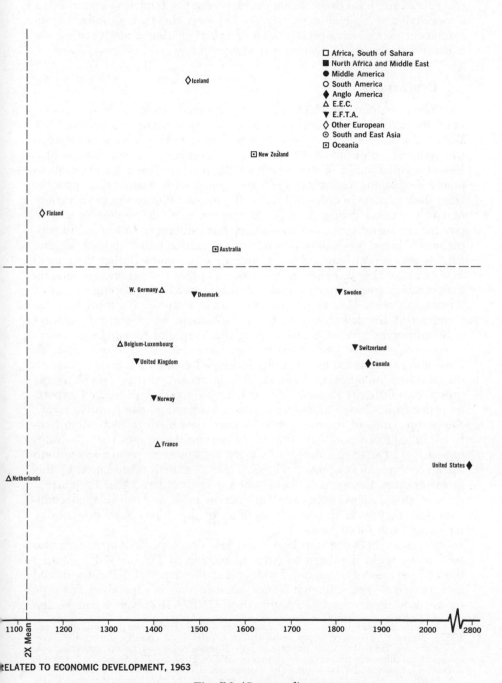

RELATED TO ECONOMIC DEVELOPMENT, 1963

Fig. 5.9 *(Continued).*

ucts and agricultural commodities. A comparison of these results with a measure of the level of economic development has tended to confirm that a decided inverse relationship exists between the two, despite certain prominent exceptions. Specialization of exports is thus a matter of significance for the study of economic development.

Conclusions

Every method by which we have measured world trade has underlined the differences separating two of the three categories of countries. Recent years seem to have brought a widening in the disparities between the trade of non-Communist, developed countries and non-Communist, less developed lands, to the benefit of the former. Trade is important to newly developing countries, since they must earn as much as possible from their exports in order to finance the importation of the great variety of costly capital goods required to modernize their economies and to pay for the many consumer goods they must obtain from abroad to supplement a home production which is as yet inadequate.[20] Indeed, lagging exports may seriously retard the growth of an economy during the critical first stages of the development process.[21] Despite the general recognition that earnings from exports are essential to a newly developing economy, however, a close look at international trade statistics discloses that the countries at the lower end of the development scale are experiencing only indifferent success in maintaining this source of national income.

The evidence we have cited in the preceding pages shows that, although only a handful of the underdeveloped countries failed to increase the absolute amounts of their exports in recent years, a much larger group—two-fifths of those in this category—recorded decreased exports on a per capita basis. Moreover, when considered in comparative terms, the performance of these countries is even poorer, since more than two-thirds failed to keep up with the rise in the world average. This illustrates one of the adverse effects of excessively high rates of population growth upon economic development. The obstacle to growth represented by this factor appears the more ominous when it is considered that the current rates of population increase are greater in most underdeveloped countries than they were in equivalent stages of development of present-day technically advanced lands.[22]

Differences between developed and less developed countries are also seen when trade is related to national income (GDP or GNP). During the early stages of economic development the export/GNP ratio should be expected to rise, although it may later decline as expanding domestic industry brings an accelerated growth in GNP.[23] However, a comparison

[20] Gunnar Myrdal, *Rich Lands and Poor* (New York: Harper and Brothers, 1957), pp. 95-6. The very heavy demands for capital by a country during the "Preconditions for Take-Off" stage are stressed by Rostow, who assigns an important role to exports in this early period of development. W. W. Rostow, *The Stages of Economic Growth* (London and New York: The Cambridge University Press, 1962).

[21] Charles P. Kindleberger, *Foreign Trade and the National Economy* (New Haven: Yale University Press, 1962), 208-11.

[22] Rostow, *op. cit.*, p. 140.

[23] Kindleberger, *op. cit.*, p. 183ff.

of 1963 data with similar information for 1953 discloses that only a few of the newly developing countries have enjoyed such increases in export/ GDP ratios, all of the others having experienced decreases. Most of the developed countries of Europe, by contrast, have increased their export/ GDP ratios. The decrease in this ratio in the less developed part of the world has occurred despite the fact that those countries have also failed to keep pace with average world rise in per capita income. As the latter figure is the denominator of the fraction, we must conclude that the numerator is also increasing at a very slow pace. This conclusion provides us with one more indication of the relatively limited gains in the trade of these poorer lands.

Specialization of exports appears to be a normal companion of underdevelopment. Of the very few technically advanced lands having specialized exports, none is an important manufacturing nation. Specialization usually means an emphasis upon the sale abroad of primary goods, such as minerals and agricultural commodities, mainly in an unprocessed state. Students of economic development disagree on whether an "emerging" country should strive for balanced development, with equal attention to growth in primary and secondary production, or whether it should concentrate its efforts upon secondary activities and neglect the primary. Obviously, such a decision is reflected in the character of the country's exports. Myrdal insists that underdeveloped countries receive the poor end of the trade bargain, that trade has a bias in favor of the rich.[24] Prebisch agrees, arguing that the long-run terms of trade operate against the less developed countries.[25] The less developed countries' shrinking share of world export earnings has been evident from each method we have used to assess them. Although the demand for minerals and the prices paid for them have fluctuated greatly (due to conditions outside the control of the producing countries), there has been limited demand for agricultural commodities, the prices of which have remained weak because of oversupply and competition from substitutes. The world trade in manufactured goods, meanwhile, has been consistently advancing both in quantity and price, to the benefit of the technically advanced countries.

In Chapter 4 it was shown that, although still generally below levels prevailing in the technically advanced, non-Communist west, the trade of Communist countries has increased rapidly since its low point at the end of World War II. Concerning that group of countries, the knowledge added by this present chapter has been limited by inadequate information. To supply meaningful conclusions based on the methods used here, the sample of Communist countries for which data are obtainable from United Nations sources is both too small and too unrepresentative. Nevertheless, the information provided by those few Communist countries for which we have sufficiently detailed trade statistics suggests certain signifi-

[24] *Op. cit.,* p. 28 *et passim.*
[25] Raul Prebisch, "The Role of Commercial Policies in Underdeveloped Countries," *American Economic Review, Papers and Proceedings,* Vol. 44, May, 1959. By "terms of trade" is meant the difference between unit prices paid per unit for imports of a country as against unit prices received per unit for its exports.

cant possibilities. We have found, for example, that the Communist countries of eastern Europe have experienced rapidly rising per capita exports much as their non-Communist neighbors have done, with the poorly developed members of the group starting from lower bases. Cuba, the lone Communist country in the western hemisphere, has declined in per capita exports, following the pattern of other Latin American exporters of food and beverage crops, although in this case the decrease was accentuated by political problems. Thus, our limited information suggests that Communist countries may possess trade characteristics which are related less to their particular form of economic organization than to their regional locations and stage of economic development, especially the latter.

Regardless of the political and economic system to which it subscribes, then, a country appears to enjoy the benefits of a high level of dependably profitable international trade roughly in proportion to its position on the scale of economic development. Accompanying that development, and an integral part of it, are the highly intricate organizational arrangements which have evolved for conducting international trade. In hierarchical fashion the mechanism of world trade encompasses the individual trading concerns and the variety of service agencies upon which they depend, the great trading center complexes through which the flow of trade is funneled, the elaborate techniques and numerous agencies by which national governments attempt to influence the size and character of trade movements across their borders, and the growing list of international organizations devoted to facilitating or channeling the trade of countries. It is to a consideration of this organizational aspect of world trade that we turn in the two chapters which follow.

CHAPTER 6 *logistics and mechanics:*
trading concerns and commercial centers

Along with the growth of trade among the countries of the world, there has evolved an elaborate system of mechanical arrangements by means of which this international flow of goods is conducted, channeled, and controlled. Normally the transfer of products across international borders is a matter of greater complexity than the domestic movement of such goods. Such movement consequently requires the assistance of many private agencies, employs the facilities of various kinds of service centers, and receives the attention of numerous national and international organizations. Although operations are highly specialized at each level, the whole trading process constitutes a closely integrated mechanism.

So smoothly does this mechanism perform that only the occasional malfunctioning of one of its more sensitive parts draws attention to it, as in the case of a maritime strike. Consequently, this aspect of international trade has been accorded little recognition by writers on the subject, except for those within that closely-knit fraternity directly concerned with day-to-day importing and exporting operations. Nevertheless, there are at least two reasons why a knowledge of this apparatus is of value to the student of the geography of international trade: (1) a close relationship exists between the mechanism of trade and the factors which produce that trade and (2) the operations are spatially organized.

Just as the international trade mechanism is a product of the need to exchange goods, so does that mechanism itself influence the flow of those goods. The growth of commercial and governmental agencies in response to the requirements of active trading partners is best illustrated by the arrangements and facilities which have evolved to serve the North Atlantic trade. At both ends of this route are found the largest and most elaborate port works, the most highly developed international banking facilities, and the largest and best organized export and import brokerage houses in the world, all connected by the most frequent steamer sailings of all the ocean routes. By contrast, regions of the world generating little international traffic have but poorly developed facilities of these types. In turn, the flow of merchandise is affected in pattern and, to some degree, in total volume by the institutional arrangements which have grown up over a period of many years. Some of these effects will be noted in a later section.

Of particular interest to the economic geographer is the manner in which the organizational aspects of international trade are distributed in space. These activities are highly concentrated in certain gateway junctions, among which seaports are especially important. (See Frontispiece.) Situated at that point where land and ocean routes meet, the seaport is clearly the preferred location for those public and private agencies concerned with the international exchange of merchandise. In addition to such focal points as the port, the pattern of routes connecting the world's traffic generating areas also interests the economic geographer, who seeks explanations for the direction and varying intensities of trade flow.

Since an adequate understanding of the geography of international trade thus logically includes an appreciation of the mechanism by means of which that trade occurs, a survey of the subject will occupy this chapter and the next. The present chapter will treat the first two levels of operation: (1) individual concerns participating in world trade and (2) centers of international commerce. The following chapter will consider the methods by which countries influence the flow of merchandise across their borders and the international arrangements which have evolved for trade purposes.

Commercial Concerns

Individual enterprises participating in international trade—the firms engaged in selling or buying as well as those which serve them—vary greatly in size, ranging from the small family-owned importing house in Santo Domingo to the great tire company headquartered in Akron and from the Chicago freight forwarder with five employees to the ocean cargo carrier with 2,500.

TRADING COMPANIES

Exporters.   In the non-Communist world several types of firms engage in exporting. In the case of such industrial raw materials as mineral ores, the exporter may also be the producer of the goods, and often is a partly or wholly owned subsidiary of a refining and fabricating concern in the country of final destination. This is largely true, for example, of iron ore exports of Canada, Venezuela, Chile, and Liberia, crude oil exports of Venezuela, and copper ore exports of Chile and Peru. Also representative of this group are pipeline shipments of petroleum and gas across international boundaries, as occurs between Canada and the United States. By contrast, other commodities, such as fats, oils, and grains, are collected from thousands of producers and exported by specialized storage and brokerage firms, whose facilities are usually located in such port areas as Quebec, Houston, or Bayonne, New Jersey.

Exporters of manufactured products are even more varied in type. Many large manufacturing concerns maintain dealer organizations abroad and export directly, preparing their own shipping documents and making their own transportation arrangements. Location of the fabricating facilities of such a company may occur at whatever point is most favorable for that operation, but its exporting division will probably maintain its offices in some large commercial center, such as New York or Chicago, where specialized services are to be found at hand. Some exportation of manufactured items, particularly to underdeveloped countries, is conducted by specialized engineering firms which collect equipment from many sources and make consolidated shipments of complete installations, such as electric power plants or telephone systems. Another type of exporting arrangement is represented by the domestic concern which purchases from a manufacturer in its own country the supplies and equipment required by its overseas subsidiaries. As a variant of this procedure, a manufacturer in one country may buy materials through a purchasing agent in another country. In such a case the purchasing agent may also perform the exportation. This list is selective, including only the more common of the innumerable arrangements by which individual concerns engage in exporting.

It was stated earlier that in most cases only the larger firms regularly engaged in international trade prepare their own export documents and take care of the other details of making shipments abroad. This fact reflects the nature of exporting procedures, which are of such complexity that only the most capable and highly trained personnel are employed in this specialized work. Among the requisites are a knowledge of commercial papers, foreign banking procedures and instruments, and the documentary requirements of both the country from which the shipment is being made and the country to which it is bound, as well as a familiarity with export packing specifications and the alternative transport arrangements which may be available. The import regulations of the customer's government often present a special problem for firms having world-wide operations, since every country has its own unique arrangements and the related documents, especially import licenses, are usually in the native language. Each detail of these operations must receive the most careful attention, since an incorrect figure on an invoice or an overlooked expiration date on an import license or letter of credit can result in serious losses.

A company deeply engaged in exporting must possess a highly developed marketing organization abroad. The various outposts in this network of distributors or affiliated companies generally receive regular visits from the parent firm's traveling representatives, who must not only have training in exporting procedures equal to that of the home office personnel but must also have a superior knowledge of the company's products as well. The field worker combines the functions of analyst, salesman, teacher, and mechanic as he makes his rounds developing new markets, appointing and training new distributors, solving special problems of customers, and supplying the parent organization with a continuous flow of intelligence reports.

Importers.   As in the case of exporters, companies engaged in the importing of foreign merchandise are of many types. Some of the largest importers in terms of tonnage are manufacturers who import raw materials or supplies and equipment for their own use. The latter include large steel companies operating at coastal sites, such as the Bethlehem Steel Company, which imports enormous quantities of ore for its gigantic plant at Sparrows Point, Maryland, or the rapidly expanding Cornigliano steel works at Genoa, Italy, which receives virtually all of its coal and ore from overseas sources and imports much of its machinery as well. By contrast, such commodities as oils and fats, grains, and vegetable fibers are imported by brokers for resale.

Another common type is the distributor of imported goods, a specialist found in most countries of the non-Communist world. In the newly developing countries this kind of importer is particularly well represented and plays an essential part. The importing firm provides the usual channel through which such a country obtains articles not yet manufactured by the newly emerging modern sector of the economy and which are required in ever greater quantity and variety during the earlier stages of industrial development. The distributor frequently holds exclusive franchises for all or part of the country, depending upon the latter's areal extent and economic development. In a typical operation the principal office is located in the most important commercial city and branches are maintained in smaller regional centers. Often the company handles a number of noncompeting but related lines of merchandise. Thus a distributor may, for example, specialize in engineering goods, ranchers' supplies, or hardware merchandise, in this way making it possible to supply a variety of items to the same customers and to provide more knowledgeable service. Distributors of imported goods include not only small family enterprises but also some large corporate groups, the latter being well represented in market areas of greater potential. Most distributing organizations confine their activities to a single country, but there are notable exceptions, such as the London-based W. H. Brady and Company, with its operations in India, Malaysia, and elsewhere in Asia. Another large firm engaged in this type of work is the W. R. Grace Company, which not only distributes imported goods in several Latin American lands but also has innumerable interests in agriculture, mining, transportation, banking, and insurance in that area. Also an exception is the large exporting firm which markets its own products through overseas subsidiaries. The latter usually specialize in distributing the parent firm's merchandise and may also manufacture certain of its products for local sale.

In their unique methods of conducting international trade, the Communist countries have followed the example of the Soviet Union, which channels all of its external transactions through foreign trade corporations. These governmental agencies are usually highly specialized, each being responsible for the sale or purchase of a single commodity in foreign markets. Because of the unrealistic values which Communist states tend to place upon their monetary units, the foreign trade corporations employ barter or the currencies of other countries in most external operations. At least in the past, these corporations have apparently not been troubled by the necessity of making a profit. Instead, their chief purpose has been to correct imbalances in home production as determined by the official plan. Furthermore, as arms of the government, the foreign trade corporations must at times undertake transactions for political reasons, as in the case of the Soviet Union's sugar purchases and certain of its mineral sales.

Regardless of the economic and political systems prevailing in their home countries, concerns engaged in exporting and importing adhere to a body of conventional terminology to reduce the possibilities for error due to ambiguity. Important among these are the "terms of shipment" employed to indicate which of the costs of shipment will be borne by the seller and which by the purchaser. The symbols FOB and FAS, accompanied by the designation of some location such as the factory, a conveyance, or a port of shipment, indicate that the cost of shipment from the point cited is to be borne by the buyer. C & F or CIF, together with the name of a port or other location within the country of destination, indicate that shipping expenses up to that point are to be paid by the seller (see the Glossary for a more detailed explanation of these expressions). When a prospective purchaser receives a quotation in which one of these symbols follows the stated price of the merchandise, he can ascertain the exact delivered cost and is thus able to make comparisons with the prices of other suppliers. The nature of the expenses incurred in transporting goods from the mine or factory of the seller to the warehouse of the importer will become apparent in the next section, which discusses the service agencies of international trade.

ANCILLARY SERVICE AGENCIES.   In that division of labor which characterizes the mechanism of international trade, exporters and importers are highly dependent upon a number of service agencies. This is true of even the largest trading firms, although their reliance upon others is not so extreme as that of their less well-equipped competitors. The service organizations perform specialized functions at a number of points along the route of shipment, their precise locations being closely oriented to the markets for their services and the availability of the facilities upon which they depend. A long corporate existence typifies certain of these agencies, especially the international banks and insurance companies, some of which are venerable institutions. Among some categories of service organizations, severe competition prevails, and the mortality rates are high. In a line of business where the demands are exacting, the one item that these businesses have to sell is service. Thus success depends upon the quality of that service, its dependability and efficiency.

Service agencies participating in international trade include combination export managers, foreign banking companies, insurers of international commerce, freight forwarders and brokers, and commercial carriers. Providing a service which makes foreign sales feasible for firms unable to support their own export departments because of the irregularity or the small scale of their foreign business, combination export managers simultaneously care for the overseas trade of several companies. When an order is received from overseas by one of the companies subscribing to this service, the order is prepared for shipment; and the packing slip, import license, and other pertinent materials and information are given to the combination export manager, whose staff complete the export documents and make all the arrangements for exportation. Of fairly recent development, this convenient type of service promises to add substantially to the trading potential of those areas where it is available. Combination export managers are found in principal seaboard cities and in major inland transport centers such as Chicago.

Whether the exporting company has its own foreign department or depends upon outside help for this function, it finds indispensable the services of foreign banking companies. Especially in the United States, where branch banking is restricted, institutions providing this type of service are largely confined to major ports and other large commercial centers. Barclay's Bank, the First National Bank of Chicago, The First National City Bank of New York, and The Bank of America typify the very large institutions engaged in international banking operations. Some banks in this category concentrate upon servicing international trade; others maintain foreign banking departments as but one of their major functions. In the performance of their chief role—transmitting funds, making collections, and financing international transactions—such banks must have some type of representation in the major overseas financial centers with which they do business. Several of the large institutions, such as Barclay's Bank (DC & O) and the Bank of Nova Scotia, maintain numerous branches in foreign lands; others depend for their representation abroad upon "correspondent" banks, which are independent institutions in other countries. Networks of such reciprocal relationships are to be found throughout the principal trading areas of the world.

Together with their responsibility for making collections and transmitting payments from one country to another, banks act on behalf of their customers in numerous ways. Banks are sometimes required by their importer customers to exercise detailed control over shipping arrangements such as packing, insurance, choice of carrier, and type of bill of lading. Enforcement is achieved by means of certificates which must be presented with other shipping documents before payment can be received by the shipper. The legal document employed when such control is desired is the letter of credit, of which there are several types. Because the letter of credit also provides a strong measure of protection for the shipper, he is frequently the one who requires such payment terms. The advantage to the exporter of this form of payment is the fact that the usual type of letter of credit constitutes a firm guarantee of payment by a bank in his own country. Thus the letter of credit constitutes the strictest terms of payment short of "cash in advance" and is most commonly specified in cases where there is uncertainty concerning the customer's ability to pay or the political or economic stability of his country. Other terms of payment used in international trade, in decreasing order of stringency, are "sight draft," "time draft," and "cash against invoice" (see glossary for definitions). Except for "cash against invoice" and "cash in advance," these payment terms require transmission of all shipping documents by the exporter's bank to a bank in the country of ultimate destination.

Export shipments may range in value from a few dollars for a parcel post package of spare parts to several hundred thousand dollars or more for the shipment by sea of a complete factory. Regardless of value, however, the exporter and his customer rarely gamble on the safe arrival of a consignment. Such uncertainties are assigned to large financial institutions whose business it is to provide marine insurance, credit insurance, and other types of risk coverage for firms engaged in international trade. Such international centers of trade and finance as London, New York, and Philadelphia are the favored locations for the headquarters of the great marine insurance companies, but branch offices and brokerage houses extend into all major cities from which export shipments originate.

The choice of the type of insurance coverage and of the company from which it is to be purchased may be made by either the exporter or his customer, but in any case the insurance declaration forms describing the merchandise and giving its value are prepared and forwarded to the collecting bank by the seller or his representative. Most shipments are insured against all risks—theft, total loss at sea, damage from fire and water, and the other hazards to which goods moving from one country to another may be subject. Included in such coverage is protection for shippers against their liability for a portion of the cost of repairs to the ship if it should be damaged while carrying their merchandise. If, for example, a vessel's propeller should be damaged by scraping against the banks of the Chesapeake and Delaware Canal, a pro-rated assessment, called a "general average," would be made against the owners of all cargo on board at the time.

The willingness of shippers to make extensive use of insurance is enhanced by the rates, which in time of peace are very low. When international tensions rise, however, as occurred during the Suez crisis of 1956, rates may be increased sharply and suddenly, dropping just as quickly when the danger passes. Aside from these general rate changes, there is also a considerable variation in individual rates prevailing at any given time, depending upon the loss record of the shipper, the character of the merchandise, and the nature of the transport medium, especially the age and tonnage of the vessel.

When a consignment reaches the port, it comes under the care of an agency known as a foreign freight forwarder. Much depends upon this agency's skill in threading the maze of details associated with getting the merchandise on board a vessel. The very important functions of the forwarder will be reviewed at some length later in this chapter.

As integral parts of the mechanism of international trade, the organizations just described represent only the major ancillary services and do not include numerous lesser but useful cogs, such as the translating services and stevedoring concerns. Also omitted has been a group whose obvious importance is sufficiently great to merit separate treatment: the commercial carriers of internationally traded goods.

Commercial Centers

We have seen that a disproportionate contribution to total world trade is made by a few pre-eminent areas of production, which are tied to each other and to their main raw material suppliers by well-defined transport routes. Even the air and sea lanes are concentrated within narrow bands despite their relative freedom from physical restraints. Each of these avenues of commerce terminates at a point having special significance for international trade: the seaport, airport, or some other form of gateway. Paralleling the transport hub in importance, complementing it in function, and often sharing its space is that command post of trade, the world market center. These two categories of focal points will occupy our attention for the remainder of the chapter.

PORTS.   In function, the various types of ports are similar. Not only does each act as a focus of transport lines, but it also provides entry to or exit from a national territory. Furthermore, the port area usually contains a concentration of the many specialized services which contribute to the efficient flow of exports and imports.

The seaport.   Located where ocean and land routes meet, the seaport exists primarily for the purpose of effecting a transfer of goods and passengers from the one transport medium to the other. Harbors—protected, deep-water anchorages for ships—are important features of most, but not all, seaports. Ports without natural harbors are fairly common along smooth coasts wherever a compelling need for their services exists, as the man-made harbor at Los Angeles testifies.

Estimates of the number of seaports in the world vary considerably, ranging from 1,700 to approximately 7,000; [1] yet it is apparent from the map of ocean routes (Frontispiece) that a relatively small number of ports receive a major part of total trade. According to one study, only 150 ports recorded more than two million net tons of shipping entered; four of these—Antwerp, London, New York, and Rotterdam—were credited with receiving more than twenty-five million tons each. [2]

Why one seaport prospers while its neighbors languish, assuming that all possess harbors of adequate physical qualities, may be explained by any of several factors. A first requirement for success is frequency of sailings. The number of vessels calling at a port reflects the demand for ocean transport prevailing there, since ship owners understandably favor ports having the most cargo offerings. Although several ports may provide access to a rich area, one will ordinarily attract more cargo from the traders of that region than will the others. The result, then, ultimately turns upon the collective decisions of many exporting and importing con-

---

[1] F. W. Morgan, *Ports and Harbours*, 2nd ed. (London: Hutchinson University Library, 1958), p. 14.
[2] *Ibid.*, p. 20.

cerns. When choosing among several ports, however, the trading firm first considers the quality of the steamer service provided by each. This service having itself been much influenced by the volume of cargo offerings, the result is a form of circular causation in which success begets still more success. Some special advantage dating to an earlier period has often supplied the momentum for this self reinforcing dominance as it is enjoyed by several world ports.

Steamer service is judged not only on the basis of the frequency of sailings to the desired destination but also on the directness of the connection. For example, most cargo ships serving the Atlantic coast of the United States call at more than one port along that coast—usually New York, Philadelphia, and Baltimore, and sometimes Norfolk-Newport News or Boston. Since upwards of a week may be consumed in making all of these stops, cargo loaded at the last port before the vessel starts its trans-Atlantic crossing will have the shortest elapsed time on its journey to the ultimate destination. Not only does New York enjoy more frequent sailings than its competitors, but it is most often the last port-of-call on the outbound voyage. Indeed, New York occasionally has the double advantage of being both the first and last port-of-call. On such a schedule the vessel comes directly to New York from overseas, discharges its cargo, and then calls at each of the other Atlantic ports before returning once more to New York for that port's cargo and then setting out for Europe or the Far East.

The shipper's decision also considers the nature of transport connections from factory or warehouse to steamer, including relative shipping costs and the speed and frequency of inland transport service. Much depends also upon the transfer arrangements at the port, whether railway cars can go directly onto the pier for unloading, as at Baltimore, or must be unloaded at a railhead and transported by truck or lighter [3] across the harbor to the steamer dock, a time-consuming procedure often necessary at New York. In many instances, the need for specialized equipment determines the choice of a port. Special equipment is also required for loading and unloading coal, grain, and ores, and for shipments employing piggy-back or van arrangements.

The availability of certain port services must also be considered. Especially important is the availability of efficient freight forwarders, as well as consular representatives of foreign governments, international banking facilities, and marine insurance brokers. Quick access to consular and banking services may be decisive in cases where licenses or letters of credit are about to expire.

These are the principal factors which influence a shipper's decisions and, in some cases, continue to do so after basic conditions have altered. The resistance to change embodied in the mechanism of international trade is illustrated by the continued dominance of the port of New York in the handling of internationally traded goods moving to and from the

---

[3] A barge or other small craft used for loading or unloading vessels which for any reason must anchor at a distance from the wharf and for transporting cargo from one part of a harbor to another. A lighter may or may not be equipped to accommodate railway cars.

Midwest of the United States long after the historical reasons for this supremacy have disappeared and despite today's generally lower inland freight rates to such excellent Atlantic ports as Baltimore and Philadelphia. The same type of inertia is partly responsible for the delay being experienced by the St. Lawrence Seaway in realizing the potential earlier predicted for it. In each case much time is required for exporting and importing firms to become fully aware of changed conditions, for service agencies to be established, and for ocean carriers to alter their routes.

The operations of a port, as these affect the merchandise passing through this gateway of international commerce, may be better understood by examining the role of the foreign freight forwarder, who provides one of the ancillary services to which reference was made earlier in this chapter. Acting as agent for various exporting firms within a port hinterland, the forwarder assumes a variety of responsibilities in connection with the intricate task of making an ocean shipment. In this highly competitive business his success depends upon the quality of the service he renders, particularly as it reflects his dependability, efficiency, and resourcefulness. Although the functions he must perform depend upon the nature of the transaction, the forwarder is usually entrusted with securing cargo space on an outbound vessel, arranging for delivery of the goods to the steamer, completing the documents sent to him by the exporter, preparing the ocean bill of lading, having the documents "consularized" (stamped) by a representative of the government of the country for which the shipment is bound, passing the export declaration through customs, and finally presenting the completed shipping papers to the collecting bank.

The agency's other major role, that of customhouse broker for importers, entails similar duties. These include clearing through customs the documents relating to an inbound shipment, paying the duties, taking possession of the merchandise, and arranging for transporting it to the customer. The work is extremely exacting and requires a superior knowledge of international trade processes. The procedures outlined here are characteristic of operations at ports of the United States and would differ in detail in some other countries. The main outline, however, is fairly standard in the technically advanced lands of the non-Communist world.

The international airport.   Like the seaport, the international airport stands at the meeting point of two unlike forms of transport, in this case land and air. It also resembles the seaport in providing physical facilities for the servicing and protection of the craft and for the transfer and care of cargo and passenger. Both types of transport centers supply services required for conducting international trade.

For the adequate performance of these functions the international airport must occupy a site meeting certain physical requirements, the first of which is an expanse of level, well-drained land. The area covered by the airport must be sufficiently great to accommodate the web of 9,000-foot paved runways required by today's jet aircraft. This space requirement, plus the necessity for avoiding heavily built-up residential areas for reasons of safety and noise control, inflict upon the commercial airport one of its principal handicaps—the sometimes long and tedious ground journey to and from the city it serves. Ideally the airport site should also be relatively free from climatic conditions tending to obscure visibility. In addition to these site specifications, the international airport requires a hinterland capable of generating substantial export and import traffic, and it must lie on direct routes leading to other trading countries.

Airport procedure for handling internationally traded goods is generally simpler than that of the seaport. After the package and its attached shipping documents have been picked up from the customer and carted to the air terminal, the airline's representative takes care of any consular formalities which may be required by the receiving country and presents the export declaration to customs. The merchandise is then placed on board that airline's first available flight to the required destination. Incoming parcels are cleared through customs and otherwise processed in much the same manner as ocean shipments.

As one of the world's leading international air terminals, London Airport possesses many special advantages and some problems as well. Located west of London on a well-drained terrace of the Thames, this airport is the eastern terminus for a large portion of the trans-Atlantic air crossings. Its heavy traffic reflects London's great size and its role as Britain's political and economic control center, main surface transport hub, cultural capital, and principal tourist attraction. Among the airport's disadvantages are frequent periods of poor visibility and the hour-long journey into the city. Other important international airports of the British Isles are those at Prestwick, Scotland, and Shannon, Ireland, both of which are jumping-off points for the Atlantic crossing. Each of the major cities of continental Europe has a busy international airport, a notable example being Rotterdam, the home of KLM Royal Dutch Airlines and the chief distribution center for the heavy air cargo traffic transported by this carrier.

Except for the fact that it does not serve a major political capital, New York City's Kennedy International Airport bears a remarkable similarity to London Airport in its assets and liabilities, even to the visibility problem associated with its twelve-foot elevation above sea level.[4] Probably the largest of all international airports is Chicago's O'Hare Field, which occupies more than eleven square miles. With the coming of jet transports, most of Chicago's long-range flights were moved to O'Hare from Midway airport, since the latter is confined to a one-square-mile area by encircling residential and industrial land uses. O'Hare Field's former isolation has been overcome by the construction of a new expressway which provides thirty-minute access to the central business district of Chicago. A number of other airfields are important to the international trade of the United States, especially the international airports at Miami and New Orleans, which participate actively in the air cargo traffic with Latin America.

Free ports.   Despite the implications of the name, only a few free ports exist as separate and independent entities, examples being the West

[4] Kenneth R. Sealy, *The Geography of Air Transport* (London: Hutchinson University Library, 1957), p. 185.

Indian ports of Charlotte Amalie and Willemstad and the Asian ports of Hong Kong and Singapore. The typical free port of a technically advanced land is merely an incidental feature of an international trade center. Although most free ports are found within the confines of seaports, they are beginning to appear at international airports as well.

The principal purpose of the free port, a device of ancient roots, is to provide docking, storage, and other port facilities for goods of foreign origin which are intended for reconsignment to a third destination or are to be sorted or processed before being imported without the necessity of incurring high tariffs or submitting to complicated customs procedures of the host country unless or until the shipper wishes to do so. Duties are assessed only if and when it may be decided to complete the formal entry of such goods into the country within which the free port lies. Because of the special privileges attending its use, the free port area is fenced off from the remainder of the sea- or airport with which it is associated.[5]

The free port has a long tradition in northwestern Europe, where Hamburg has maintained such a function since its membership in the Hanseatic League. Among other North Sea and Baltic ports providing facilities of this type are Bremen, Gothenburg, and Stockholm. Free ports are also found in the Adriatic. Under the name "foreign trade zone," this device has been the subject of experimentation at several American ports, notably New York and New Orleans. In many other parts of the world there are free ports of considerable variety, including not only the examples from the Caribbean and Asia cited earlier but also several ports providing access to the sea for landlocked countries, as does Arica, Chile, which performs that valuable function for Bolivia.

Although it is common for goods to be on display in a free port area, most sales are in wholesale lots. Exceptions to this are found at several of the Caribbean ports, where the tourist trade supports a brisk retail business. A similar situation obtains at Shannon International Airport in the Republic of Ireland, where air travelers may purchase a great variety of duty-free European merchandise before setting out for North America.

Added considerations.   This discussion of the gateways through which imports and exports of countries are funneled has emphasized those two categories found where land transport meets air or water together with a special feature which may be found at either, the free port. In addition there are certain other points of entry and exit for internationally traded goods, especially those occurring at border crossings of railways, highways, and waterways. Although large volumes of merchandise are exchanged by these means, especially in Europe and North America, little need be added concerning the procedures they entail. Border formalities differ only slightly from those previously mentioned except that they are much simplified in the case of all-surface transport by the fact that it is usually not necessary to transfer cargo from one conveyance to another. If cargoes must be shifted, as is required for L/C/L (less-than-carload) or L/T/L (less-than-truckload) shipments

---

[5] Richard S. Thoman, *Free Ports and Foreign Trade Zones* (Cambridge, Maryland: Cornell Maritime Press, 1956), pp. 6-8.

across the United States-Mexican border, the ensuing complications may require the services of a forwarder or broker.

These centers devoted to the physical handling of exports and imports are paralleled by others which are primarily concerned with transferring title to international merchandise and with financing transactions—the world market centers—whose role in international trade will be considered next.

INTERNATIONAL MARKET CENTERS.   The flow of international trade requires not only the facilities for transferring goods from one country to another but also some means of contact among prospective buyers and sellers of a given product. Although the producers and their customers may be widely scattered within their respective countries, the trade is often directed from important world centers. These centers, usually great cities, provide the institutional arrangements needed for such trade: financial organizations, transport (including port facilities), communication media, and a wide range of specialized services, some of which have been discussed previously in other contexts. Because of the many advantages offered by world trade centers, they are favored as locations for the headquarters of large manufacturing concerns and of trading firms. Thus the great market centers are the principal control points for international trade of all kinds. There are special classes of merchandise, however, which are particularly dependent upon such centers for their exchange.

Although manufactured goods are bought and sold mainly by means of bilateral negotiations between importer and exporter, as was described earlier, raw materials and other bulk commodities are traded in a very different fashion. The dissimilarities between these methods of trading result principally from the contrasting character of the two types of merchandise. By means of trade-marks, manufactured products are closely identified with the maker and possess unique qualities (upon which the manufacturer's sales efforts lay great stress); on the other hand, commodities are seldom characterized by any significant degree of product differentiation and rarely bear the names or marks of their producers, who may number many thousands. For these reasons quality, quantity, and price are the only major concerns among commodity traders. Prices result from the interaction of innumerable interested individuals and firms—the great numbers of independent producers, the large corps of middlemen who collect, clean, sort, and grade the commodity, and the many buyers, acting through their agents. Ultimately, commodity prices conform closely to the relationship between supply and demand, the merchandise flowing from one place to another, always in the direction of the strongest demand. It is in the great commodity markets, located at important trading centers, that prices are determined, and it is upon these points that international movements of raw materials and bulk goods focus.

During the period of European empires the largest commodity markets became established in the principal consuming countries, reflecting the initiative of buyers as well as the conditions of colonial control. Although markets have also arisen in producing countries—and in recent times such markets have tended to increase in size and importance—trading in most lines continues to be dominated by the older centers, where tradition exerts a strong influence. Custom governs the procedures at these older markets, exacting its conformity of all who participate and incorporating usages so old that no one knows their origins. Over the many years, trade in any one commodity tends to become concentrated within a particular section of a city and to attract highly specialized traders and brokers, banking houses, transport experts, and insurance concerns.

Depending upon the type of goods and the circumstances of particular transactions, there are three principal methods of commodity trading. Concerning the first of these, individual sale—exemplified recently by the huge grain transactions involving Canada, Australia, and the United States on one side and the Communist countries on the other—little will be said here because of the unique character of such events. Instead, attention will be focused upon the other two, the commodity auction and the commodity exchange, both of which are found in well-established market centers.

International commodity auctions.   The oldest method of selling raw materials and other bulk commodities in large quantities, the commodity auction, was probably initiated in its present form by the Dutch East India Company, although its roots doubtless extend into antiquity.[6] Adopted since by the British and others, the auction has become the principal method for trading certain types of commodities. Among these are such nonstandard items as furs, diamonds, and wool, which are difficult to grade; perishable commodities such as vegetables and fruits; and seasonally produced goods of all kinds. Because of their variation in quality and their irregular appearance on the market, these products must be physically present at the sale; hence the characteristic use of the auction for their disposal.

Procedures followed at the great international auctions are subject to varying degrees of government regulation and supervision, and the instruments and warranties employed, whether written or implied, have legal force. As in the case of the Hudson Bay Company fur sales in London, some auctions are conducted by the owners of the merchandise; in the main, however, these are under the auspices of licensed brokers who serve as auctioneers and act as agents of the owners. Customarily the sale is preceded by a public announcement giving the date, time, place, conditions of sale, and a description of the goods. Buying is most often conducted by brokers, who possess an expert knowledge not only of the product but also of the intricate procedures characteristic of that particular market. At the sales, bidding is free and open, prices being determined in a competitive fashion.

The commodity auctions of greatest international importance are held in some of the world's leading port cities. London and Liverpool are noted for their rubber, fur, wool, tea, and coffee auctions; Rotterdam, Amsterdam, and Antwerp specialize in auctioning various tropical commodities,

[6] J. Anton de Haas, *Foreign Trade Organization* (New York: The Ronald Press Company, 1923), p. 231.

including coffee, tea, rubber, spices, and cacao, as well as diamonds and tin. Other leading international commodity auctions within consuming countries are held at Hamburg and New York. In producing countries there are important sales in the principal ports and market centers, as, for example, the rubber auctions at Singapore and the tea auctions in Calcutta and Colombo.

International commodity exchanges. Called by various names— "burse" or "bourse" on the continent of Europe, "exchange" in Britain, and "exchange," "board of trade," or "chamber of commerce" in the United States—the commodity exchange is the principal means for trading those bulk goods which are easily classified, not subject to deterioration, produced in many parts of the world, and marketed throughout the year. Sugar, cotton, wheat, and metallic ores are some of the products fitting this description. Although there is some overlap between the commodities sold at auction and those traded on exchanges (coffee and rubber, for example), the two methods of selling are distinguished particularly by the fact that products sold on the exchanges are not physically present and may in fact be a continent away or not even in existence as yet. The importance of the great commodity exchanges relates not only to their function as places of sale but also to their role in establishing world prices and their usefulness for insulating manufacturers and other interested parties from wide fluctuations in price. How the two latter objectives are accomplished exceeds the scope of this present discussion.

By contrast with auctions, exchanges meet regularly to match "buy" and "sell" orders for commodities. Transactions are of two types, those resulting in an immediate exchange of title to the product ("spot" sales) or those promising to trade at some specified later date ("futures" sales). In the former case, the evidence of ownership is a negotiable instrument known as the warehouse receipt. Most exchanges are controlled and operated by private corporations which are subject to varying degrees of government supervision. Membership is strictly limited, and "seats," which entitle their holders to trading privileges, are bought and sold at high prices, depending upon the condition of the market at any given time.

Several (but not all) large exchanges in continental European countries trade in a wide range of items, not only commodities but also stocks, bonds, and foreign currencies. The general exchanges, typified by those at Amsterdam and Rotterdam, are less common elsewhere, especially in the United Kingdom and the United States, where exchanges tend to specialize to a greater or lesser degree. Of an intermediate type is the New York Produce Exchange, the world's largest, which was founded in 1862 and deals in grain, fats, oils, cotton seed products, and other commodities of a like nature. A still more highly specialized type of exchange deals in only a single commodity or class of commodities. In this category are the London Metal Exchange, the Chicago Board of Trade (grains), and the New York, Liverpool, and New Orleans Cotton exchanges. Specialized exchanges of this type are particularly numerous in London and New York.

CHAPTER 7 *logistics and mechanics:*
countries and international organizations

The importance of international trade to the countries of the world and to their citizens was indicated in Chapter 1, where it was also shown that most modern governments are well aware of this method of realizing a profit from their surpluses and making good their production deficiencies. In order to derive the maximum benefit from this international exchange of goods, governments have developed arrangements for influencing the volume and direction of the flow. Methods employed toward this end by individual governments will be discussed in the first part of this chapter, and international organizations established for this same purpose will be examined in the remainder of the chapter.

The Commerce of Countries

Although generally in agreement concerning the benefits of international trade, governments differ in conceiving their own roles on the trading scene. Their differing viewpoints result in a variety of official policies.

GOVERNMENTAL TRADE POLICIES.   The history of international trade contains examples of governmental interference ranging in degree from rigid control to the near absence of control. This variation in official attitude may be explained in any of several ways. To some extent a country's stage of economic development may influence its governmental policy toward trade with the rest of the world. The British shift from a mercantilist to a free trade outlook was prompted by the Industrial Revolution, which provided that country with unique monopolistic opportunities for trade. The protectionism adopted by the United States during its earlier years, and more recently by newly industrializing Mexico, represents a different response to economic development in the absence of the monopolistic advantage afforded by an early start.

Government trade policy often results from the political control of a special interest group, such as landowners, merchants, or manufacturers, whose ascendancy may or may not be associated with the stage of economic development. The business cycle can also affect policy, particularly when a country attempts to reduce unemployment by means of trade control measures. Considerations of national defense influence the trade of many countries as they stockpile vital imported raw materials and subsidize import-competing industries in an effort to reduce vulnerability in the event of war. Likewise, some countries seek international political advantage through trade with small but strategically situated countries. This aim has been apparent in the sugar purchases of both the Soviet Union and the United States.

A consideration in international trade policies since mercantilist times, the state of the balance of payments continues to influence many government decisions. The balance of payments has been defined as "a systematic record of all economic transactions between the residents of the reporting country and residents of foreign countries during a given period of time." [1] All payments for goods and services, capital and gold transfers, and miscellaneous adjusting items are included in a country's balance of payments; its balance of trade, on the other hand, refers only to the difference between the money value of its merchandise exports and imports. Since exchanges of gold constitute the ultimate means by which imbalances in payments and receipts are adjusted, governments continue to scrutinize carefully the levels of their gold reserves, even though the hoarding of gold for its own sake is no longer an acknowledged policy of most governments. Thus, while West Germany was for a time finding some embarrassment in what was regarded as excessive gold and foreign currency reserves, the United Kingdom and the United States have had to restrict foreign spending in order to stem gold-draining deficits in their international financial accounts.

Shaped by such considerations as these, government trade policies are reflected in the variety of agencies and techniques which have evolved for the purpose of implementing national aims. Some of the measures adopted by governments may be positive in purpose, being intended to promote trade, particularly exports. Other measures may be restrictive in character, having as their purpose the limiting of imports and, occasionally, of certain *types* of exports.

GOVERNMENT ASSISTANCE TO TRADE

Trade promotion. One way in which a government may influence trade positively is to promote the foreign sale of goods produced by its citizens. To this end, consulates maintained by larger countries in the major cities of other lands often perform valuable services for their nationals. Traveling representatives of exporting firms depend upon the

---

[1] Charles P. Kindleberger, *International Economics,* rev. ed. (Homewood, Illinois: The Irwin Series in Economics, 1958), p. 16.

personnel of their government's consulates for assistance in assessing local market conditions, locating business prospects, and securing guidance in other matters concerned with selling their products. Some countries, such as the United Kingdom, use this method of increasing foreign sales so effectively that they have acquired a special reputation among trading firms for the quality of business assistance provided by their consular officials.

Most governments sponsor or participate in trade fairs at which the goods of their countries may be exhibited and demonstrated. Some European fairs have a venerable tradition and attract world-wide attention. Certain countries also send exhibits of their products abroad, a technique currently practiced by the United States Department of Agriculture, which uses this method for promoting the consumption of American wheat, rice, and meat products. West Germany has employed traveling caravans and exhibits to bring its wares to the attention of prospective purchasers in foreign lands; one such group completed an 8,000-mile tour of Central and East Africa. Still another method of assisting trading firms is the government-sponsored foreign trade mission, essentially an organized tour for the representatives of companies having goods to sell or wishing to make purchases abroad. This is a technique favored by Communist countries, whose missions are composed of members of state trading corporations.

Financing and underwriting.   Governments of many countries seek to increase their exports by means of financial assistance to trading firms, often in the form of direct or indirect subsidies. Exporters of cotton from the United States find it possible to compete with foreign sellers only through a government subsidy which enables them to purchase the product at a price below that prevailing on the domestic market. West Germany offers its manufacturers a tax rebate on all exported goods, thus providing them with a strong incentive to enter international trade and with a favorable competitive position in world markets.

During the postwar era an increasing share of the international market has been secured by countries which have been quick to take advantage of a large source of previously unsatisfied demand. Recognizing that many export sales were being lost because prospective buyers did not have established credit ratings or operated in countries suffering from political instability or a shortage of foreign exchange, the West German government, among others, has assisted its exporters by credit guarantees of as much as twelve years in length. Under the pressure of a persistent gold outflow, the United States is placing greater emphasis upon this method of increasing exports. The Export-Import Bank of Washington, which had for some time guaranteed certain types of export credit transactions through commercial banks, inaugurated in 1961 a new program which extended financial backing to a much wider range of export sales and greatly simplified the procedures for securing such assistance. In that year the Bank sponsored the formation of the Foreign Credit Insurance Association, comprising a number of marine, casualty, and property insurance companies, which have joined with the Bank to underwrite short-term (180 days or less) and medium-term (181 days to five years) export transactions. The Export-Import Bank assumes all of the political risks and shares equally with the FCIA the commercial risks.

Inter-governmental grants and credits.   It has long been common for countries to extend loans or gifts to their allies during a war. The United States has provided examples of this practice with the Lend-Lease and Mutual Aid programs of World War II, which were succeeded by the postwar European Recovery Plan ("Marshall Plan") and other devices to assist devastated lands in their return to economic, political, and psychological health. The inter-governmental aid supplied during this period differed from that of earlier occasions not only by its far greater magnitude but also by its inclusion of former enemies. As recovery came to the countries which had participated in the war, an even more significant departure from the past occurred with the introduction of large-scale aid to less developed areas, most of which had newly emerged from colonial status.

Although inter-governmental aid of the type now being received by the underdeveloped countries is not intended primarily as a means of increasing trade, a substantial flow of goods results from such assistance. Some of this movement is one-way, consisting of machinery, foodstuffs, and other merchandise supplied on credit to promote economic development and to improve the standard of living in the receiving country. Development of an economy, however, may also be expected to yield an absolute increase in that country's normal trade with the rest of the world as it begins to produce exportable surpluses and as its needs and wants multiply. Eventually the rate of trade increase may diminish when the domestic economy becomes sufficiently developed to supply a greater number of those goods previously imported (see Chapter 5).

The first to develop a broad program of foreign aid and still the leading source of such assistance, the United States has more recently been joined in this work by several other countries. In terms of the proportion of its gross national product devoted to foreign aid, the United States has actually been surpassed by two other western countries. In 1963 some of the percentages of GNP so employed were: Portugal, 1.41; France, 1.37; the United States, 0.65; the United Kingdom, 0.53; Canada, 0.14; and Denmark, 0.12. As could be expected, most of the aid is being contributed by technically advanced countries; yet it is of interest to note that one donor country, Portugal, is not classified as technically advanced according to most measures. Another, Communist China, itself belongs to the underdeveloped group. Of the $8.5 billion allocated for aid in 1962, all but $400 million came from the western world.

GOVERNMENTAL CONTROLS AND RESTRICTIONS.   The regulation of trade crossing its borders is generally considered the prerogative of a national government. The extent to which this authority is exercised varies widely throughout the world, as does the complexity of the machinery set up to perform the task. Any of several purposes may be served by governmental controls. Some measures are purely economic in character, being intended to provide governmental income, to assist in the development of the national economy, to save declining industries, to stem a drain on gold reserves, or to conserve natural resources. In many instances, however, interference with foreign trade, whether positive or negative, is politically motivated. Thus restrictive trade policies may result from pressures exerted by special interest groups within the country, or exceptional concessions may be accorded certain other countries with whom particularly friendly relations are maintained. Trade controls may even be employed for military ends, as when a country prohibits the export of goods which might enhance the war-making potential of a rival government. A country may also regulate exports and imports for the purpose of gaining relative self-sufficiency and thus increasing its military strength. An emphasis upon attracting strategic industries is usually an important part of such a policy. Trade policies may be influenced by any one of these considerations or by a combination of several.

Numerous techniques exist for controlling the trade of a country, some being at least partly interchangeable. The principal devices in current use include tariffs, quota restrictions, exchange controls, and state trading. Of these, the leading method prior to the 1930's was the tariff, which has remained a much debated issue from its inception—possibly in Medieval Spain—down to the present.

Tariffs. The term "tariff" usually refers to a *schedule* of taxes or duties to be paid upon various classes of goods when transported across national borders, although it may also apply to a particular duty or, in the plural, to a collection of such duties. Payment is more commonly required for imported merchandise, tariffs on exports being less usual. Indeed, export tariffs are prohibited by law in the United States. During its long history, this device for controlling trade has acquired a variety of forms and disguises; nevertheless, when classified according to purpose, most tariffs fall into one of two main categories: tariffs for revenue and protective tariffs. The two are not mutually exclusive, however, as a tariff may perform both functions.

When intended as a source of governmental revenue, a tariff must be kept low enough not to stifle trade, or else it would be self-defeating. Tariffs of this type are important to less developed countries, for which they often constitute the largest single item of public income. This was true of the United States during its first sixty years, for example. The attractiveness of tariffs to such countries derives in part from the ease of collecting tolls on tangible merchandise as compared with the difficulty of taxing incomes recorded by primitive accounting methods. For technically advanced lands the tariff is normally a minor, though significant, means of public support; the United States receives less than two per cent of its government income from this source.

Protective tariffs constitute a form of special government help for a sector of an economy or for a particular industry within that economy. Newly industrializing countries—and some others as well—often use the "infant industry" argument when granting tariff protection to economic activities which require insulation from the world market during the period in which they are becoming established. The tendency, however, is to continue such tariffs long after the protected industry has developed sufficient strength to compete unaided. Countries frequently impose tariffs to induce foreign suppliers of certain imported goods to locate production facilities within their borders. This is a favored means of saving foreign exchange and increasing the national product at the same time. Such tactics are normally most successful with industries making consumer goods or other products having a strong attraction to the market. Under certain circumstances, however, even industries oriented toward raw materials may be drawn to a country in this manner, as in the case of Venezuela, which has attracted petroleum refineries by means of an export tax on crude oil. Tariffs are sometimes used to prolong the lives of declining industries, especially when the group in power has a special interest in their preservation. Thus the tariff is highly susceptible to political influences.

Tariffs have a variety of other uses as well, particularly in efforts to overcome balance-of-payments deficits. Tariffs are also a common means for combating the effects of a major downturn in the business cycle, at which times they may be used to stimulate domestic employment at the expense of imports. Another function of tariffs is to supply protection for domestic industries of strategic importance, such as shipyards and aircraft factories.

A single government agency is usually responsible for administering a country's tariffs. In the United Kingdom this is Her Majesty's Customs, in the United States it is the US Customs Service, and in Canada it is the Department of Customs. At all international seaports, airports, and other points of entry and exit are stationed customs officials under whose control all goods immediately pass until the importer—or, more commonly, his agent, the customs broker—complies with the procedure which has been prescribed for the shipment's release or "entry." In the United States, Canada, and most other non-Communist countries the customs broker must file at the customhouse a set of documents including the bill of lading, the commercial and customs invoices, and an entry form. After the customs officer has examined the merchandise to make certain that the goods are in compliance with the documents, he determines the amount of duty owing. When this amount is paid, the goods are released to the broker for forwarding to the importer.

The method of determining the amount of duty differs greatly from one country to the next. Every country has its own classification scheme, some using broad categories and others extremely detailed schedules with thousands of individual items. Despite this wide variation in classification, assessment usually results in either or both of two principal types of duties, *specific* and *ad valorem*. Specific duties are assessed at so much per unit of weight, measurement, or some other indicator of quantity, whereas ad valorem duties are based upon the monetary value of the product. The methods of determining the latter are varied. Often the total duty exacted is a combination of both types plus possible surcharges and "anti-dumping" duties.[2]

A number of undesirable results of tariffs have been noted by students

---

[2] Many countries assess special penalties for "dumping," that is, importing goods at prices below those prevailing for the same items in the country of their manufacture.

of international trade. One such problem is the distortion of national resource use, as inefficient operations are artificially preserved and stimulated. Tariffs also tend to limit total consumption of goods because of the high prices they create. Furthermore, when one country imposes tariffs, other countries frequently retaliate in kind, the end result being a reduction in total trade and lower standards of living everywhere. Although other techniques for controlling trade have gained prominence since World War I, the tariff still continues to be the most common device. This persistence is due partly to the respectability it has gained through long use and partly to its impartiality, since it merely changes prices and thus affects all importers of a given product alike. Nevertheless, other methods have gained increased acceptance in recent years because of such advantages as greater versatility, administrative flexibility, and effectiveness, especially for combating emergency conditions and solving temporary problems. One technique which possesses these qualities is the quota restriction.

Quotas.   As a device for controlling international trade, the quota produces direct and immediate results. It constitutes the placing by a country of specific limits upon the quantity of a product that it will permit to be imported or exported. Import quotas are esteemed by government administrators because they are so quickly and easily applied when a sudden need for control arises. Whereas tariffs become deeply entrenched in the system, are difficult to change, and are uncertain in their effects, quotas yield predictable consequences without delay. The main disadvantage of quotas from the administrative standpoint is that, unlike tariffs, they do not produce government revenue except in special cases.

The popularity of import quotas with officials is not matched, however, by the attitude of many of those affected. Since a quota limits the quantity of a product admitted to a country, those importers who are privileged to receive such a commodity enjoy greater profits as a result of its scarcity. Thus the possibilities for official corruption are great. In addition to criticism for their arbitrary character and their tendency to produce monopoly conditions, quotas are often opposed on the ground that they are expensive to both buyers and sellers.

To minimize unfairness and dishonesty, many countries devise elaborate systems for administering import quotas. Usually this system includes the issuing of import licenses in some manner which provides for equitable distribution among importers and possibly among producing countries as well. In some instances, however, licenses may be granted on a first-come, first-served basis, in accordance with the importers' or suppliers' traditional share of the market, or by means of public auctions conducted by the licensing authority. Elements of all but the last of these methods are found in the United States sugar system. Only the public auctions yield revenue to the issuing government. Some quotas are determined in general outline by legislative action, which is then supplemented by detailed procedures drawn up by the administering agency; others, however, are specified by the terms of elaborate international agreements. Licenses covering individual transactions are issued to importers by the administering authority and accompany the shipping documents (see Chapter 6).

The uses of import quotas are generally similar to those of tariffs, except that the former are more effective. This was the main reason for their introduction during World War I to control shipments of strategic merchandise. Prior to that time, quantitative restrictions had generally been prohibited by international agreement.

One of the principal peacetime uses of quotas has been to limit the importation of agricultural commodities. Tariffs are often of little avail in controlling the entry of such goods, since their world supply may not respond to tariff-induced price changes. Thus quotas on agricultural goods were much used during the interwar depression years and have since continued as a means for protecting threatened producers of both agricultural and industrial goods. Today such quotas are often imposed informally, as in the case of Australian beef and Japanese textiles, whose exporters were "persuaded" to accept voluntary limits on quantities shipped to the United States. Since World War II several countries, especially the newly developing ones, have depended upon quota systems to maintain favorable balances of payments and to combat inflation.

The mixed reaction received by import quotas is paralleled by that accorded export quotas, which are used by countries to control the quantities of their products reaching world markets. Export quotas are intended either to ensure high world prices for a country's goods or to conserve scarce resources. Ordinarily they are applied to agricultural commodities, minerals, and other primary goods, although they are occasionally imposed on manufactured items, especially during times of national emergency. During the Korean War the United States employed this means of controlling strategic exports, and it has since continued to limit sales to Communist countries in this fashion. Export licensing is the normal method of administering such quotas.

Enforcement of export quotas is also accomplished by state purchase and resale, especially of agricultural commodities. This is the procedure Brazil has followed in its attempts to influence world prices of rubber and of coffee. In the latter instance, surplus supplies were actually destroyed. Primary producers have repeatedly made attempts of this sort to control world prices despite the serious obstacles to their success, including buyer resistance to price changes of such luxury goods as cacao and coffee and the availability of alternative sources of supply, as in the case of Brazilian rubber and Chilean nitrates.

Despite the advantages quotas have for certain uses, especially in emergencies, they share many of the weaknesses of tariffs and have certain disadvantages of their own as well. It is interesting to note that some of the countries which have used quotas with least success are among those employing still another technique, exchange controls.

Exchange controls. A number of countries require that all foreign exchange earned by their exporters be channeled to central banks or other official agencies, which then ration these foreign currencies to importers according to some prearranged scheme. Exchange control arrangements of this type trace their origins to the problems of the depression era of the 1930's, when exchange deficits were widespread.

One method of controlling foreign exchange is through clearing arrangements, by means of which a country matches its exporters' claims to a given currency with corresponding debts contracted by its importers. Another practice which is very common today is the use of multiple exchange rates. A country engaged in this practice will have two or more different rates of exchange for its national currency, each corresponding to a particular purpose or to a specific category of merchandise. Exports requiring aid to compete successfully in world markets are permitted to be sold at low exchange rates, whereas high rates are exacted for products in demand. Multiple exchange rates are much used to enforce an order of priority for imported goods, higher rates being applied to luxury items and lower rates to those items designated as necessities. Many countries accomplish this aim by importing necessities at relatively low fixed (or "official") rates and admitting nonessentials at "free" rates which are permitted to fluctuate according to conditions in the world market and which are consequently higher than the pegged official rates. The net effect, in any case, is to influence strongly the composition and volume of trade of those countries using this device.

Although introduced during a period of world economic chaos, exchange controls continue in use wherever trade is imbalanced, severe inflation prevails, or governmental finances are otherwise in disarray. Exchange controls of various types are common in southeast Asia and among the countries of Central and South America, especially Brazil, Colombia, and Chile.

State trading.   Usually associated with Communist trading methods but also occurring in such non-Communist areas as western Europe, state trading represents another means by which governments regulate their flow of trade with the rest of the world. As its name suggests, state trading constitutes the buying and/or selling of internationally traded goods by an official arm of government. Such transactions are usually conducted on a large scale and deal in bulk quantities. Regardless of the political coloration of the government concerned, the impact of state trading upon foreign commerce is considerable. In capitalistic countries the effects are particularly noticeable where a government maintains a monopoly—usually with substantial profit—over the retail sales of certain items in broad demand, such as liquor, salt, sugar, or tobacco. At the least, state trading provides government revenue; at the most, it constitutes a potential weapon of economic warfare.

As should be expected, the purest examples of state trading are provided by the Communist countries, where foreign trade is but one aspect of an economy wholly controlled by the state. As a government monopoly, the external trade of Communist countries serves as a cautious link between world commerce and a domestic economy otherwise tightly insulated against outside influences. Foreign trade has been regarded by the Soviet Union as a mere supplement to the development of the domestic economy, with national self-sufficiency the ultimate goal. Emulating this example, the eastern European satellites at first likewise attempted to achieve autarky; unlike their Soviet model, however, these smaller countries lacked the resources to succeed in this goal and have turned actively to promoting external trade since the death of Stalin in 1953.[3]

In both the Soviet Union and its satellites, trade with other countries falls under the jurisdiction of the Ministry of Foreign Trade, which conducts all trade planning, negotiates inter-governmental trade agreements, and exercises direct control over the trading mechanism. Actual implementation of the plans and general agreements devised by the ministry, however, is delegated to individual foreign trade corporations or enterprises, which are government agencies responsible for the commercial details.

Until recently, each such corporation specialized in a single commodity and competed in no way with other similar agencies. They had little if any contact with the domestic units whose products they sold, nor did they have any role in disposing of the goods they imported, their domestic relationships being confined to the various ministries and internal trading organizations. In response to the liberalizing trend of the post-Stalin era, the foreign trade corporations have enjoyed some increase in domestic communication and a decrease in specialization. Their operations are, however, still complicated by the arbitrarily and unrealistically pegged national exchange rates, which usually make it necessary for them to use barter, gold, or currencies other than their own when buying or selling abroad.

Other restrictive practices.   The ingenuity of the world's nations in devising means for regulating their foreign trade does not end with tariffs, quotas, exchange controls, or state trading, although it is these which attract much of the interest of writers on this subject and absorb the attention of delegates to international conferences. Very nearly unnoticed by all but the trading concerns which must cope with them daily are countless other devices often capable of effects quite as drastic as the better known techniques. Included among these are import regulations—often numbering in the hundreds—intended, at least ostensibly, for the safeguarding of the health, safety, morals, and rights of a country's citizens. Often, however, such measures go beyond these stated ends to provide a particularly effective form of trade protection to certain classes of domestic producers. In some cases this is the result intended by those conceiving the measure; often, however, the protectionist effect is inadvertent, stemming perhaps from failure to respond to changed conditions.

Health and sanitation measures produce a heavy impact upon world trade in agricultural goods, in both raw and processed states. It is here that some of the most severe pressure is exerted by domestic producers for what amounts to hidden protection for their commodities. Complex import regulations, which differ widely from one country to the next, govern the types and amounts of food coloring, preservatives, and other ingredients. Rigid inspection of meats is common, with strict attention paid to sanitation and freedom from disease, often enforceable by whole-

---

[3] Frederic L. Pryor, *The Communist Foreign Trade System* (Cambridge, Mass.: The Massachusetts Institute of Technology, 1963), p. 32.

sale exclusion of all imports from a particular source area on the basis of a single doubtful shipment. Indirectly, foreign suppliers of agricultural products are much affected by legal requirements stating that domestically produced foods, such as bread, must contain a minimum amount of homegrown ingredients.

Among other regulations are special packaging requirements, which may discriminate against importers in cases where foreign manufacturers or processors are tooled up for a quite different kind of packaging. Restrictions intended to protect property rights of a country's nationals—for example, copyrights, patents, and trade-marks—are susceptible to discriminatory application as well.

Not the least effective, however, are the administrative procedures employed by many countries when admitting imports. Innumerable opportunities exist here for discrimination against imports and thus for concealed protection of domestic producers. Regulations such as those governing health and sanitation inspection are frequently applied more rigorously to imports than to domestic goods. Much discrimination of this type is doubtlessly unintentional, resulting from the fact that all imports are subject to examination whereas competing domestic goods may more easily escape detection. Sometimes this effect is achieved merely by failure of a country's customs service to remove outmoded requirements from its list of regulations. Furthermore, importers bear an extra cost resulting from unnecessary delays in making inspections and processing documents, an expense which is customarily reduced in some lands by a system of bribery.

Among these miscellaneous restrictions on trade—only a few of which have been mentioned here—are many which are so drastic as to prohibit trade in certain goods altogether. The effect on total trade is unmeasurable but must be great. Some aspects of the problem would be solved by establishing international standards, toward which some efforts have already been directed.

We have seen that, in attempting to influence their trade with the rest of the world, countries customarily employ two approaches. The first of these seeks to increase trade, mainly through promoting one's own exports, whereas the other attempts to restrict trade, largely by controlling imports. For international trade as a whole, which is highly sensitive to political pressures, the probable net effect of government policy and practice has been to reduce total trade.

Many students of international trade insist that the greatest benefit for the world would come from removing trade restrictions. This argument is based on the supposed inherent efficiency of the price system when conditions are provided for its uninhibited operation. Although this viewpoint does not take into account the peculiar disadvantages that many analysts believe free trade has for the less developed countries (see Chapter 1, p. 9; Chapter 5, pp. 118-119), some variation of this idea appears attractive for the world as a whole.

In the past, numerous attempts have been made to promote a freer flow of international trade, and such efforts appear to be increasing in the present period. Gaining in popularity are various plans for regional groupings of trading countries, a natural response to the success enjoyed by certain ventures of this type within the past dozen years. Enthusiasm for regional groupings is tempered, however, by a growing realization that such limited steps are inadequate and, from the international viewpoint, possibly restrictive and disruptive. By contrast, increased consideration is being given to plans for a world-wide approach to trade development. We shall devote the remainder of this chapter to a review of both regional and global efforts to organize for trade purposes.

International Agreements and Organizations

Headline attention greets most formal efforts to increase cooperation among the world's governments in promoting trade. The European Economic Community, with its recurring crises and frequent ministerial conferences, has been an almost constant subject of commentary not only in the press but also in the periodical and academic literature. Only back-page notice, however, is accorded a more prosaic but nonetheless effective form of international cooperation: the system of organizational arrangements to be found among private concerns participating in world trade.

ASSOCIATIONS OF COMPANIES. Trading firms, and the various service agencies associated with them in the international exchange of goods, maintain a high degree of coordinated effort. It is not possible to assess the precise importance of these non-public forms of trade cooperation, but there are indications that their effect is great. It is also difficult to distinguish strictly private activity from that of governments, in view of the fact that certain countries own or control at least some of the trading concerns and transport companies under their jurisdiction.

The flow of goods from one country to another is much benefited by the sharing of product and market information among traders. One important way in which this occurs was described in Chapter 6 (pp. 123 to 124), where the distributorship method of selling goods abroad was described. The typical large exporting firm has a network of such marketing companies, usually at least one agency for each country with which it does business.

If the exporter is the manufacturer of the goods it sells, it may also maintain production facilities in its larger foreign markets. In many cases manufacturing facilities in other countries are only partly owned and controlled by the parent firm, which shares this responsibility with local capital and management personnel. Complex corporate structures are typical of such arrangements. Although the building of foreign factories is often cited as an example of substituting exports of capital for exports of merchandise,[4] there is evidence that such capital flows can promote the movement of goods as well. Indeed, the United States Department of Commerce has reported that nearly one-fourth of all that country's exports are sent to foreign companies controlled by domestic concerns.

[4] R. A. Mundell, "International Trade and Factor Mobility," *American Economic Review*, Vol. 47, No. 3 (June, 1957), 321-35.

Machinery and equipment, raw materials, and semimanufactured goods account for most such shipments.

International arrangements among companies making the same or similar products is a type of cooperation which has existed for many years but which has taken new forms in recent times. One such voluntary association of companies is the cartel, which is an international business agreement "to regulate price, division of markets, or other aspects of competition." [5] Because combines which divide international markets among giant producers mitigate against national self-sufficiency and thus tend to present problems upon the outbreak of war, the term "cartel" has acquired an unfavorable connotation. The usual net effect of such arrangements is to restrict trade, and for this reason conditions for the regulation of cartels are explicitly stated in several agreements among trading countries, including the General Agreement on Tariffs and Trade and the Treaty of Rome, by which the European Economic Community was created. [6]

The label "cartel" (the exact definition of which is a matter of some disagreement) is often applied to certain other types of international business agreements that probably tend on the whole to increase trade. These include arrangements for pooling and licensing patents and for joint ventures, such as the international consortium which operates the Abadan refinery in Iran. Cooperative undertakings of this sort permit the sharing of risks and the exploitation of resources which might not otherwise be used.

International cooperation also prevails among transport agencies, which are usually subject to severe competition. The steamship conference, of which there are several hundred in existence, is one of the oldest of such arrangements, dating back to the latter half of the nineteenth century. The conference, a voluntary association of steamship lines operating over the same route, sets freight rates, regulates the number of sailings of each line, and defends its members against outside competition. Similar functions are performed by the International Air Transport Association, the membership of which includes more than thirty cargo-carrying airlines from at least twenty countries.

INTER-GOVERNMENTAL AFFILIATIONS.   Gaining prominence in recent years has been a trend toward greater cooperation among world governments for the purpose of expanding their trade with each other. The main question to be resolved concerns the best way to accomplish this end with the least injury to heretofore heavily protected sectors of national economies and with a minimum loss of national sovereignty. Most of the plans being proposed and implemented are not of recent origin; indeed, several are of considerable age. What is new is the widened acceptance of the feasibility, and even necessity, of such ideas in an age when communication has become instantaneous, business has become international, and political problems have become perilous.

[5] Charles P. Kindleberger, *International Economics*, rev. ed. (Homewood, Ill.: Richard D. Irwin, Inc., 1958), p. 279.
[6] Charles P. Kindleberger, *Foreign Trade and the National Economy* (New Haven: Yale University Press, 1962), pp. 132-33.

The groupings of countries resulting from this cooperative promotion of trade are being superimposed upon another pre-existing set of multinational organizations which sprang up during the payments crises following World War II. In the next few pages we shall classify under three main headings the numerous organizations which have evolved. These categories are not mutually exclusive: not only are some countries affiliated with more than one organization, but certain of the organizations are themselves logically capable of being classified in more than one way. The first category includes those blocs united either by their use of a common currency (usually that of a dominant member of the bloc) for trading purposes or to fulfill their collective requirements for settling international accounts. The second category contains groupings of countries voluntarily associated more or less as equals for their mutual economic advantage and for purposes which may transcend trade alone. Finally, we shall examine several organizations which, by contrast with the limited membership of groups in the first two categories, are worldwide in their scope and composition.

Currency blocs. In an effort to alleviate the exchange shortages that hampered international trade during the early postwar years, large organizations of trading countries were formed. These were the sterling area, dollar area, European Payments Union countries, Latin American area, and ruble bloc. Certain other countries remained unaffiliated. Because such arrangements eased the financing of trade among members of the same "area" or "bloc," the flow of goods within the group was much stimulated; however, there was little to facilitate trade with members of other similar organizations. There was thus at first a tendency for intrabloc trade to grow at the expense of trade with the rest of the world. More recently, the currency bloc has declined somewhat in importance as the US dollar and the British pound have strengthened in world-wide acceptance and the currencies of most non-Communist countries have become convertible.

Three of the areas merit special comment here. Within two of these there is common use of a single currency for most international transactions. The third is sometimes referred to as a currency bloc, although its bonds are more political than financial. Indeed, to varying degrees the currency arrangements in all three groups reflect historical as well as political and economic relationships characterized by the overwhelming dominance of one country. In each instance it is the currency of that dominant member which gives its name to the bloc.

One of the three blocs constitutes what is mainly the remnant of a great colonial empire, within which strong economic interdependence had evolved. The second represents a grouping of countries whose economic interests have centered upon a single giant trading partner, the economic power of which has at times produced political consequences. The other bloc has through historical events been joined by a common ideology that partially isolated the group from the rest of the world and forced its members at least temporarily to look to each other for markets and raw materials. Although all three groups have developed institutional arrangements for trade purposes, intragroup trade ties are more or less informal, based mainly upon self-interest and, in the case of one of the blocs, a degree of loyalty and sentiment.

One of the largest groupings of countries engaged in world trade is the British Commonwealth, whose members comprise the major part of what was once the British Empire. In addition to the United Kingdom, the Commonwealth includes the now wholly self-governing dominions and republics which have elected to retain this mainly informal affiliation with the mother country, together with Britain's remaining colonies, protectorates, and United Nations trusteeships. As a whole the group constitutes an important element in international trade, accounting for one-fourth or more of all world trade in most years. Less than half of this trade is with other members of the bloc, however, due in part to the external trade ties of Canada. This second largest trader in the Commonwealth depends upon the United States for the majority of its exports and imports (see Chapter 3, pp. 31 to 39). The main emphasis of the British Commonwealth as an organization is political, which contrasts with the commercial functions of another grouping of some of these same countries, the sterling area.

Membership in the sterling bloc is similar to that of the British Commonwealth except for the exclusion of Canada—which instead has chosen membership in the dollar bloc—and the inclusion of such non-Commonwealth countries as Ireland, Iceland, Iraq, Jordan, and Burma. These countries have been united by their dependence upon Britain for finance and trade, although the latter is tending to become less important as a cohesive force. Member countries keep a large part of their monetary reserves in London and maintain convertibility of their currencies with that of the United Kingdom. Thus London serves as banker for the group, and sterling is generally used for settling international accounts throughout the bloc. Although institutional arrangements are informal, the group is further drawn together by an interlacing network of bilateral agreements, including, in some cases, preferential tariff treatment. The sterling area is in relative decline on the world scene (Table 2.1, p. 12).

Besides the United States, the dollar bloc, strictly defined, includes Canada, Mexico, and Venezuela, all of whom maintain convertibility of their currencies with United States dollars. Prior to the Castro régime, Cuba also belonged to the group. All the members of the bloc are heavy traders, especially with each other.

There is a third group which is sometimes labeled with the currency of its leading member, although this practice is not entirely appropriate. The so-called ruble bloc, which appears actually to make only limited use of the Soviet Union's currency for settling its international claims, is held together mainly by ideological kinship. The group consists of the Soviet Union and its Communist neighbors of eastern Europe, together with Outer Mongolia and Cuba, the latter being a recent addition. Since the Sino-Soviet schism, China and her Asian satellites have curtailed somewhat their commercial relations with the ruble area, despite the similarities of political and economic systems. The ruble bloc, with its nonconvertible currencies and its heavy dependence upon barter, bears little resemblance in its trading methods to the dollar and sterling blocs.[7] Because the Soviet-bloc countries have been attempting to develop a tighter economic organization, with purposes going beyond the requirements of trade, we shall reserve further consideration of this group for the next section.

Most of the countries lying outside these three blocs hold membership in one of two other groups which are not specifically tied to a single currency. The European Payments Union, an outgrowth of the Marshall Plan, is one of these. In 1950, fourteen non-Communist countries of Europe, including one sterling bloc member, the United Kingdom, formed this organization for the purpose of clearing international payments and eliminating artificial restraints on trade among member countries. The second group is made up of those independent Latin American republics having traditional trade ties with western Europe and lying outside the dollar bloc. In addition, there are several countries which have remained unaffiliated, the most important in world trade being Japan. A regrouping of countries belonging to the five blocs is currently in progress.

Combinations for trade and economic integration. Doubtless the most common type of international trade cooperation in past years has been the bilateral (occasionally multilateral) trade agreement, which has characteristically taken one of two forms. The first is an agreement for the exchange of specific quantities of particular commodities, whether for cash or barter. This is a trading device much used by the Communist countries (see pp. 144-145). The other is the tariff treaty, which provides for mutual concessions on import duties and is exemplified by the United States reciprocal trade agreements program under the Act of 1935.[8] These traditional, narrowly conceived devices are rapidly becoming eclipsed by a number of organizational arrangements much broader in scope and farreaching in their consequences.

Now attaining prominence in several widely scattered parts of the world is a category of international association bound by relatively strong ties and having purposes which in some cases transcend the needs of trade, as these have been conceived in the past. One aim which is implicit or explicit in nearly all cases is the attainment of some degree of economic integration—that is, uniting two or more individually small economies into a single large one. After a flurry of experiments with economic integration during the nineteenth century, the limited attempts of that era had been largely abandoned, with certain notable exceptions, by 1900. Sparked by the problems remaining from World War II and encouraged by a revolutionary change in attitudes, interest in the subject of economic integration has been rekindled in the present period.[9]

Several conditions combined to focus attention upon this method of international cooperation, especially in Europe, where the need was most

[7] See Chapter 4 for a discussion of the trade of Communist countries.

[8] Charles P. Kindleberger, *International Economics* (Homewood, Ill.: Richard D. Irwin, Inc., 1958), pp. 251-53, also p. 227 *et passim.*

[9] Bela Balassa, *The Theory of Economic Integration* (Homewood, Ill.: Richard D. Irwin, Inc., 1961), pp. 3-6. This valuable work, together with Jacob Viner's classic, *The Customs Union Issue* (New York: Carnegie Endowment for International Peace, 1950) has provided much of the information appearing on the next several pages.

urgent or, at least, most obvious. During the interwar period, Europe, the home of the nation-state, had begun to feel the worst effects of its multiple divisions. The excessive political fragmentation of the continent had produced new extremes of economic fragmentation—accomplished by means of high tariffs, rigid quota systems, and discriminatory freight rates—as each national economy sought to seal itself off from the others. As a result, some countries achieved a relatively high degree of national self-sufficiency, with a consequent loss of the efficiencies possible through large-scale production. Thus between the two world wars intra-European trade was decreasing steadily, even though trade with other parts of the world, especially with the less-developed suppliers of industrial raw materials, continued to grow. The immediate cause of this stifling of intra-European trade was the need to combat depression, but a related factor was the aggressive nationalism which preceded World War II.

By the end of the war, many Europeans had come to recognize the nature of the problem and the necessity for a cooperative solution. Through joint efforts they hoped to eliminate intra-European rivalry, with its potential for producing war; to accelerate recovery of their war-devastated economies; to develop means for combating future depressions; and to provide for continued economic development. This need for a united effort toward economic growth became particularly urgent because of the threat of further encroachment by a Stalinist Soviet Union. Further stimulus came from the United States, which in 1948 specified that Marshall Plan aid be carefully coordinated in order to make optimal use of European resources. The concrete expression of this American prodding was the Organization for European Economic Cooperation, composed of eighteen countries in western and southern Europe, including Turkey. Concerned with a broad range of matters centering upon European economic recovery and development, the OEEC was replaced in 1961 by the Organization for Economic Cooperation and Development, a group which added the United States and Canada as members but which restricted its functions to problems of trade and payments, including some financial assistance to less developed areas that will enhance world trade.[10]

Out of this beginning have sprung a rapidly growing number of co-operative ventures, which have spread from Europe to other parts of the world, with important implications for international trade. Their main organizing concept is economic integration, with its promise of the benefits of size. Proponents of integration often point to the dynamic economy of the United States as an example of this advantage.[11] If a number of smaller countries can agree to remove barriers to the movement of

[10] William Diebold, Jr., "The Process of European Integration," *Current History* (March, 1962), reprinted in *The Common Market: Progress and Controversy*, ed. Lawrence B. Krause (Englewood Cliffs, N.J.: Prentice-Hall, Inc., 1964), pp. 30 and 38.

[11] Sidney Dell, taking a minority view, considers the experience of the United States to be an inadequate argument for size as a basis for economic success and insists that other factors have possibly been of greater importance in the growth of that country's economy. "Economic Integration and the American Example," *Economic Journal* (March, 1959), reprinted in *The Common Market: Progress and Controversy*, ed. Lawrence B. Krause (Englewood Cliffs, N.J.: Prentice-Hall, Inc., 1964), pp. 75-89.

goods among them, it is argued, such exchanges will assume all the advantageous characteristics of domestic trade within the United States. If, in addition to this freeing of trade, restrictions on the movement of the factors of production are eliminated, then the resulting larger market can be expected to increase manufacturing productivity through improved opportunities for specialization and economies of scale. As illustration of this point, it is often noted that the optimal size of many large manufacturing establishments yields an output exceeding the entire requirements of some European countries and dwarfing the demand in many Latin American lands. Enlarged market size is also expected to raise the efficiency of producers because of an increase in the competition among them. It is further suggested that these efficiencies will tend to become diffused throughout the territories of the member countries and help remove regional differences in productivity and standard of living.

A number of incidental benefits are also expected from union. For one thing, the enlarged market should attract greater investment, not only from domestic sources but also from abroad. Other important factors are the possibilities for enhanced bargaining strength in dealings with non-member countries, opportunities for savings in administering trade, and a wider choice for consumers at more attractive prices. It is worth noting that these hoped-for benefits are of interest not only to technically advanced countries but also to those which are less developed and, in some respects, to Communist countries as well as non-Communist.

It is not anticipated that integration will bring equal benefits to all attempting it. Several considerations may influence the success that a particular group of countries should expect from union. One of these is complementarity—that is, the degree to which member countries produce unlike goods. Complementarity is usually regarded as conducive to the success of a union because of the production efficiencies it should bring,[12] although it has been suggested that competitive economies can also experience savings as a result of integration.[13] Furthermore, the larger the total area included within the group, the better the results ordinarily expected from association, due to the greater opportunities for division of labor. A related factor is the size of individual member countries. A union of many small economies is considered more beneficial, both in total effect upon world trade and from the standpoint of the individual country, than is an association of two large ones.[14] This idea is explained by the smaller country's lesser capabilities at the outset and thus its greater possibilities for improvement.

A final characteristic, probably the most important of all, is propinquity. If a number of contiguous countries form a union of compact shape, the opportunities for transport cost savings and the likelihood of increased commerce are much enhanced, especially if the artificial barriers to movement were great before union occurred. Such results are to be expected because of the greater probability of similar tastes and awareness of business opportunities in neighboring populations. Associations of widely

[12] Viner dissents from this commonly held view. *Op. cit.,* p. 51.
[13] Balassa, *op. cit.,* p. 32ff.
[14] *Ibid.,* p. 39.

scattered countries may suffer from disadvantages in all these respects.[15]

Just as there is much variation in these characteristics from one group to the next, so also are there many differences in forms of organization being adopted. The latter have been classified into five categories, according to the degree of economic integration intended by each.[16] The type having the least strict form of integration is the free-trade area, in which tariffs and other trade restrictions among member countries are eliminated, although each country continues to maintain its own tariffs on the goods of countries outside the group. Somewhat higher in the scale of economic integration is the customs union, an arrangement by which all barriers to intragroup movements of goods are removed but a common system of tariffs is applied to the imports of nonmembers. A common market also maintains a uniform tariff wall against the commodities of outsiders; however, it eliminates barriers not only to the movement of merchandise among member countries but also to the movement of the factors of production, especially capital and labor. A still greater degree of economic integration is achieved by an economic union, which, in addition to the features of a common market, provides for the synchronization of national policies on economic matters. The fifth and highest level is complete economic integration, in which member countries unite their economic and social policies and submit to the binding decisions of a supranational authority.

We may ask what considerations could be expected to influence the choice of organizational type that a group of countries may make. Judging by past decisions, it seems probable that an association of countries widely separated from each other will form a union providing for a minimum of economic integration, such as a free-trade area. Minimal forms of integration also appear to be the preference of states having proud traditions of neutrality and independence, as well as those countries already possessing strong political, economic, or sentimental ties with nonmembers. It may be noted, for example, that members of the British Commonwealth have formed no other connections stronger than a free-trade area.

By contrast, a high degree of integration seems preferred by groups whose members are contiguous to each other and which have few if any strong ties to nonmember countries. It might be expected that complementarity of production would be conducive to the formation of highly integrated organizations, but this assumption is not confirmed by the examples which have appeared to date.

The list of multinational groups adopting this solution for their economic ills is currently a growing one. During the postwar period of intensified interest in economic integration, the initial impulse came from the Benelux countries—Belgium, The Netherlands, and Luxembourg—which on September 5, 1944 signed an agreement to form a customs union, later broadened into an economic union. In 1953 France, Italy, and West Germany joined the Benelux countries in an experiment with the sectoral approach to economic integration, and the European Coal and Steel

[15] *Ibid.*, p. 40.
[16] *Ibid.*, p. 2.

Community came into being. The success of this venture prompted the same six countries to establish a common market, the European Economic Community, under the terms of the Treaty of Rome, signed in March of 1957.[17] A companion document, agreed upon at the same time, created the European Atomic Energy Community (Euratom) among these countries. After the failure of negotiations for a wider grouping of European states, the United Kingdom led six other countries [18] in the formation of the European Free Trade Association, initiated on July 1, 1960. Meanwhile, the Soviet bloc countries had in 1958 reacted to the Treaty of Rome by strengthening their Communist Council for Mutual Economic Assistance (Comecon), an association which in its earlier form actually antedates the EEC by more than eight years.[19]

The European example has been emulated elsewhere, most notably in Latin America. Much of the stimulus there has come from the Economic Commission for Latin America (ECLA), one of four such regional economic study groups maintained by the United Nations in various parts of the world. The ECLA has assisted in forming two organizations and a possible third. The two are the Latin American Free Trade Association [20] and the Central American Common Market,[21] both of which became operative in 1961. In addition to these two presently functioning, another Latin American organization, a West Indian customs union (or possibly a common market) is under consideration.

On January 1, 1965 an Arab Common Market, composed of several Middle Eastern states, became effective,[22] and shortly thereafter four Moslem countries of North Africa formed the Maghreb Economic Community.[23] Various combinations of countries in southern Asia and in the portion of Africa south of the Sahara have also made moves in the direction of economic integration. Most recent of all are the Australia-New Zealand Free Trade Agreement, which came into effect on January 1, 1966, and the agreement of Canada and the United States to integrate their automobile manufacturing industries. The latter, of course, affects only one sector of the two economies concerned. (See Chapters 3 and 4 for a discussion of the trade of certain of the above groups.) The accompanying map, Fig. 7.1, shows the locations of the various organizations just mentioned.

Upon examining specific features of each type of organization, we note

[17] Greece and Turkey have subsequently joined as associates, with plans for eventual full membership.

[18] Norway, Sweden, Denmark, Austria, Switzerland, and Portugal. Finland became an associate member in March of 1961.

[19] Included in Comecon are the Soviet Union, East Germany, Poland, Czechoslovakia, Hungary, Bulgaria, Rumania, and the Mongolian Republic. Albania has suspended its membership in the group. Other Communist countries have at various times participated as observers, although this practice has apparently been discontinued.

[20] Argentina, Brazil, Chile, Colombia, Ecuador, Mexico, Paraguay, Peru, and Uruguay. At last, late in 1965, Venezuela reached a decision to apply for membership also.

[21] El Salvador, Guatemala, Honduras, and Nicaragua were the founding members. Costa Rica has joined subsequently, and Panama is still studying such a move at the time of this writing.

[22] Iraq, Jordan, Kuwait, Syria, and Egypt. Kuwait dropped its membership later that year.

[23] Algeria, Morocco, Tunisia, and Libya.

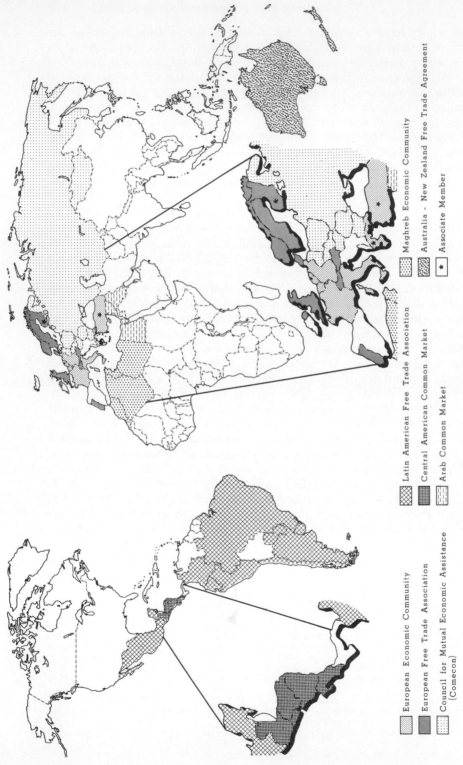

Fig. 7.1. *Trading blocs experiencing some degree of economic integration.*

European Economic Community

European Free Trade Association

Council for Mutual Economic Assistance (Comecon)

Latin American Free Trade Association

Central American Common Market

Arab Common Market

Maghreb Economic Community

Australia - New Zealand Free Trade Agreement

★ Associate Member

a tendency for those groups on each level to assume gradually some of the characteristics of the next higher level. The reasons for this will be found in certain inherent weaknesses of the lower forms. Thus the free-trade area, although providing individual member countries with much freedom in external commercial relations, may create distortions in the patterns of trade, production, and investment within the group, unless safeguards are employed. Because each country continues to set its own tariffs on imports from non members but pays no tariffs to others within the group, goods will tend to be attracted to that member country having the lowest external tariffs. This result will occur especially in the case of raw materials and semimanufactures, which may be drawn to the low-tariff member for processing and for distribution of the finished goods throughout the bloc. Thus, to diversion of trade is added diversion of manufacturing and investment. Although complex systems of taxes and compensating duties may be used to minimize this effect in free-trade areas, the problem has not wholly disappeared, and as a result there is some pressure upon the higher-tariff members to reduce their duties to the lowest level prevailing in the group. Ultimately, therefore, a common external tariff may take effect throughout the bloc. This development, plus the incentive for coordinated commercial policies which follows the elimination of internal duties, may cause the organization to acquire some of the characteristics of a customs union, or even a common market.[24]

Such propensities became apparent in free-trade areas from the first. One early group of this type, formed by Sweden and Norway in the nineteenth century, foundered in part because of trade-diversion problems. The first modern example, the European Free Trade Association, appears to be skirting this danger. Although hampered by the barriers of distance and dissimilarities of culture and tradition separating some of the members, the EFTA has attained some degree of cohesiveness through skillful planning and adroit use of certain fortunate advantages inherent in the group. For one thing, the EFTA, in common with the EEC, has used a gradual approach in making its internal tariff and quota adjustments. (Nonetheless, these have been accomplished so smoothly that all such barriers to industrial goods were reduced to zero by the end of 1966, three years ahead of schedule.) [25] Although some agricultural and fisheries products are specifically exempted from these reductions, nearly all are covered by bilateral trade treaties. Indeed, one of the most advantageous characteristics of this group is the complementarity of production among its members, a factor tending to reduce diversion problems. Such dislocations are further minimized by imposing tariffs upon internally traded goods of less than 50 per cent EFTA origin. The success of these measures is expected to facilitate rapprochement with the EEC, an avowed purpose of this organization.

Similar weaknesses of the free-trade-area approach are evident in the Latin American Free Trade Association. For a number of reasons, past trade among these countries has been meager. A serious disadvantage of

[24] Balassa, *op. cit.*, pp. 69-79.
[25] Having become associated with EFTA a year late, Finland is permitted an additional year to complete its part in the program.

LAFTA has been the scattered locations of its members (see Fig. 7.1), a problem made all the more difficult by the characteristic Latin American settlement pattern. Their economically effective areas often comprising mere enclaves surrounded by vast, little-used territory, these countries have few surface interconnections overland, being separated from each other by sometimes formidable physical barriers. It is little wonder that commercial relations among them are so poorly developed and that a free-trade area should be their choice when deciding upon a cooperative trade venture. Unlike the EFTA, the Latin American countries are competitive in their traditional export lines, which are composed mainly of primary commodities. This characteristic, which is often cited as a fatal flaw in the LAFTA, should be recognized as mainly a function of underdevelopment. The problem is expected to diminish as industrialization occurs and each member establishes its own manufacturing specialties under the influence of the free-trade area, which was formed in large part for this particular purpose. Such specialization has in fact already begun to appear in the more advanced members of the bloc. Because of the great differences among these countries in their systems of external tariffs and other trade barriers, the possibilities for deflection of imports, production, and investment are serious. The group is much aware of this problem, however, and harmonization of such differences is planned, the free-trade area being intended as merely a first step toward a customs union.[26] Thus, we have another example of a group moving to a higher level of economic integration.

The intentions of Australia and New Zealand in this regard have not yet been indicated as they begin the implementation of a free-trade area. Their choice of this lower form of integration is related doubtlessly to their isolation from each other and from the rest of the world and possibly to their Commonwealth ties. At present, many of the commodities they export are competitive, particularly the animal products, but much of their current production is complementary, presenting opportunities for new kinds of interchange between them. New Zealand, for example, is eager to find new markets for her forest products and vegetables, which are much needed in Australia. The latter, on the other hand, has surplus production of metal products, machinery, and vehicles which are not currently manufactured in New Zealand. Additional types of manufacturing specialties are expected to emerge as the effects of union appear.

A somewhat different set of advantages and disadvantages characterizes the customs union, another product of the nineteenth century. Certain of the earlier examples are still in existence, especially one variety known as the "customs accession." In this type of union one member, being of much greater size than the others, assumes entire responsibility for administering customs functions.[27] Current examples are France and Monaco, Switzerland and Liechtenstein, and Belgium and Luxembourg. In certain historic instances, customs unions have resulted in permanent political unions, as illustrated by the German Zollverein, a customs union

[26] *Ibid.*, p. 77.
[27] Viner, *op. cit.*, p. 83.

which was initiated in 1819 and had by 1867 incorporated all the German states which became the German Empire in 1871. The Union of South Africa had similar origins.[28]

In addition to simplifying customs administration, the formation of a customs union provides increased bargaining power and a stronger attraction to foreign investment, both resulting from the creation of an enlarged market through the erection of a single tariff wall. The common tariff also eliminates the problems of internal dislocations to trade and production characteristic of free-trade areas. Indeed, union should help rectify previously existing distortions to the location of production, as commodity flows assume their natural directions with the removal of old barriers to trade. On the other hand, unlike the free-trade area, with its tendency toward reduction of external trade barriers, the customs union appears subject to pressures for higher tariffs on goods of nonmembers. A union of this type may encourage efforts toward group self-sufficiency, although such a result is not entirely feasible unless economic policies are closely coordinated, thus drawing the group into a still higher form of economic integration. This is one of the important reasons for the number of customs unions which have strengthened their ties in recent times.

Several groups formed since World War II have labeled themselves "common markets," but most have become more integrated than the term implies. For this reason we shall consider all of the existing higher forms at one time. These have several advantages that customs unions do not. First, they are better coordinated because of the harmonization of economic policies, which is an aid to reducing dependence upon external trade. Another, and particularly important, source of strength is the free intragroup movement of the factors of production, which permits a high degree of efficiency in production. With fewer but larger establishments, which are able to choose the most advantageous locations within common market territory, substantial economies of scale and savings in transport costs are theoretically possible. Social gains may also be expected, as coordinated investment policies and unimpeded migrations of labor reduce local pockets of poverty. To the small countries of Europe these features appear to offer much promise.

Formed as a customs union near the end of the war, Benelux was from the outset intended to become an economic union ultimately. The incentives for such union were great for these three very small, densely populated countries, all heavily dependent upon international trade.[29] Despite certain problems of adjustment, particularly those resulting from the somewhat competitive agricultural sectors of Belgium and The Netherlands, Benelux experienced substantial gains in both external and internal trade during its first decade—much greater, in fact, than the rise in gross national product of these countries.[30] The other countries of west-

[28] *Ibid.*, pp. 97-98.

[29] This dependence is shown by the very high export coefficients of these countries—38.4 in the case of The Netherlands and 38.0 for Belgium-Luxembourg, as compared with only 4.3 for the United States. All three coefficients are based upon 1963 data. See Chapter 5, Table 5.1.

[30] Balassa, *op. cit.*, p. 52.

ern and northern Europe did not fail to note this striking example of the advantages of bigness which cooperation can bring to small countries. Several imitators quickly followed.

Although the larger group of countries which formed the European Coal and Steel Community were at first willing to attempt only a sectoral approach, they contemplated a very high order of integration for those industries affected. The six countries agreed not only to the free movement of raw materials and products within these sectors but also to full mobility of capital and labor, all subject to the binding decisions of a supranational executive, legislative, and judicial apparatus. Coal and steel provided an attractive opportunity for the experiment because of the apparent complementarity of member countries in these industries. France's iron ore reserves were very large, whereas Germany's were inadequate; Germany's coking coal was of good quality and in good supply, but France and Belgium were poorly endowed; Italy and The Netherlands were virtually lacking in both resources but had growing steel industries and, at that time, an excess of labor. In practice, these countries have continued to draw heavily upon outside sources for these raw materials—iron ore from Sweden and coking coal from the United States, for example—but the coordinated development of the steel industries of ECSC has been highly successful in terms of both production and trade.

Nevertheless, the sectoral method has a number of defects. It is capable of causing harmful effects in those industries not liberalized, and it can produce balance-of-payments difficulties for high-cost producers of those goods included in the agreement if compensating benefits are not possible from other sources. There may also be conflicts of interest between producers and consumers within the high-cost countries, the former opposing integration and the latter favoring it.[31] Such problems were eased for the ECSC by the prompt expansion of integration to all industrial sectors through the formation of the European Economic Community, with which ECSC and Euratom are now merging.

Although it can be shown that trade among the EEC countries was rising rapidly prior to the signing of the Treaty of Rome,[32] this trade has increased at a phenomenal rate subsequently and has been accompanied by numerous other benefits as well. The six countries have several characteristics conducive to the success of this type of union, one of these being their contiguity. Except for the enclave formed by Switzerland and Austria in their midst (see Fig. 7.1), the group forms a compact unit occupying a position of remarkable centrality in the heart of one of the most economically active regions of the world. These countries, having small to moderately small economies, had much to gain from a union which would permit their industries to commence operation at optimum capacity and which would at last provide them with a strong voice in world councils. Increased attraction to foreign investment because of the common tariff was another expectation, one which has been amply confirmed by

[31] *Ibid.*, pp. 15-17. The newly formed Canadian-American auto agreement is already beginning to produce such strains.
[32] See Alexander Lamfalussy, "Europe's Progress: Due to Common Market?" in *The Common Market: Progress and Controversy*, ed. Lawrence B. Krause (Englewood Cliffs, N.J.: Prentice-Hall, Inc., 1964), pp. 90-107.

recent experience. Members of the group have found cooperation much easier because their transportation and communication systems had already become standardized and had in each case previously been nationalized. Although the national economies of the six were ostensibly more competitive than those comprising the EFTA, they were in fact much specialized within individual sectors (each having its own steel specialties, for example). At the outset there was also complementarity of labor supply, as mentioned above. A further complementarity is found in the agriculture of the group, reflecting a wide latitudinal range extending from the subtropical Mediterranean to the cool Baltic, to which is added the tropical production of the eighteen associated African states.

The EEC has shown greatest progress in the production and trade of industrial goods, with substantial benefits to consumers as well as to industrialists. The gains have accompanied (and in some cases actually preceded) internal reductions of industrial tariffs, which are to reach zero in 1968, and the adoption of common external tariffs, which are to become an arithmetic average of the four systems in existence when the treaty was signed (Benelux, France, Germany, and Italy). By contrast, agriculture has predictably proved a source of much difficulty, reflecting the conflicting interests of the members. This is true particularly of France and Germany, whose agricultural situations and farm policies are very different. Whereas France favors agricultural autarky for EEC, thus solving very cheaply France's problems of farm surpluses, Germany needs external markets for her industrial products and must buy agricultural products from those customers to provide them with the necessary exchange. The Bonn government must, however, never lose sight of the powerful Bavarian farm vote, secured with the aid of high agricultural subsidies.

A second fundamental difference confronting the six has been the conflicting national attitudes toward the degree of integration desired. Five of the countries insist upon a literal interpretation of the Treaty of Rome, which indicated an ultimate aim of complete integration economically, socially, and politically. The trappings of a super state, with which the treaty endowed EEC, include an executive branch, the nine-member Executive Commission, which in its day-to-day operations is free of national control except for a policy-making group known as the Council of Ministers; a legislative branch referred to as the European Parliament, composed of members from the various national parliaments of the six; and a judicial branch, the Court of Justice, whose decisions are binding upon members.[33] The sixth country, France, in accordance with the political philosophy of President de Gaulle, has objected to the supranational character of EEC. As this is being written, the issue between the two factions has been temporarily compromised but not permanently resolved.

Despite this conflict of aims, the six countries have already accepted many features of economic integration going beyond those of a common market. These include attempts at harmonizing (1) tax laws, where these might cause economic distortion; (2) economic legislation, covering such

[33] George Kish, "European Economic Community," *Focus*, December, 1962, p. 2.

matters as patents, property laws, and cartels; (3) social legislation; (4) policies with regard to transportation, energy production and use, and such matters as education and vocational training; and (5) policies concerned with economic development. In addition to these, the group has made efforts to devise a common monetary policy, possibly to include a "European reserve unit." [34] Of all the postwar attempts at economic integration, the European Economic Community is by far the strongest and would become immensely powerful if it should be merged with the European Free Trade Association, which now appears more possible than at any time since the United Kingdom's ill-fated attempt to join in 1963.

Moving quietly in the shadow of EEC is another organization of similar character, which, during its brief history, has also shown remarkable results. The Central American Common Market is composed of countries which had previously existed in virtual economic isolation from each other, even though they are contiguous. Formerly most railways and roads served only to connect capital cities with their principal seaports, links between countries being few; now, however, the five are joined by the new Pan-American highway, which has received increasing use. The growth of commercial relations is also aided by the common language, religion, and ethnic composition of these countries, whose problems are further simplified by the fact that all are starting from levels of economic development that are equally low, or very nearly so. The Central American area, which was a single political unit for a brief time following independence from Spain in 1821, contains a relatively homogeneous population.

Perhaps second only to the benefits of contiguity and homogeneity of populations is the advantage resulting from the fact that the CACM is a union of several very small countries. [35] None is large enough to support most types of modern manufacturing establishments, but together they form a market of 12 million, quite enough to absorb the output of many types of secondary production. For this and other reasons, the possibilities for gains from economies of scale are considered by some authorities to be relatively greater for the CACM than for European integration experiments. [36] Thus, although the five countries have previously shown little if any complementarity of production or exports, consisting mainly of primary goods, the opportunities for developing industrial specialties are much increased by union. A new oil refinery and numerous new factories, making such products as basic chemicals, metal containers, textiles, irrigation equipment, refrigeration equipment, cables and wires, and a wide variety of consumer goods, all give evidence of such an effect.

Although foreign aid has provided support for some of these enterprises, private financing, both domestic and foreign, has been substantial. Capital has come especially from the United States, West Germany, Ja-

---

[34] "The Common Market's Action Program," *Community Topics, No. 10*, European Community Information Service (July, 1963).
[35] Populations for 1963 were as follows: Costa Rica, 1,344,000; Nicaragua, 1,541,000; Honduras, 2,024,000; El Salvador, 2,721,000; and Guatemala, 4,095,000. Total of the five was thus 11,725,000. United Nations, *Demographic Yearbook, 1963* (New York, 1965).
[36] Balassa, *op. cit.*, p. 141.

pan, and even Mexico, whose investors are eager to enter this enlarged market enclosed by high tariff barriers that are rapidly approaching a common level. The effects have already appeared in the trade figures of these countries. Intrabloc export trade was only 3 per cent of the total in 1955, but by 1963 it had risen to 11.9 per cent, and by 1970 it is expected to reach 25 per cent. Between 1959 and 1963 total exports increased 30 per cent, matched by an almost identical rise in gross national product; however, during this same period intrabloc trade increased approximately 139 per cent.

A high degree of integration is planned for the CACM, as reflected in its elaborate institutional arrangements. As in the EEC, a supranational organization has been erected, including executive, legislative, and judicial arms. In addition, the five have established a Central American Bank of Economic Integration, operating with capital provided by the members as well as by the United States Agency for International Development and the Inter-American Development Bank. CACM has also sponsored an integrated program for universities, technical schools, and an institute for business management; and it has initiated various other cooperative ventures.[37] Of all the current experiments in economic integration, the Central American Common Market appears to provide the most nearly ideal laboratory conditions.

The two groups which have recently emerged in North Africa and the Middle East are so new that there has been time for them to do little except to give some indication of their potentials. Both groups have planned fairly high degrees of integration, for which they have certain advantages. The Maghreb Economic Community countries are contiguous and form a compact unit; the Arab Common Market states, on the other hand, are somewhat scattered, being separated especially by their old enemy, Israel. The members share a common religion in each instance, together with certain similarities of culture. As producers and exporters of primary commodities, all have small economies at low levels of development. Consequently there would appear to be much for them to gain from integrated industrialization, with resulting opportunities for specialization and economies of scale. Internal financial resources of some substance are available to each group from members whose wealth from oil helps to balance the poverty of their partners. The success of the two associations is not assured by these assets, however, if the repeated failures of past unity efforts of these proudly independent and politically volatile states are taken as evidence.

In our discussion of multinational groups brought together for increased efficiencies of production and trade, we have left to the last an organization which does not fall neatly into any of the categories we have used. In view of the ideological considerations which shape the economic and social systems of the Communist countries of which it is composed, the Council for Mutual Economic Assistance could be expected to exhibit some unique features. Nevertheless, CMEA (or Comecon, as it is known in the West) has acquired a number of elements of economic

[37] John H. Nelson, "The Central American Common Market Makes Further Progress," *Foreign Trade*, Vol. 124, No. 13 (Dec. 25, 1965), 8.

integration, which have tended to grow stronger and to multiply with the passage of time, just as in the non-Communist counterparts of this group.

There were no signs of such tendencies, however, when the organization was formed in January, 1949 as the Communist answer to the Marshall Plan and the OEEC. That being a time of unquestioned Russian control of its satellites, CMEA was cast in the mold of the Soviet Union under Stalin. This meant an effort on the part of each member to build an economy which was as nearly self-sufficient as possible but which also placed great emphasis upon heavy industry, especially the basic metals. During this period the Soviet bloc countries were virtually cut off from trade with the non-Communist world and had very little trade with each other, except for a certain amount of bilateral barter. Stalin's death in 1953 relaxed the previously rigid pattern of production, terminated the attempts at economic autarky, and brought renewed trade with western Europe. At the same time, the CMEA countries began to trade more with each other and undertook their first halting attempts at multilateral clearing of intragroup payments balances.[38]

The greatest change came in 1958, when the Communist countries began to fear the loss of their newly found trade with the West because of the formation of EEC and EFTA. Also profiting by the example of these experiments in integration, Comecon abandoned its past methods and drew up a charter (it had had none before) which called for the specialization of each of its members in those lines of production for which its advantages were greatest. A number of institutional arrangements were made then, and subsequently, to implement the provisions of this document.[39]

The Comecon countries have a number of attributes, both positive and negative, which affect their prospects for success in integrating their economies. Clustered about their dominant member, the Soviet Union, they form a contiguous group which is compact in shape. Coordination among them is further aided by the political-economic-social system which all share and by the similarities of tradition and language which characterize certain of the group. In other respects, however, they have less to favor group efforts. They range widely in level of economic development, with the industrialized Soviet Union, Czechoslovakia, and East Germany at the upper end of the scale, Hungary and Poland at an intermediate level, and mainly agrarian Rumania and Bulgaria at the bottom of the European sector of the community. Having a largely primitive pastoral economy, Mongolia occupies a lower class of its own. Despite the complementarity of resources within the association, the degree to which most members depend upon foreign trade is low, though rising at an increasing rate, especially with the West (see Chapter 4, pp. 71-74).

In accordance with Marx's view of socialism, the remodeled version of Comecon has been conceived by its architects as the nucleus of a

[38] Michael Kaser, *Comecon: Integration Problems of the Planned Economies* (London: Oxford University Press, 1965), p. 69. This work has provided much of the information which follows in this section.
[39] *Ibid.*, p. 79.

socialist commonwealth which would extend to all members the benefits of an international division of labor.[40] In this role it is intended to produce equality of national development among its constituent states and to promote a rapid rate of growth for the group as a whole. To accomplish these ends, CMEA is unable to rely upon a supranational authority to give its purposes cohesiveness, because its members have from the outset resisted strenuously any encroachment upon their sovereignty. Furthermore, all decisions must be unanimous, with one vote per member. Nevertheless, there are several features of Comecon which indicate a fair degree of integration. One of these is the provision for free movement of the factors of production, especially capital, which is evident in the several joint undertakings within Comecon. Free movement of labor is provided for also, which seems natural in view of the acute shortages in Czechoslovakia and East Germany and the surpluses in other countries; however, there are apparently obstacles to such flows, because almost none have occurred to date.[41] Integration is also implied by the recent formation (January, 1964) of a CMEA bank to which the members have subscribed, each according to its abilities. Other shared activities include a common electric grid, the "Friendship Pipeline" for distribution of Soviet oil, a freight car pool, and widespread dissemination of technological information, including joint publications. Some of these features of Comecon resemble the higher capitalistic forms of economic integration.

In a more circuitous fashion, CMEA has achieved certain customs union effects, without the aid of a tariff structure in the usual sense. This has been possible because of the fact that in each case all trade, domestic and foreign, is a monopoly of the government through its ministries and trading corporations. The instrument by which CMEA manages to erect a common wall to outsiders is its pricing policy. Prices to other CMEA members are currently tied to world prices, a Soviet bloc customer being assessed transfer charges equal to half the difference between the shipping costs from a possible outside source and the costs actually incurred from the point of origin within the bloc. Although this does not in practice result in lower delivered prices for all intrabloc shipments, the customs union effect is further strengthened by what amounts to mutual agreement to disregard outside offers. Among the incentives for giving such preference to other members are the assured markets the latter provide.[42]

As an experiment in economic integration, Comecon has not had the success its sponsors had hoped for. One of its most persistent problems has been distortions in the location of production inherited from the Stalinist era of economic autarky. Because a factory, once built, must be used and markets for its products found, the inefficiencies of uneconomical production tend to perpetuate themselves, and much of the resulting trade consists of merely disposing of surpluses. Another fundamental problem results from Communist adherence to the Marxist labor theory

[40] *Ibid.*, p. 159.
[41] *Ibid.*, p. 165.
[42] *Ibid.*, pp. 142-44.

of value, which undervalues land- and capital-intensive goods and over-values labor-intensive products. Because of this bias, CMEA members are never sure whether they are gaining by trade or not. One of the most serious causes of intra-Comecon dissension, however, has been the dissatisfaction of the less developed members, especially Rumania and Bulgaria, with their assigned roles as suppliers of raw materials. Mainly because of these difficulties, much of the Soviet-bloc trade increase noted in Chapter 4 has taken place with the outside world.

In this brief summary of the leading experiments in economic integration now in progress, we have indicated the several benefits expected by members of such groups. It must again be stressed that the mere formation of such groupings of countries provides no assurance that they will in fact achieve the objectives intended for them. At the time of this writing only the two organizations in western Europe and the one in Central America have produced results that are measurable in economic terms. Where the effects of economic integration are beginning to appear, however, profound changes in space relations are occurring, a matter of obvious interest to the economic geographer. Already these changes are becoming manifested in the re-orientation of production and the re-routing of trade flows. Concern that serious dislocations will occur, that many countries outside the major integrated units may suffer, and that total world trade may in the end be reduced (or at least fail to reach its full potential) has brought a search for some means of alleviating these possibly harmful results of integration.

To date the product of these efforts has been twofold. We have already seen the defensive response whereby a number of countries, finding themselves excluded from a newly formed organization, establish a rival association of their own. EFTA and Comecon, both conceived in answer to EEC, exemplify this approach to the problem. The second response is to create a world organization, open to all countries, which will systematically work to reduce trade barriers generally.

World organizations for trade.   A global effort to remove obstacles to the flow of trade has during the past two decades been promoted most effectively by the United States, which, paradoxically, had previously been one of the high-tariff countries. United States interest in freeing world trade has intensified with the creation of the EEC, which threatens American trade. In particular there is a fear of lost markets in the EEC itself as the Common Market uses its own industrial raw materials more efficiently, as the common external tariff attracts American capital in the place of American goods, and as the group gains in agricultural self-sufficiency.[43] Of the various world-wide organizations which have formed since the war, several have been concerned with easing the flow of trade, a few directly, others indirectly. We shall confine our attention to the former, including the stillborn International Trade Organization (ITO), the more successful General Agreement on Tariffs and Trade (GATT),

[43] Irving B. Kravis, "The U.S. Trade Position and the Common Market," in *The Common Market: Progress and Controversy*, ed. Lawrence B. Krause (Englewood Cliffs, N.J.: Prentice-Hall, Inc., 1964), pp. 147-52.

and the newly forming United Nations Conference on Trade and Development (UNCTAD).

So severe were the trade restrictions of the inter war years that world trade managed to survive during that period mainly through a tangled web of bilateral agreements. So intricate had the arrangements become that any improvement in trade required a wholly new approach. To this end the United States suggested in 1945 the establishment of a new association of the world's trading countries to accompany the United Nations.[44] To be called the International Trade Organization, it would replace the unwieldy and complex net of bilateral trade treaties with a single multilateral agreement. This instrument would enable world trade to reach its true potential by reducing or eliminating quantitative and other non-tariff restrictions on the movement of goods, especially those of a discriminatory nature; by lowering gradually the general world level of tariffs; by setting up administrative arrangements for supervising these treaty provisions, and by sponsoring periodic meetings at some central location where trade problems could be systematically reviewed.

In 1947, at Geneva, 23 contracting parties negotiated a consolidated trade agreement which was intended as a preliminary step in the formation of the ITO. This was referred to as the General Agreement on Tariffs and Trade. At the same time a temporary secretariat was set up to supervise implementation of the treaty. At the historic Havana conference of these countries, held in 1947 and 1948, the delegates produced a document, since called the Havana Charter, which was to serve as the constitution of the ITO. The charter was never ratified by the participating governments, however—due in large measure to opposition within the Congress of the United States—and ITO failed to come into being.

Many important provisions of the Havana Charter have subsequently been incorporated into GATT, and the "temporary secretariat" still carries on in Geneva, even though it had never been intended that GATT should become the basis for a formal organization. To date, five "rounds" of tariff negotiations have been concluded by GATT, with 64,000 items affected.[45] GATT has successfully brought about a substantial reduction in the general level of tariffs,[46] and much of the postwar increase in world trade cited in Chapter 2 has been attributed to this cause. Today 62 countries are signatories of the pact, while 13 others participate indirectly.

The sixth round of GATT negotiations, which began in May, 1964, is usually called the "Kennedy Round," in reference to the former President's sponsorship of the United States Trade Expansion Act of 1962. This legislation gave the president authority for five years to reduce United States tariffs by as much as 50 per cent in the GATT conferences then planned. In February, 1966, negotiations were still under way but were hampered by internal dissension within the EEC. The final outcome

---

[44] W. S. and E. S. Woytinsky, *World Commerce and Governments* (New York: The Twentieth Century Fund, 1955), p. 255.

[45] Negotiating conferences were held in Geneva (1947), Annecy, France (1949), Torquay, UK (1951), Geneva (1956), and Geneva (1960-62).

[46] For example, during the 1930's the average level of United States tariffs was 50 per cent, whereas today it is approximately 11 per cent.

is uncertain, despite the great optimism with which the talks began. This doubt is reinforced by the wave of protectionism which has accompanied recent balance-of-payments problems of several principal trading countries.

It is too early to assess the effects of the United Nations Conference on Trade and Development, which came into being on the last day of 1964 by vote of the General Assembly. UNCTAD is intended as a vehicle for attacking the trade problems of the less developed countries as these problems relate to economic growth. Headquartered at Geneva, the organization comprises a 55-member trade and development board (which meets twice annually) and four subsidiary committees, each dealing with a particular commodity group. UNCTAD is to study commodity price problems and to sponsor conferences of commodity producers.[47]

As we have seen, the organizational approaches to world trade are exceedingly varied. Some, more limited in scope, would promote a freer flow of trade among a few countries. Considering the trend toward ever tighter economic integration within such groups, their result could conceivably be a dividing up of the world into tight compartments. Other organizations would encompass all or nearly all of the world in an effort to remove as many obstacles to international trade as possible. All of these attempts at international organization of trading countries are being superimposed upon, and to some degree modify, the pre-existing trade mechanisms of national governments. Meanwhile, the commercial world adapts its own intricate but flexible arrangements to each change in international conditions.

To the geographer the mechanism of trade is of direct concern as he attempts to uncover and to explain the present pattern of commodity flows. With an appreciation for the dynamic character of this apparatus, he can better understand the changes which are beginning to appear in this pattern and possibly anticipate to some degree the future international movement of goods and location of production. In the final chapter we shall consider some of the implications which this changing scene holds for the field of economic geography.

[47] The Cocoa Conference, held in October, 1965, is to be the forerunner of a series of such meetings held under UNCTAD auspices.

CHAPTER 8

retrospect, prospect, and assessment

This chapter is a review of findings as to actual conditions in the international trading scene, a projection of those findings into the years just ahead, and a statement of the need for more geographic effort in the field of international trade.

Retrospect

TRADING CONDITIONS

Rapid growth.   Developments since World War II that have affected international trade can be grouped under two headings: trading conditions and problems. The most important conditions, in turn, have been associated with change—rapid change in certain areas of the world and little or no change in others (Chapters 1-4). The accelerated growth of world trade since 1945 after a wartime stagnation has been due in part to postwar recovery by war antagonists. This has been true particularly of Japan, Western Europe, and the Soviet Union. However, growth of these countries has proceeded far beyond the recovery period, and a new impetus has been projected from that period. Benefiting from the internal dynamism of the countries in question, this new impetus has thrust such countries forward at unprecedented rates of absolute growth and sometimes of percentage growth as well. Meanwhile the United States, Canada, and other technically advanced countries which emerged from the war with undamaged and active physical plants have also expanded, but at slightly slower rates. The total volume of world trade thus has grown very speedily in the past quarter century, with the developed economies, including the Soviet Union and certain countries of eastern Europe, setting the pace.

In addition to economic growth in certain countries, a second factor contributing to the increase in world trade has been the reduction of artificial barriers to such trade. Whether at the multilateral level of observation, or the level of trading groups, or under bilateral arrangements, certain tariffs, quotas, and other restrictive influences have declined in importance since the war (Chapter 7). Indeed, even the Iron Curtain, which arose after the war as a sharply drawn political barrier to all kinds of exchange, has softened in recent years—although smaller "curtains" have appeared in unexpected places, both within the centrally planned economies and within other cooperating groups.

Still a third factor in the rapid growth of postwar trade has been the growth of populations in certain developed economies, notably the United States and Canada, where such growth has been accompanied by economic expansion and hence has resulted in acceleration of total demand.

Differential growth.   Economic growth, however, has not been uniform (Chapters 2-5). The centrally planned economies have moved forward especially fast, though from moderately low bases of calculation (1945 conditions). Developed countries other than the centrally planned group also have expanded at rates generally above the world average, which, because of their heavy trade, they influence very strongly. The less developed countries generally have not kept pace, even in percentage calculations that rest upon low initial foundations. Furthermore, there has been uneven growth within each of these groupings: the Soviet Union and parts of Eastern Europe have emerged as dynamic traders, not only with each other but increasingly with noncentrally planned economies, whereas the trade of Communist China and its Asian associates has fluctuated in an uncertain, although rising, trend. The developed countries that are not centrally planned have expanded their trade more consistently and uniformly. The less developed group again stands out in that some of its members, particularly those exporting mineral products needed by either of the other two groups, have prospered while others have languished and still others have managed to maintain a kind of subsistence equilibrium.

Still another aspect of the uneven growth of world trade concerns changes in trading partners (Chapters 2-5, 7). The evidence indicates especially an increased trade within and among certain technically advanced and centrally planned groups. The European Economic Community, the European Free Trade Association, and to a lesser degree the Council for Mutual Economic Assistance (Comecon) are examples of formalized groupings which have increased internal trade. In contrast, the traditional bonds of the sterling area have weakened over the past quarter century, exemplifying once again the decreasing roles of less developed countries in world trade (Chapter 2). Whether trading associations recently formed in the less developed portions of the world will result in a further weakening of ties between the advanced and less developed countries remains to be seen (Chapter 7).

Changing composition.   Change in world trade has not been limited to volume and direction, but also has involved composition (Chapter 2). Trade in manufactures, notably machinery and transportation equipment, is increasing. To a lesser extent, trade in minerals, including sources of energy, also is on the rise, especially when measured by tonnage. Trade in agricultural products, while growing absolutely, has declined sharply in a relative sense during the past quarter century.

PROBLEMS.   The most severe problems associated with international trade during the past quarter century have been those of the less developed economies. To be sure, problems of the developed and centrally planned economies have not been insignificant; but, especially because of the very development and planning policies of each of these groups plus a sizable resource endowment and/or capital accumulation in at least the larger economies of each group, those problems are being treated.

In contrast, few of the less developed countries possess sufficient reserves of natural resources, educated and trained human resources, and capital to keep pace with world growth in development and trade. Serious problems in deteriorating terms of trade, over-specialization in the export of a few primary products, lack of adequate investment capital and of the means of raising such capital, and low levels of technology all mitigate against the chances of these economies moving forward toward what might be regarded as their logical places in the world scheme of things (Chapter 5).

Moreover, the very high rates of population growth in many of the less developed countries further weakens their positions in world trade as they are forced to substitute food crops for commercial crops in agriculture, to sell their limited mineral resources from weak bargaining positions, to invest heavily in consumer goods industries when producer goods industries are so vitally needed for long-term development, and to concentrate on labor-intensive types of production when capital-intensive output has demonstrated a superiority except where wages of labor are low and efficiency high. The aggregate results of these and associated problems are that most of the less developed countries are trapped in economic conditions, sensitively reflected in world trade, over which they have little control and from which they cannot hope to rise without generous assistance from the outside.

Prospect

The pronounced changes that have affected the volume, pattern, and composition of world trade can be expected to continue. Reviewing these changes, one becomes wary of forecasts. Geographical, economic, technological, demographic, sociological, and still other change has become interwoven so fully into the fabric of the international trading scene that a long-range evaluation is foolhardy and a projection into even the intermediate future, the next quarter century, is tenuous.

Volume.   From the record, however, we can derive some threads of continuity, at least into the immediate future, or the next decade. The first involves expansion. With allowance for major fluctuations during the depression and war years, for minor cyclical adjustments, and for inflation, we find that world trade has grown impressively during this century and probably will continue into the next decade, and possibly into the next quarter century, at a rate not substantially below the six-to-seven per cent per year (constant prices) of the 1953-1963 period.

Pattern.   There also is evidence that the developed economies, including the more active of the centrally planned group, will continue to dominate world trade. Transition from less developed to developed status is a slow process, even if one accepts the Rostowian thesis that the actual "take-off" involves only a few years. Therefore, because both world demand and supply are so highly concentrated in the developed areas, these areas will continue to be the major places of world trade generation and termination, although such trade may become compartmentalized more sharply into groups (EEC, EFTA, etc.) that have been formed rather recently. The less developed areas will supply crude materials not available in the developed countries and will accept as many manufactured products as they can afford over and above their domestic production. Unless some kind of effective assistance becomes available from the developed countries, coupled with major efforts discouraging population growth in certain less developed countries, there is little reason to expect the gross world trading pattern to deviate soon from the present framework.

Composition.   Past trends in composition of world trade also can be projected into the immediate future. The growth of manufactures and mineral products at the relative expense of agricultural commodities appears likely to continue. Within manufactures, one may question whether the present heavy emphasis on capital goods now being traded among developed economies will continue into the intermediate future. Goods currently being exchanged among these economies, especially machinery and transportation equipment, involve sectors in which the purchasing country or group is weak in domestic production. When, therefore, these producer goods are integrated into the economies of the present buyers, they will be in competition with present suppliers. With minor exceptions, the flow of capital goods to less developed economies will not be affected in this way. If a greater degree of equilibrium and range of capital goods production is achieved in the developed group, exchange of manufactures probably will involve, to a greater degree than now is true, precise specialties that cannot be detected in coarser classifications of commodity trade but become apparent only upon inspection of fine or even ultrafine classifications. (This condition would indicate a need for continued reliance upon Ricardo's Theory of Comparative Advantage in understanding the subtleties of such specializations.)

With depletion of the highest quality mineral reserves that are accessible to major consuming economies, choices will be made increasingly between beneficiating easily available reserves of intermediate to low grade ores and obtaining high grade deposits from more distant sources. Frequently, although not always, the high grade materials will be sought from the less developed areas. We can expect, therefore, that minerals will play an important and very probably an increasing role in world trade for both the coming decade and the coming quarter century. Inasmuch as the reserves of such resources are finite and are being used at increasing rates, it is possible that further problems of availability may arise, despite current capacities for beneficiation of lean materials and for substitution of one material for another.

For the next decade, it appears likely that agricultural products, while rising in actual volume, will continue a relative decline in world trade— a circumstance caused by a marked rise in demand for international exchange of manufactured and mined products. It is very possible, however, that within the next quarter century, or beyond, agricultural commodities may regain at least a portion of their formerly prime position in world trade. Several sets of conditions indicate this possibility.

First of all, the planned agricultural progress of the Soviet Union and Communist China, as well as of some of the smaller countries having centrally planned economies, has not met specified target levels, and the Soviet Union especially has accumulated substantial capital for purchasing agricultural commodities in the world market place. Therefore, the Soviet Union may embark upon an agricultural importation program similar to that long followed by the United Kingdom. By purchasing needed agricultural commodities from abroad, the Soviet Union could at once maintain a minimum supply and enhance its position in world economic and political affairs. Secondly, the unification plans for western Europe include an emphasis upon "Buy European" in agricultural production as well as in manufacturing output. If, therefore, western Europe were to initiate a successful effort toward this end, its position as a purchaser of farm commodities in other parts of the world would decline relatively if not absolutely. Also, the United States and Canada are currently surplus producers with respect to certain agricultural commodities, and yet they have substantial internal markets for agricultural produce they cannot grow at home. Export trade of these countries currently is a two-way movement, some of it constituting assistance to less developed countries. If the populations of these countries were to become large enough to absorb their domestic agricultural production, they would cease to be exporters at the current scale but would retain and even increase their roles as importers of tropical agricultural produce. All in all, therefore, the circumstances involving agricultural trade indicate that the intermediate future of agricultural commodities in world trade can be projected with only a certain degree of accuracy and that any of a number of alternatives may develop.

Assessment

Only in the last thirty years have economic geographers come to appreciate the importance of flow phenomena, especially the movement of goods, people, communications, and currency. Even this appreciation has been manifested in studies of flows within and between urban and farming units, and within and between regions that are components of countries. Only a minimum of attention has been given to international movement of these phenomena.

It is important to end this treatise on international trade with an expression of the need for more detailed and complete geographical work in this realm of interest. Such work can well be focused on theoretical and practical approaches to three overlapping sets of ideas: the flows themselves, their causes, and their results and implications. Some specific questions which have occurred to the authors have included not only the points raised in preceding paragraphs, but also the following:

1) What is the exact composition, at at least a four-digit detail level, of the trade of each of the world's major trading routes, and how has this composition changed in the past quarter century?

2) What relationships exist between the movement, especially of goods and people, and the transportation media and routes responsible for that movement? To what degree does transport efficiency affect commodity and passenger movement, and what will be the effect of anticipated technological change in transportation upon that movement?

3) How is international trade influenced by ideology and government policy? Do geographical aspects of international trade involving the centrally planned economies differ substantially in volume, pattern, and composition from what might be expected if the means of production, exchange, and distribution were under a larger measure of private management?

4) What are the implications of the two contrary movements in the reorganization of current international trade—the creation, on the one hand, of trading blocs and, on the other, of such world-wide general arrangements as GATT?

These are but four of a number of very important and intriguing questions which await detailed analysis by geographers. The review of conditions presented in this volume is envisaged as an initial stage in what can be a major channel of geographic effort.

appendix

The Lorenz Curve has long been recognized as a useful and convenient device for measuring diversification or, conversely, specialization of a variety of phenomena.[1] Probably the first to recognize its potential for geographical analysis was J. K. Wright, who described this device, together with certain others, in a methodological work written in 1937.[2] It has subsequently been used by geographers principally as a measure of diversification;[3] in this present work, however, it serves as a gauge of specialization. A detailed description of the method used for calculating the index of export specialization follows.

The first step is to separate the data into distinct categories, the number of such classes preferably being kept fairly small. For calculating the indices used in this book the ten first-digit categories of the United Nations Standard International Trade Classification have been used (see Chapter 5, pp. 106-108). Next we construct a cumulative frequency table for the exports of each country, as illustrated by the 1963 data for Denmark shown in Table A.1. This is accomplished by first converting the

[1] For a recent discussion of the mathematical properties of the Lorenz Curve, see Taro Yamane, *Statistics: An Introductory Analysis* (New York: Harper & Row, Publishers, 1964), 28-29. The Lorenz Curve, as the subsequent discussion of this technique will show, involves a measurement of area and thus differs from certain other related methods requiring only the addition of cumulated frequencies. An example of the latter is the "crude index of diversification" calculated by Allan Rodgers who then converted it to a "refined index" by means of a correction factor based upon a national norm. "Some Aspects of Industrial Diversification in the United States," *Economic Geography*, Vol. 33, No. 1 (January, 1957), 16-30.

[2] J. K. Wright, "Some Measures of Distribution," *Annals of the Association of American Geographers*, Vol. 27, No. 4 (December, 1937), 177-211.

[3] Examples are to be found in Frank H. Thomas, *The Denver and Rio Grande Western Railroad: A Geographic Analysis*, Northwestern University Studies in Geography No. 4 (Evanston, Ill.: Northwestern University Press, 1960), and Edgar C. Conkling, "South Wales: A Case Study in Industrial Diversification," *Economic Geography*, Vol. 39, No. 3 (July, 1963), 258-72.

Table A.1.   Calculation of Export Specialization Index
Denmark, 1963

(1) SITC Code	(2) Percentage of Total Exports, by Value (Ranked in Ascending Order)	(3) Cumulative Per Cent	(4) Area Beneath Curve
9	0.53	0.53	2.65
3	0.62	1.15	8.40
4	1.15	2.30	17.25
1	1.28	3.58	29.40
5	4.66	8.24	59.10
2	6.42	14.66	114.50
8	6.56	21.22	179.40
6	7.58	28.80	250.10
7	21.23	50.03	394.15
0	49.98	100.00	750.15
Total Area Beneath Curve			1805.10

values of the ten categories into percentages of the total exports of that country, arranging these in ascending order of magnitude (column 2), and, cumulating them (column 3). The cumulative values are then converted to graphic form, as shown in Fig. A.1, a diagram in which the vertical and horizontal axes have been made of equal length. The cumulative percentages of exports are plotted on the Y-axis against the ten categories of the SITC, the latter having been arranged in ascending order of magnitude and spaced at equal intervals along the X-axis. Next a diagonal, *c,* is extended from the origin, 0, to point *P.* If all of Denmark's ten major categories had been of identical value, the cumulative frequency curve, *d,* would have coincided with the diagonal, *c,* indicating that Denmark's exports were completely diversified. Conversely, if all of that country's exports had been concentrated in one or a few categories, the resulting cumulative frequency curve would have approached more closely to sides *a* and *b,* suggesting a high degree of specialization. In fact, Fig. A.1 shows that Denmark's cumulative frequency curve falls somewhere between these two extremes.

Having constructed the diagram, we are now prepared to derive a quantitative measure of specialization. Had we wished a value for diversification, this could easily have been obtained by measuring the area beneath the curve, *d.* The concept of interest to us here, however, is specialization, which we interpret for this purpose as the opposite of diversification.[4] Thus it is the area between the curve and the diagonal, *c* (shaded portion of Fig. A.1), that we require, since this measures the extent to which the cumulative frequency curve of exports *fails* to approach the diagonal. In order to find the latter value we first calculate the area beneath the curve, bounded by the sides *a, b,* and *d,* and then

[4] For a detailed theoretical discussion of diversification with its various possible meanings, together with its converse, specialization, see E. C. Conkling, "The Measurement of Diversification," in *South Wales in the Sixties,* ed. Gerald Manners (Oxford: Pergamon Press, 1964), pp. 161-183.

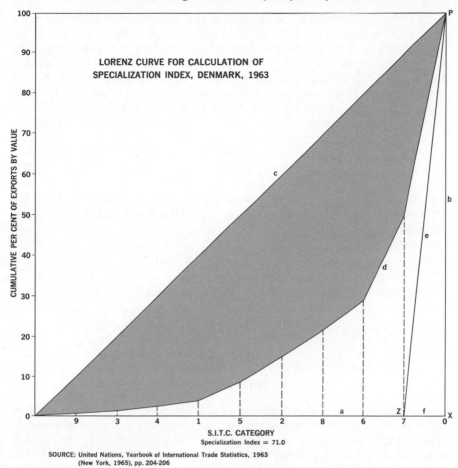

LORENZ CURVE FOR CALCULATION OF
SPECIALIZATION INDEX, DENMARK, 1963

S.I.T.C. CATEGORY
Specialization Index = 71.0

SOURCE: United Nations, Yearbook of International Trade Statistics, 1963
(New York, 1965), pp. 204-206

Fig. A.1.

subtract this value from the total area of the triangle lying beneath the diagonal. To measure the area under the curve, *d*, we begin by dividing it into segments. Each segment is bounded on two sides by parallels consisting of the cumulative per cents of adjacent SITC categories, on the third side by the related portion of the curve *d*, and on the fourth by a horizontal representing the distance separating the categories on the X-axis (equal to a value of ten, that is, one-tenth of the total length of the axis). The first segment on the left is a triangle, since the origin, 0, is its left-hand limit. The other segments are all trapezoids. After the areas of all the segments have been calculated (column 4, Table A.1), they are totaled. For Denmark the total area beneath the curve equals 1805. Next we determine the triangular area beneath the diagonal, *c*, which gives us a value of 5000 (i.e., $100 \times 100 \div 2$), and subtract from this the previously obtained area below the curve ($5000 - 1805 = 3195$, in the case of Denmark). This gives us a numerical value indicating the country's degree of export specialization.

In order to convert this value into a more convenient index form, we may express it as a per cent of total possible specialization. This is accomplished by dividing the area between the curve and the diagonal (the raw specialization value) by the area which would have been obtained had specialization been complete, that is, if all exports had been concentrated in a single category. This maximum specialization would in all cases give an area bounded by sides *a*, *c*, and *e*, the value of which can be obtained by computing the triangular area within sides *e*, *f*, and *b* ($100 \times 10 \div 2 = 500$, when 10 categories are employed), and subtracting this from the total area under the diagonal as found above. Complete specialization would then have yielded an area of 4500 (i.e., $5000 - 500$). Dividing Denmark's specialization value of 3195 by 4500 and multiplying by 100 to remove the decimal gives a specialization index of 71.0. Expressed as a formula, calculation of the specialization index would appear as follows:

$$S.I. = \frac{abc - abd}{abc - efb} \times 100$$

In the case of Danish exports for 1963, this would give

$$S.I. = \frac{5000 - 1805}{5000 - 500} \times 100$$

$$= \frac{3195}{4500} \times 100$$

$$= 71.0$$

We might say, then, that Denmark's exports represent 71.0 per cent of total possible specialization, which is fairly high for a European country. The calculation of such an index is quickly accomplished, and in this case the procedure has been further simplified by the use of exactly ten categories. Actual construction of a curve is not required for deriving the index; it has been done here only to explain the graphic basis of the method. Furthermore, only the value of *abd* need be calculated anew for each country, since the other quantities in the formula are constant so long as ten categories are used.[5]

---

[5] This is but one of several ways in which the area under the curve can be computed. Thomas, *op. cit.*, used a planimeter to measure the area, from this deriving his index. Michaely accomplished the same thing by means of the Gini Coefficient, obtained from the following formula:

$$\sqrt{\overline{\sum_i^n \left(\frac{x_i}{X}\right)^2}}$$

in which

        n = number of export goods
        x_i = annual value of exports of any good, *i*
        X = annual value of total exports of the country.

(Michael Michaely, "Concentration of Exports and Imports: An International Comparison," *The Economic Journal*, Vol. 68 [December, 1958], pp. 722-736). The main advantage of the Gini Coefficient is that it permits the use of statistical tests of

The inexact nature of international trade statistics restricts the use of highly refined techniques, and the specialization index is admittedly a rough measure. The broad categories upon which it is based tend to combine some commodities sufficiently unlike to have merited possible separate classification. Conceivably, the use of a limited number of classes could produce an index as low for a country exporting only a few items within each of several major categories as for a country with many items in each of the categories. In practice, however, this problem has not proved serious, since those countries having exports well distributed among the ten categories have a strong tendency toward differentiation of exports within classes, and vice versa. The ranking of countries by specialization indices (see Tables 5.4 and 5.5) generally corresponds well with results of studies using other techniques based on more classes, even where the latter made use of data now several years old.[6] Although the specialization index distinguishes clear differences between countries, we have nevertheless applied the results on a broad scale in this book as a precaution against reading too much significance into minor variations.

---

significance (see Gerald J. Glasser, "Variance Formulas for the Mean Difference and Coefficient of Concentration," *Journal of the American Statistical Association,* Vol. 57, No. 299 [September, 1962], pp. 648-54). The disadvantage of both the planimeter and Gini Coefficient methods is that they are very time consuming. The technique employed in this book produces results identical to those of the Gini Coefficient but in much less time. It is both quicker and more accurate than the planimeter method.

   [6] Michaely, *op. cit.*

glossary

Ad Valorem Duty: A *tariff* assessed on the basis of monetary value.

Anti-Dumping Duty: A tariff applied as a penalty for the importation of a good at a price below that prevailing in the country of origin.

Balance of Payments: The net difference in a country's national accounts resulting from the total of all monetary transactions with other countries at any particular time.

Balance of Trade: The difference between the aggregate value of a country's imports and exports of merchandise.

Board of Trade: See *commodity exchange*.

Bourse: See *commodity exchange*.

Cartel: An agreement among companies, usually in the same industry, for any of several purposes, including the division of markets, fixing of prices, or exchange of information.

Chamber of Commerce: See *commodity exchange*.

Commodity Auction: A public sale of commodities at which the goods are physically present, a condition usually required by the non-standard character, perishability, or seasonality of the commodities to be exchanged.

Commodity Exchange: A place where merchants meet to exchange "buy" and "sell" orders for specific quantities and grades of bulk commodities such as grains, vegetable oils, and fibers. The merchandise is not physically present, being represented by warehouse receipts or other evidence of ownership. Also, an association of merchants for the purpose of conducting such transactions. Sometimes called *bourse, board of trade,* or *chamber of commerce*.

Common Market: A union of countries in which all barriers to the movement of goods and the factors of production are eliminated and a common wall is maintained against the goods of non-member countries.

Currency Bloc: An association of countries using the same currency for the settling of international accounts among members. The Dollar Bloc (United States Dollar) and the Sterling Bloc (British Pound Sterling) are the leading currency blocs.

Customs Union: An association of countries having as its main purpose the elimination of all intragroup barriers to the movement of goods and the maintenance of a common set of conditions governing the importation of products from nonmembers.

Draft: A written order for payment of a specified amount of money, prepared by the creditor and forwarded to a bank for collection from the debtor.

Dumping: The importation of a product at a price below that for which it would sell in the country where it was produced.

Economic Integration: A combination of two or more countries for the purpose of forming a single supranational economy. Also, in the scale of such integration, the highest degree of unification, including political and social as well as economic ties.

Economic Union: An association of countries for the purpose of eliminating all intragroup restrictions on the exchange of goods and the movement of the factors of production, maintaining uniform conditions for the importation of merchandise of nonmembers, and establishing a common economic policy.

Exchange Controls: A systematic arrangement by which a country distributes its supply of foreign currencies among its importers.

Foreign-Trade Zone: See *free port.*

Free Port: A piece of land, usually a carefully guarded enclosure within the confines of a port area, to which imported goods may be admitted free of duty and where they may be further processed or stored pending re-export to some third country or sale within the host country. Only in the latter case is payment of duty required. Sometimes known as a *foreign-trade zone.* See Richard S. Thoman, *Free Ports and Foreign-Trade Zones* (Cambridge, Maryland: Cornell Maritime Press, 1956), p. 159.

Free Trade Area: A loose association of countries the chief feature of which is the gradual elimination of intragroup trade barriers of all kinds with the retention of full freedom on the part of individual members in their international transactions with nonmembers. The lowest degree of *economic integration.*

Futures Sale: A commodity transaction specifying an exchange of title to the product at a stated price on some specified future date.

Gross Domestic Product (GDP): A measure of a country's output of goods and services. As employed by the United Nations Statistical Office, GDP is based upon either *market prices* or *factor cost.* The former is defined as "the market value of the product, before deduction of provisions for the consumption of fixed capital, attributable to factor services rendered to resident producers of the given country. It is identically equal to the sum of consumption expenditure and gross domestic capital formation, private and public, and the net exports of goods and services of the given country." The latter is "the value at factor cost of the product, before deduction of provisions for the consumption of fixed capital, attributable to factor services rendered to resident producers of the given country. It differs from the gross domestic product at market prices by the exclusion of the excess of indirect taxes over subsidies." In either case, GDP excludes net factor incomes from abroad, which distinguishes it from *gross national product. Yearbook of National Accounts Statistics, 1964* (New York, 1965), p. xi.

Gross National Product (GNP): One of several measures of the value of goods and services produced by a country. *Gross national product at market prices* is defined by the United Nations Statistical Office as "the market value of the product, before deduction of provisions for the consumption of fixed capital, attributable to the factors of production supplied by normal residents of the given country. It is identically equal to the sum of consumption expenditure and gross domestic capital formation, private and public, and the net exports of goods and services plus the net factor incomes received from abroad." *Yearbook of National Accounts Statistics, 1964* (New York, 1965), p. *xi.*

Hidden Exports: Income from abroad received by a country from sources other than the export of merchandise. Such earnings may result from supplying to foreigners such services as transportation, communications and finance, or they may represent income from investment in other countries.

Letter of Credit: A document, usually issued by a bank, in which the issuing agency agrees to make payments of certain sums of money to a specified party upon the latter's compliance with conditions stated in the document.

National Income: A commonly used indicator of a country's output of goods and services, based upon value at factor cost, of its normal residents, before deduction of taxes and including factor income from abroad. United Nations Statistical Office, *Yearbook of National Accounts Statistics, 1964* (New York, 1965), p. *xi.*

Quota: A limitation on the quantity of a good that may be imported or exported.

Specific Duty: A *tariff* assessed on the basis of weight or measure.

Spot Sale: A commodity transaction which specifies immediate exchange of title to the merchandise.

State Trading: The importing or exporting of goods by a government agency, particularly where the state maintains a monopoly on such transactions.

Steamship Conference: An association of steamship lines operating over the same routes. Among its purposes are the setting of rates, regulating frequency of sailings, and combating outside competition.

Tariff: A schedule of taxes or duties levied by a country against goods being transported across its borders. In the singular, *tariff* refers to the duty to be assessed against a particular commodity or good. Most commonly applied to imported merchandise. *Protective tariffs* are those imposed primarily for the purpose of aiding home industry in its competition with foreign producers. *Tariffs for revenue* are exacted principally in order to provide government income.

Terms of Payment: Conditions governing time and method of payment for a given shipment, as agreed upon by buyer and seller. Following are the most frequently cited terms, listed in order of decreasing stringency:

Cash in advance: Payment is to be received by the seller before shipment will be made.

Letter of credit: Payment is to be made under mutually satisfactory conditions specified in a *letter of credit,* the latter to be in the seller's hands before shipment will be made. (See *letter of credit.*)

Sight draft: Payment is to be made by the customer immediately upon his being presented with a *draft* for the amount of the shipment. (See *draft.*)

Time draft: Payment is to be made by the customer within a specified period of time after his being presented with a *draft* for the amount of the shipment. (See *draft.*)

Cash against invoice: Payment is to be made directly by the customer to the seller upon arrival of an invoice for the amount of the shipment.

Terms of Shipment: Agreed conditions betwen seller and buyer governing the allocation of transfer costs on a particular shipment. Four standard sets of terms are customary:

FOB: Literally, "free on board." Often followed by the name of a transport medium and a specific location in the country of origin—as, for example, "FOB railway cars New York"—this terms indicates to the customer that all charges from that point forward are for his account. These may include cartage, forwarder's fees, marine insurance, ocean freight, etc.

FAS: "Free alongside steamer." *FAS*, plus the name of a port of loading, indicates that the customer is to pay all transfer costs from the steamer dock to the ultimate destination, all charges up to that point being borne by the shipper.

C & F: "Cost and Freight." All transfer charges (except insurance) up to some specifically designated point in the customer's country are included in the amount quoted.

CIF: "Cost, Insurance, and Freight." All transfer charges up to some designated point in the buyer's country are included in the amount quoted.

bibliography

ALEXANDER, JOHN W., "International Trade: Selected Types of World Regions," *Economic Geography,* Vol. 36, No. 2 (1960), 95-115.

BALASSA, BELA, *Changing Patterns in Foreign Trade and Payments.* New York: W. W. Norton & Company, Inc., 1964.

———, *The Theory of Economic Integration.* Homewood, Ill.: Richard D. Irwin, Inc., 1961.

BLAKE, GORDON, *Customs Administration in Canada.* Toronto: University of Toronto Press, 1957.

BRZENK, ELEANOR, "Patterns of Trade Between the Common Market and Eastern Europe," *The East Lakes Geographer,* Vol. 1 (1964), 21-28.

CAVES, RICHARD E., *Trade and Economic Structure: Models and Methods.* Cambridge, Mass.: Harvard University Press, 1963.

CHIPMAN, JOHN, "A Survey of the Theory of International Trade," *Econometrica,* Vol. 33, No. 3 (1965), 477-519; Vol. 33, No. 4 (1965), 685-760; Vol. 34, No. 1 (1966), 1-76.

The Common Market's Action Program, Community Topics No. 10, European Community Information Service, July, 1963.

CONKLING, E. C., "The Measurement of Diversification," in *South Wales in the Sixties,* ed. Gerald Manners. Oxford: Pergamon Press, 1964, pp. 161-83.

———, "South Wales: A Case Study in Industrial Diversification," *Economic Geography,* Vol. 39, No. 3 (1963), 258-72.

CORDEN, W. M., *Recent Developments in the Theory of International Trade,* Special Papers in International Economics No. 7. Princeton, N. J.: Princeton University Press, 1965.

DE HAAS, J. ANTON, *Foreign Trade Organization.* New York: The Ronald Press Company, 1923.

ELLIOTT, G. A., *Tariff Procedures and Trade Barriers.* Toronto: University of Toronto Press, 1955.

Euratom's Second Five-Year Research Program, 1963–1967, Community Topics No. 7. European Community Information Service, January, 1963.

GINSBURG, NORTON, *Atlas of Economic Development.* Chicago: The University of Chicago Press, 1961.

GLASSER, GERALD J., "Variance Formulas for the Mean Difference and Coefficient of Concentration," *Journal of the American Statistical Association,* Vol. 57, No. 299 (1962), 648-54.

GROTEWALD, ANDREAS, *A Selective, Annotated Bibliography of Publications Relevant to the Geographical Study of International Trade.* Columbia, Missouri: Department of Geography, University of Missouri, 1960.

————, "Can We Have Better Trade Statistics?" *The American Statistician,* Vol. 18 (1964), 38-40.

————, "What Geographers Require of International Trade Statistics," *Annals of the Association of American Geographers,* Vol. 53, No. 2 (1963), 247-52.

————, "World Exports of Non-Mineral Primary Products, I," *The American Journal of Economics and Sociology,* Vol. 25, No. 2 (1966), 153-62.

HABERLER, GOTTFRIED, *A Survey of International Trade Theory,* Special Papers in International Economics No. 1. Princeton, N. J.: Princeton University Press, 1961.

HANSON, J. L., *The Structure of Modern Commerce.* London: MacDonald & Evans Ltd., 1955.

HORN, PAUL V., *International Trade: Principles and Practices.* Englewood Cliffs, N. J.: Prentice-Hall, Inc., 1936.

How the European Economic Community's Institutions Work, Community Topics No. 11. European Community Information Service, August, 1963.

JOHNSON, H. S., *International Trade and Economic Growth.* Cambridge: Harvard University Press, 1958.

KASER, MICHAEL, *Comecon: Integration Problems of the Planned Economies.* London: Oxford University Press, 1965.

KENEN, PETER B., *International Economics.* Englewood Cliffs, N. J.: Prentice-Hall, Inc., 1964.

KINDLEBERGER, CHARLES P., *Foreign Trade and the National Economy.* New Haven: Yale University Press, 1962.

————, *International Economics* (rev. ed.). Homewood, Ill.: The Irwin Series in Economics, 1958.

KISH, GEORGE, "European Economic Community," *Focus,* Vol. XIII, No. 4 (1962).

KRAUSE, LAWRENCE B., ed., *The Common Market: Progress and Controversy.* Englewood Cliffs, N. J.: Prentice-Hall, Inc., 1964.

LEVIN, JONATHAN V., *The Export Economies: Their Pattern of Development in Historical Perspective.* Cambridge: Harvard University Press, 1960.

MAIZELS, ALFRED, *Industrial Growth and World Trade.* Cambridge: The Cambridge University Press, 1963.

MICHAELY, MICHAEL, "Concentration of Exports and Imports: An International Comparison," *The Economic Journal,* Vol. 68 (1958), 722-36.

MORGAN, F. W., *Ports and Harbours* (2nd ed.). London: Hutchinson University Library, 1958.

MUNDELL, R. A., "International Trade and Factor Mobility," *American Economic Review*, Vol. XLVII, No. 3 (1957), 321-35.

MYRDAL, GUNNAR, *Rich Lands and Poor*. New York: Harper and Row, Publishers, 1957.

NELSON, JOHN H., "The Central American Common Market Makes Further Progress," *Foreign Trade*, Vol. 124, No. 13 (1965), 8.

NURSKE, RAGNAR, *Patterns of Trade and Development*. New York: Oxford University Press, 1961.

OTREMBA, ERICH, *Allgemeine Geographie des Welthandels und des Weltverkehrs*. Stuttgart: Franckh'sche Verlagshandlung, 1957.

PREBISCH, RAUL, "The Role of Commercial Policies in Underdeveloped Countries," *American Economic Review Papers and Proceedings*, Vol. 44 (1959).

PRYOR, FREDERIC L., *The Communist Foreign Trade System*. Cambridge: The Massachusetts Institute of Technology, 1963.

ROBERTSON, B. C., *Regional Development in the European Economic Community*. London: George Allen & Unwin Ltd., 1962.

RODGERS, ALLAN, "Some Aspects of Industrial Diversification in the United States," *Economic Geography*, Vol. 33, No. 1 (1957), 16-30.

ROSTOW, W. W., *The Stages of Economic Growth*. London and New York: The Cambridge University Press, 1962.

SEALY, KENNETH R., *The Geography of Air Transport*. London: Hutchinson University Library, 1957.

THOMAN, RICHARD S., *Free Ports and Foreign Trade Zones*. Cambridge, Md.: Cornell Maritime Press, 1956.

————, "Trade Relationships Between the European Economic Community and the United States," *The East Lakes Geographer*, Vol. 1 (1964), 29-39.

THOMAS, FRANK H., *The Denver and Rio Grande Western Railroad: A Geographic Analysis*, Northwestern University Studies in Geography No. 4. Evanston, Ill.: Northwestern University Press, 1960.

United Nations Statistical Office, *Demographic Yearbook, 1963*. New York, 1965.

————, *The Growth of World Industry, 1938–1961: National Tables*. New York, 1963.

————, *Yearbook of National Account Statistics, 1964*. New York, 1965.

————, *Yearbook of International Trade Statistics, 1963*. New York, 1965.

United States Department of Commerce, *Statistical Abstract of the United States, 1965*. Washington: U.S. Government Printing Office, 1965.

VINER, JACOB, *International Trade and Economic Development*. New York: The Free Press of Glencoe, Inc., 1952.

————, *The Customs Union Issue*. New York: Carnegie Endowment for International Peace, 1950.

WOYTINSKY, W. S., and E. S. WOYTINSKY, *World Commerce and Governments*. New York: The Twentieth Century Fund, 1955.

WRIGHT, J. K., "Some Measures of Distribution," *Annals of the Association of American Geographers*, Vol. 27, No. 4 (1937), 177-211.

index